Palgrave Studies in Cybercrime and Cybersecurity

Series Edit
Marie-Helen
Department of Security, Fire
and Emergency Management
John Jay College of Criminal Justice
New York, NY, USA

Thomas J. Holt
Michigan State University
East Lansing, MI, USA

This book series addresses the urgent need to advance knowledge in the fields of cybercrime and cybersecurity. Because the exponential expansion of computer technologies and use of the Internet have greatly increased the access by criminals to people, institutions, and businesses around the globe, the series will be international in scope. It provides a home for cutting-edge long-form research. Further, the series seeks to spur conversation about how traditional criminological theories apply to the online environment. The series welcomes contributions from early career researchers as well as established scholars on a range of topics in the cybercrime and cybersecurity fields.

More information about this series at
http://www.palgrave.com/gp/series/14637

Angus Bancroft

The Darknet and Smarter Crime

Methods for Investigating Criminal Entrepreneurs and the Illicit Drug Economy

Angus Bancroft
School of Social and Political Science
University of Edinburgh
Edinburgh, UK

Palgrave Studies in Cybercrime and Cybersecurity
ISBN 978-3-030-26514-4   ISBN 978-3-030-26512-0   (eBook)
https://doi.org/10.1007/978-3-030-26512-0

This Palgrave Macmillan imprint is published by the registered company Springer Nature Switzerland AG
The registered company address is: Gewerbestrasse 11, 6330 Cham, Switzerland

Acknowledgements

Dr. Kimberley Masson whose input has been fundamental to the development and final version of this book and the thinking behind it, and for many more reasons besides.

I would like to thank Liam and Palgrave for giving me the opportunity to write this book and their patience.

My deepest acknowledgements to co-author Peter Scott Reid. Versions of Chapters 9 and 11 were published with him in two journals. Without him, none of the research for this book would have begun.

A version of Chapter 3 was published in the *International Journal of Drug Policy* and of Chapter 9 in *Health, Risk and Society*.

Thank you to those who have contributed to the research and thinking behind this book: Alex Voss, Ilia Lvov, Rebecca Hewer, Andreas Zaunseder, Ben Collier, Daniel, Shivina, Fia, Francesca and Amy.

Inspiring authors and guiding lights: Monica Barratt, David Décary-Hétu, Sarah Jamie Lewis. The many contributors to Cryptomarkets Research Hub. Their passion, tenacity and creativity have opened new ground.

Overview of the Book

In this book, I explain why criminals would benefit from having fewer friends and more acquaintances (the strength of weak ties in cybercriminal networks), why drug dealers are best working in open online spaces (when and why anonymity technologies fail), why cybercrime is sometimes moral (how criminal markets regulate and limits criminal behaviour), why internet scams need helplines (criminals and victims need to obtain expertise), and why more digital engagement means less knowledge (trust interferes with quality signalling).

This book draws on research into illicit online drug markets to examine themes of cybercrime, security, and privacy as well as the changing nature of digital societies and of drug use. Digitally mediated societies share a general problem in common: there is a range of emerging threats towards individuals and societies conducted by organisations and individuals that use digital means as their attack vectors. What these threats are, where they come from, how they are motivated and what to do about them is an area of contention. Citizens, states, non-governmental organisations and private corporations are often at a loss as to how to attribute threats to variously the effect of existing and developing technologies, the enhanced organisational capacity of malicious actors, and the weakness of existing societal institutions and norms. There are concerns about the loss of privacy and autonomy in the face of state surveillance and corporate digital feudalism, the capacity of Artificial Intelligence (AI) to be misused and of technology generally to make harmful actions low cost or costless. At the same time, societies face the creation of ungovernable spaces and the facilitating of terrorism, drug dealing and interpersonal harassment. There is at best limited agreement on what secure digital spaces mean and how safety can be improved without effectively ending liberty. Solutions are often proposed in the technical arena, such as that traceability can substitute for trust.

There are a growing number of conflicts around digital security that combine technical challenges with competing political and public agency priorities. For example, increased online surveillance might mean decreased technical security in cases where it is proposed that encryption is weakened to facilitate law enforcement surveillance. Competing demands are not necessarily reducible to a single concept of what digital security should be, nor can they be dealt with effectively on a purely technical or system level. These differences and disputes highlight the dual nature of the internet. The internet both allows new publics to emerge and also creates opportunities for state and private domination through control of the data infrastructure.

Fear of crime can mislead. The internet has its dangerous spaces, and some lawless spaces, which are not the same thing. The ungoverned and 'dark' parts of the internet can be functional and community creating. We can learn from illicit groups and the techniques used by them. Sometimes illicit groups are trying to solve the same problems the rest of us are regarding how to verify and trust information and motives, how to avoid exposure, how to validate the data infrastructure and how to assess risk. Therefore, some of the same tools can be used to assess the extent and intent of illicit activity. It also leads me to question the direction in which the internet and digital culture is changing, towards something more governed and watchful, where principles of personal ownership and control are replaced with those of rental and licensing. As digital societies change, so do the structured opportunities for criminal activity. At the moment, they are changing away from seeking out and exploiting vulnerabilities in the technical infrastructure, and towards making use of the developing social media infrastructure.

Chapter 1 sets out why we should think about criminological risks more in terms of digital crime rather than cyber crime. 'Cyber' implies a set of rules and spaces separate from the real. 'Digital' shows how embedded the internet infrastructure is with day-to-day life and other systems. This means that costs and risks of crime are distributed more widely throughout society. Work is increasingly distributed through digital platforms designed for the purpose or repurposed from other platforms. This creates opportunities for new forms of work and reward, and risks of exploitation and scamming.

Chapter 2 introduces the main case used in the book: darknet cryptomarkets. Cryptomarkets are one way in which the illicit drug market is mediated through a digital platform. The cryptomarket case is unusual because it is one area where the groups supporting the market control the backend, the front and the content. This is very different from dealers and drug users who arrange deals through social media applications where people meet and communicate such as WeChat, Snapchat or Tinder where they have a much more precarious and contingent position. The benefits lie in the development of an information-driven community of illicit drug users.

Chapter 3 discusses the context of digital drug research. The internet is a fractured place with varying, incompatible structures. The abundance of data is tempting for drug research and it must be tempered by an understanding that the digital is not society, and that there are challenges to social science norms of what makes quality research. Two developments are relevant here. There is the emergence of a citizen science movement that collects and analyses data on digital security, privacy and drug issues. Community members develop effective tools for data collection and analysis. Next, there is the development of a private data infrastructure. The latter is sometimes available to researchers, but is often opaque in terms of how it produces its results. These present opportunities and challenges for digital social science in terms of ethically navigating the data landscape and embedding itself in a community of public science.

Chapter 4 presents cryptomarkets and drug supply chains as political economies. This means understanding how harm and benefits are distributed by processes external to the criminal group or act. The changing global power structure, the emergence of regionally dominant digital payment platforms, the gig economy, the international division of labour and the deformation of the international liberal order all affect how crime is done and where it happens. These changes also affect relationships between states, law enforcement, and citizens and the sphere of criminal activity. They lead much more to semi-licit or semi-criminal activity that is not wholly distinguishable from lawful enterprise.

Chapter 5 examines how drug markets are embedded culturally and institutionally. Digital life has provided new capacities for criminal action and new ways of monitoring and surveilling criminals. In terms of the control infrastructure, it has produced new capacities for law enforcement, security services and private agencies to intervene, coerce and disrupt the activities of criminals and others outwith the normal workings of criminal justice. On the other side, cultures of crime have changed. Successful illicit markets require the creation of mutually intelligible cultural forms and scripts which I outline.

Chapter 6 sets out the different business models present in the cryptomarkets and the basis on which participants are driven towards selecting one over another. The market confers advantages on big players; thus, there is a tendency towards market concentration. Some drug vendors, however, deliberately limit the size of their business. Vendors take on bigger risks when expanding their business. Employing more people, having to deal with larger throughputs and engaging in greater blockchain exposure are all factors pushing people to limit their business size. Therefore, the market logic and the business logic tend to work against each other in many instances. The way in which business and market logics work out point to ways in which crime is structured without being organised. Organised crime implies the existence of a well-organised command system that coordinates different actors. Such mafia-like organisation is relatively rare and tend—even in those cases—to consist of coalitions of convenience rather than hierarchal power. Digital crime, however, does confer a greater ability to coordinate remote actors and resources and increases the power that small groups or individuals have. Different modes of criminal action are created. A botnet—an array of compromised computing devices—can be rented to launch an attack on public infrastructure, potentially creating significant havoc for a small outlay of time and resources. Markets also provide a way in which illicit labour and capital can be coordinated more effectively and help resolve some challenges involved in the economics of criminal activity such as coordination and price setting.

Chapter 7 examines how trust is built between users and the faith that users put into technology. There has been a significant focus on what is called trustless technology, systems that in theory allow users to make agreements enforceable by software. The blockchain used by the bitcoin cryptocurrency is a trustless technology. An core implementation of trustless technology is writing smart contracts with arrangements adjudicated by blockhain software. Venture capitalists have been keen to pour money into this area. This shows a level of faith in computer code to solve problems and allow otherwise distant or uncooperative actors to reach agreement. However, the working of trustless technologies relies on a rich lattice of communicative individuals in order to make it happen. Shared culture and meaning are needed, not only for people to comprehend machines, but for machines to talk to each other.

Chapter 8 develops the theme of faith being put in technology over community to consider the differences between automatic trust systems and drug users' and vendors' own judgements when it comes to drug quality. The chapter explores the different kinds of knowledge that are employed to assess and ensure drug quality. Some of this knowledge can be reflected in published market ratings but much has to be developed and shared between users. Drug quality is not a single attribute that can be measured by one metric. It is a multivariate element that changes depending on the purpose for which it is being used and the context in which it is being taken.

Chapter 9 examines the possible benefits that cryptomarkets have for harm reduction. The cryptomarkets are often claimed as promoting transparency about drug quality and therefore benefits both harm reduction in illicit drug use and the establishment of a model for a legalised drug market. To that end, many market players seek to promote a rational, risk-reducing consumer orientation to their actions. This chapter explores the significance for peer-supported harm reduction. As with drug quality, risk and health are not agreed-on standards, but are dependent on how the drug is used. Some users do not seek to reduce their risk to the lowest possible level. Instead harm is expected and anticipated as a 'necessary' and even beneficial cost of drug use.

Chapter 10 considers another claimed benefit of cryptomarkets, the feature that is seen as most threatening: anonymity. This chapter argues that anonymity is not the dangerous quality it appears to be. Most malicious activities do not take place using a darknet-provided cloak of anonymity. Communities can benefit from anonymity and pseudonymity. In any case, anonymity is neither an inherent quality of the darknet nor the cryptomarkets. Anonymity must be produced by the user. Even then, anonymity is contingent and temporary. It is contingent on the ability of the user to hide in the crowd, and it is temporary because of the growing capacity for various organisations to de-anonymising using blockchain analysis and other kinds of machine learning and standard investigation techniques.

Chapter 11 concludes by arguing that digital crime is something society is increasingly exposed to and, as such, it is treated as a normal threat. The changing configuration of the digital society is changing the capacity and autonomy of the citizen. Our digital lives are increasingly 'modded' by systems that have characteristics governed by the interests of the owner rather than the user (and the 'owner' and the 'user' are separate). Platforms tell us what we may say, who we may connect with, and assess us on our worth. It could be argued that this is the price of participating in a digital society. It is certainly a price that *is* being paid however much we may be aware of it while it is happening. In contrast, the most successful criminal markets tend to eschew some of the techno-fixation of wired culture and rely on social interaction to maintain resilience.

Contents

1

Crime Is as Smart and as Dumb as the Internet

… and the internet means the many versions of digital 'you' in this instance.

What is the relationship between digital society and crime? To understand this question, I have to ask firstly why crimes are committed at all and then how technology both facilitates and drives new forms of crime. When does it make sense to commit crime? Or rather, when was the last time you contemplated a crime? That torrent, online bet, or handy personal use of your employer's resources, might be tempting and apparently risk-free. Such explanation focuses on when the incentives are right, what is called instrumental rationality. Another consideration is whether it is justifiable crime, a value rationality perspective. These two perspectives are not really in opposition. Instrumental rationality is situational. One needs to cross the moral boundary first in order to begin contemplating the act (Kroneberg et al. 2010). Even the most calculating act takes place in a moral economy (Karstedt and Farrall 2006). People are morally situated towards the free market, society and the law and citizens take their cue from the structured immorality of major institutions being seen to

© The Author(s) 2020
A. Bancroft, *The Darknet and Smarter Crime*, Palgrave Studies
in Cybercrime and Cybersecurity, https://doi.org/10.1007/978-3-030-26512-0_1

'get away with it'. Beyond the cynicism that this embeds in people's own calculations, what happens when there are moral incentives to commit crime itself? This is a motivational problem. In situations where crime is a value or reward in itself, breaking the law is its own incentive. Crime then can be situationally rational, motivated and meaningful.

Cybercrime is a diminishing, though important, part of digital crime overall. Many people experience digital crime as a hybrid of in-person and internet-mediated crime, rather than solely within the online sphere. These developments are significant for crime control. If crime is rationally motivated, it can be controlled in the same way by managing disincentives and reducing opportunities. Situational crime prevention addresses chosen calculated actions rather than dispositions (Clarke 1980). However, actions must be considered in terms of people's own sense of their past and future trajectories. If the motivation is longer-term, for example, if people are prepared to take immediate losses for the promise of future gains, or to establish themselves in specific networks, or because they think what they are doing is important enough to take those risks, then situational crime prevention may be limited. Hence we see the surprising resilience of many online criminal markets. Participants want them to succeed (Ladegaard 2017). The issue is then one of cultural, social and infrastructural resilience, its achievement and maintenance, and threats to it.

In one sense, a crime victim may not even be aware that some harm has been done to them. This becomes salient in the context of technology and the ever-growing complexity of law and regulation, which rather undermines the idea that we have effective personal knowledge and responsibility. If aware, the crime victim's emotional response may be strong but not likely to make them involve the police. Many victims of remote exploitation are too ashamed to report they have been defrauded, or are not even aware that what was done to them was illegal (Goucher 2010). The perpetrator may not know when they are committing a crime. In 1976, a Virginia couple were surprised to find themselves prosecuted having taken polaroids during sex. Their child had taken the pictures to school for show and tell (Edgley and Kiser 1982). The polaroid instant photography system created a fusion of technology and sex which the Polaroid corporation cottoned onto and subtly promoted. Technology creates pathways for behaviour, and people hack it to make new things happen. Some technologies become the focus for public problems. New technologies generate new kinds of crime—in the sense of new routes for criminal activity—and also produce new ways of monitoring and criminalising speech, thought and action. This may be done because the activity's anti-social nature justifies it, or because it is now possible to track and intercept it and what gets done is what is possible (Iginio et al. 2015). Connected societies then face problems of system-generated risk that are not wholly reducible to technological weakness or lack of user awareness. Like the Polaroid couple, the technology allows for behaviours that might be harmful or merely transgressive depending on the purpose and context. Digital technology scales that up. It fuses with opportunity to create behaviour. It is adapted to human use and also shapes human capacities recursively.

In 2019, we see serious examples in which harm and crime is facilitated by technology: revenge porn spread by dedicated websites organised markets in disinfirmation; political speech criminalised by states and public space disrupted; mass-automated attempts to illegally access services. Abuse is workshopped and calculated (Squirrell 2017). Crime is platform driven (Dittus et al. 2017). Criminal markets generate new platforms and use the affordances of existing ones, their visuality, geo-localisation and reputation boosting (Moyle et al. 2019).

There is a range of crime that matters to this book, some of which is ideologically motivated, some opportunity-based. Criminal action depends on an architecture of opportunity that renders personal qualities of honesty suddenly mutable (Mayhew et al. 1976). Vulnerabilities are designed in, and opportunities produced by in the digital infrastructure. These threats are often experienced where there is an interface between different systems, like between cash and electronic money, or between electronic identification and interpersonal trust.

Digital Crime Is Global and Local

A combination of politics and power shapes the digital crime and illicit drug economy in developed and developing countries. Criminal networks can take advantage of contested political authority and state failure and are themselves exploited by political and state actors. On the other hand, digital criminality is often more widespread where there is more developed infrastructure to take advantage of. Major actors legitimate state violence against drug traffickers but ignore state violence against their own populations, activities that partly legitimise drug traffickers. They tend to assume that 'violence' only stems from the underclass. Crime follows other lines of exploitation. There is an active remote webcam industry in the developing world that has a large Western and local clientele. In the Philippines, Cam models—sex workers who operate using remote video link—can command higher earnings than prostitutes with whom they emphatically do not identify (Mathews 2017). The same technologies and systems are used for sexual exploitation. Technology then forms part of integrated harm producing systems.

Harm production systems do not necessarily have to centre the technology while working through it. There is often in public discussion and policy strategies a focus on scams that target the West and launch from the developing world. Most cybercrime and hybrid digital crime operates close to home. The targets of developing world criminals are most likely to be others in the same countries or regions (Mba et al. 2017). In South Africa, scamming is crucial in affecting how people relate to digital technology. Catfishing and phishing scams are common. One common trick is to make cloned mobile sim cards using the victim's identity. The cards can be sold and victim is landed with the bill. Crimes like this exploit the need for mobile airtime in a situation where the land-based infrastructure is weak, unreliable, untrusted or inaccessible. They exploit the poorest and most precarious, who cannot rely on other systems.

Digital crime is localised and interpersonal, though it draws on globally shared practices and systems. It is not, however, just the old ways made new. Digital crime has its own productive dynamics. The architecture of crime used to exist in the grey spaces left by the licit world. Now, criminal enterprises create their own practices, architecture and technologies and are well-adapted to people's digital needs. Increasingly, crime is responding to market-driven cost and price signals and it is also generating new logics of opportunity. Its existence is not confined to the underground; it is public, and sometimes barely even illegal. Companies use big data to evade regulation, so crime is not simply a matter of the seamy side (Zwick 2018).

Some national governments maintain arms-length stables of cybercriminals, trolls and chaos merchants (Badawy et al. 2018). Digital criminals are better able to exploit this due to their sharing of knowledge, software and hardware. Crime is becoming standardised, copied and extended, without appearing to need to very organised.

The Limits of Digital Crime

There are inherent limits of what can be known about crime, not least the difficulty of reporting some crimes, and being aware of ourselves as plausible complainants. Crime itself cannot be defined entirely by statute and precedent. Law cannot enumerate all. A 'crime' means that agreement has been reached between key persons and institutions that a particular activity should be criminalised. It must be reported, recorded and processed as such. Most crimes never get to the reporting stage. Many digital crimes go underreported which limits researchers' ability to estimate the full cost (Anderson et al. 2013). Some crimes are unnoticed, take place in large numbers but have low individual unit cost, and one category of self-interest crimes is legitimated, widespread and normalised such as copyright violation (MacNeill 2017). These do not invite any social sanctioning and require only the most cursory of self-justifications. Crime, then, is not a single, naturally occurring category, but it is a coherent body of harm, influenced by developments in digital society.

Crime is getting 'smarter' because it is becoming better integrated into—and in some cases driving—the underlying digital and financial infrastructure and it adopts key features and norms of that (Powell et al. 2018). Criminals are much better and more agile at making use of the smart infrastructure and they are growing their capacity to learn from each other. This reduces the cost of entry to criminal activity. It also draws more of the licit infrastructure into the criminal infrastructure to the point where there is not much of a distinction between them. To some extent, those involved in digital crime are as governed by similar metrics, incentives and principles as any Youtube influencer or derivatives trader. For example, much criminal entrepreneurship is put into spotting what are effectively arbitrage opportunities, exploiting price differences between different markets (Keegan et al. 2011). Others are involved in pumping their online reputation.

As well as being embedded, digital crime is also becoming more inter-dependent. If a criminal wants to sell a multi-tool piece of malware, they will also have to provide after-sales support, tying them into a longer rela-tionship with their client (Alazab et al. 2011). Ransomware targets the less computer savvy and so the criminal needs to provide instructions and sometimes telephone 'after crime support' for their victim (Kamat and Gautam 2018). There are new criminal behaviours, an extended reach of criminal activity, and also new social dynamics. The changed social struc-ture may be the most significant part of recent developments in cybercrime. The personnel, organisation and meaning of activities have all changed radically. The digital crime labour market has broadened, become more structured and differentiated between levels of skill and asset control (Holt 2013).

Producing Cybercrime

The term cybercrime is awkward as it implies something unreal, taking place in virtual space. In fact it is all happening somewhere. The internet goes through pipes, in someone's pond or yard. At one end, the length of a fibre optic cable and the nanoseconds it gives can spell the success or failure of high frequency trading (MacKenzie et al. 2012). At the other, digital technologies and platforms are ubiquitous, so it would be remarkable were a crime to take place that was not in some way informed or facilitated by the digital. Someone who steals a credit card in a pub and sells it in another pub is still manipulating a digital system.

In the early days, it was hard to get anyone to take cybercrime seriously as a phenomenon. The existence of cybercrime means a reconfiguration of crime in the context of technological development. This means it is not crime that takes place somewhere else. Digital crimes should be under-stood as melds of technical systems and social arrangements which change historically.

There are some ways in which this configuration of crime creates orig-inal, not just analogous, crimes. One is systematic theft of time. Using infected computer hosts to mine cryptocurrencies steals processor cyclers. It also means that there is a close and near real-time relationship between the changing incentive structure and developments in digital crime (Cárdenas et al. 2009). Growth in the value of Bitcoin, the decentralised cryptocurrency payment system, could be considered an incentive for malware deployment. The harms also go beyond the annoyance to the users: theft of processing cycles adds to electricity load and causes machine degradation. Another harm is theft of agency: doxxing, harassment, swatting and inhibiting someone's digital life all remove agency from them. I say this is at once both more and less novel than traditional crime. It is more novel because before the digital became ubiquitous, no woman needed worry about being verbally abused by someone on the other side of the planet because she expressed an opinion about a banknote design. It is less original because it plays into the same structured vulnerabilities with which we should be familiar. The people who were victims of harassment through the telephone system or in the public square were largely the same demographic who are threatened with rape and murder through Twitter, that is women and sexual minorities (Powell and Henry 2017).

There is a natural focus on criminal innovation and the new ways in which people can be harmed, the new methods through which illegal trades can be conducted and attacks launched. However, increasingly crime is stabilising around culturally integrated, motivated and highly reactive predatory networks (Dodge 2016), hybrid exploitation and attack platforms, and market communities.

New Configurations of Digital Crime

Definitional problems are central to what digital crime is and is not. They rely heavily on how seriously the context in which the activity is happening is taken. Online role playing games which rely on mass interaction often have economy-like features. Players must work to earn points to unlock a better spaceship, a bigger sword, usually through repetitive drudge work. A real-world economy has sprung up to service this need by engaging in 'gold farming'. Banks of players work at nothing but producing the points needed to sell to wealthier players, to enhance their online characters they are too busy to service. Is gold farming in online games criminal (Keegan et al. 2011)? It is deviant. It distorts the carefully balanced game economy with its balance of incentive and challenge. Is it a crime, or just smart? Taking advantage of rent opportunities is thought of as showing financial acumen when it happens elsewhere. The fuzziness about what defines digital crime—or even if it is a thing at all—relates to a similar and perhaps more profound disagreement about what defines security. Who is being protected from whom and, increasingly, from what? We have the straightforward problems of weakly designed devices that are ubiquitous and which generate risk and vulnerability. Internet connected devices leak data and can be turned against other targets. As ever these are part technical, part political challenges. For some there should be hard-coded limits in the reach of the state and the law.

Digital crime is being rapidly reconfigured under various influences: financial deregulation, globalisation, fragmentation of the Westphalian state order, the re-emergence of Russia and China as global powers, more adept policing, and digital platform development. The rapid reconfiguration of cybercriminal activity has been facilitated by the emergence of crime as a service (National Centre for Cyber Security 2017). There are two senses in which this matters: there is an empirical sense about how crime is being restricted socially and technologically to prioritise providing, selling and hijacking services rather than goods. Then, there is the categorical question about what crime is and where it happens.

Crime as a service has certain features: expertise can be rented rather than learnt. There are decreasing skill demands as much of the skilled work is farmed out to other services. It makes use of non-human agents such as compromised botnets and Internet of Things devices which were never intended to be human-controlled (Rossow et al. 2013). It can be automated. The majority of web traffic is non-human. Web pages are created by bots and 'viewed' by other bots. Crime also happens automatically and not all reflects the agency of its creators. Vulnerabilities and exploitation systems are shared so that users can roll their own botnet. Botnets are in competition with each other (Krebs 2016a). They make use of shared system characteristics such as cloud storage, using licit systems as force multipliers. The 'democratisation of censorship' means one individual or reasonably coordinated group can create havoc and target opponents, raising the cost of protective security work and analysis (Krebs 2016b).

Much of these developments are attributed to the effect of digital systems alone; however, they are due to developments in the capitalist economy and choices made about platform design, the distribution and impermanence of gig economy labour, and the de-globalisation of politics and the economy. Many of these developments well predate the digital society. Criminal economies are rationalised, reducing middle market costs and shortening supply chains for illegal products but—as we shall see—it is not reducible to economically rational behaviour. Crucial to these new forms of digital crime is the way they employ hybrids of the digital, the real and the human. Some money laundering value chains include a crucial money mule network for transferring cash and opening controlled bank accounts. Others that distribute malware incorporate a troll farm where users are paid to engage in reputation hacking. Digital crime now systematically engages human labour in a more structured and directed way than before.

These dimensions change the social configuration of crime. For example, illegal file-sharing started out as a university student and academic staff activity, as they had access to the fast internet connections required (Andersson 2011). It was largely confined to that social fraction. As broadband became widespread, file sharing has become more common. Criminal configurations such as file-sharing and internet drug dealing may start out among a particularly tech-savvy demographic and then spread out to a larger population as the effort and cost of participating is lowered. While expertise may be easier to fake, bake or take, there is one resource stubbornly resistant to automation, that of acquiring and maintaining a reputation (Décary-Hétu and Dupont 2013).

Players in illegal markets face various problems. They have to succeed in making their activities work together despite being disparate, remote, and only fleetingly interactive. It is a problem of ordering interaction in ways that will lead to the expected outcome. Market actors want to exchange but they want to do it at a price that suits them. This can be tricky to agree and so formal pricing mechanisms are useful. Every participant risks something, and particularly so in illicit markets. Thus they use proxies to reduce that risk, for example brand loyalty, store loyalty, markers of quality and reliability, all of which (of course) may not be that reliable. It is an oddly precarious thing when described in economic theory. Markets can only solve these problems if they are culturally, socially and institutionally involved and meaningful (Beckert 2009).

These themes come together in response to the online illicit drug trade and specifically the cryptomarkets, open markets in illicit drugs, services and other goods (Aldridge and Décary-Hétu 2014; Barratt and Aldridge 2016; Martin 2014a). Cryptomarkets use the darknet. A darknet is a set of system relays and encryption protocols that disguises the origin, content and destination of internet traffic. The most prominent of these is The Onion Router (Tor) network. It was developed so that citizens—particularly those of repressive regimes—could communicate and browse the internet anonymously (Çalışkan et al. 2015). It is still used for that purpose but can also host hidden or 'onion' services, a function for which it has become better known under its previous name of hidden services, to the chagrin of some Tor fans. Paired with the peer-to-peer payment system/economist annoyer Bitcoin, onion services allow people to exchange goods and services without their transactions being cleared through any financial institution or exposed to any external surveillance. This function first came to prominence with the launch of the Silk Road site in 2011. Illicit drugs amounted to around 70% of listings on the site (Martin 2014b). Following the closure of Silk Road in 2013, numerous other markets have sprung up. The cryptomarket economy is currently in a state of flux following major law enforcement operations which have shattered the illusion of them being untouchable (Afilipoaie and Shortis 2018). Cryptomarkets like other digital crime spaces can be thought of as spaces apart from the rest of the illicit economy and in their original conception they were. Increasingly, they are tied into it and reflect the motives and interests of players across the illicit world.

Do not Fear the Darknet

A darknet is any communication system that separates it from the open internet. Usually it means one that enables anonymous, encrypted communication and browsing. It overlays the internet infrastructure but is separate from the open world wide web. Facebook has some characteristics of a darknet as it is not part of the open web. It is a darknet that is very easy to join. And harder to leave. When talking about 'the' darknet, we usually mean the set of software systems and protocols primarily designed for anonymity and that are supported by loose movements concerned with resisting monitoring. Tor provides for encrypted, unlocated communication. Tor developers do not like the term 'darknet'. They characterise it as an encrypted, open communication system. But I like the term so I will keep using it.

The darknet is presented as disrupting decent social norms when in fact it mainly disrupts the internet's always-on monitoring and recording. It has a reputation as the origin of much malicious internet traffic, and the site of criminal behaviour and shenanigans, as the internet of hipsters. It is also a tool used by security agencies, political activists and drug users in search of community. Despite the risks involved in it and its role as the site of criminal activity the darknet can be ethically and morally attractive and protective for its users. The darknet is a social space. Some of the misconceptions about the darknet and what it is for stem from myths of the internet. If the internet is a sphere of open, democratic discussion and free action, then the only reason a darknet should exist is for people who wish to operate in the shadows. If, however, the internet is not really what its boosters say about it and is increasingly closed, suspicious, and restricting, then a darknet is a logical response. The internet in many forms looks back at its users. Providers of internet services, website administrators, and security and intelligence services can and do monitor who is using the internet and what they are using it for. Governments try and scapegoat technologies like encryption, one of the key technologies used in Tor. The problem with attacking encryption in the name of security is that either these are indivisible—and therefore security is a system characteristic—or they are not, in which case the whole system is insecure.

Browsing and communications over the internet have the inherent weakness. Even if it is impossible to discover who is saying *what*, it is possible to find out *who* is saying it to *whom* and this is called 'traffic analysis'. The connection can be enough to infer a great deal about the person doing it and can cause suspicion to fall on them or make them the target of retaliation. An example could be a resident of a totalitarian regime visiting the website of a dissident group. To protect privacy, they need to disguise both the content of communication and the fact of it happening. This is a challenge that faced security researchers for many years. The solution cooked up by a team at the US Naval Research Laboratory's Centre for High Assurance Computer Systems was called 'onion routing' (Goldschlag et al. 1999).

Onion routing is a kind of network architecture that bounces traffic between relay nodes, encrypting at each stage. Only the start node 'knows' where the traffic starts from and the final node where it is going to. The in-between nodes are only aware of the existence of the next nodes in the network. So there is no overall network picture held by any node. Because each node wraps an encryption layer or 'onion' around the message, only entrance nodes can tell the destination of traffic. Each node along the way only communicates with immediately adjacent sibling nodes so does not have this information which is hidden in an encryption layer. Traffic gets to where it is going without being exposed. Tor is an implementation of onion routing that, among other innovations, adds directory servers that control what nodes join the network (Dingledine et al. 2004).

Much discussion of whether Tor is badass or just bad focuses on its ability to provide onion hosting. It allows anyone to set up a host whose origin is untraceable, unless they mess up when setting it up, and many do. Hidden services are implicit in the design of onion routing. It is relatively simple to set up one-way anonymisation using a trustworthy starting service. The cleverness of onion routing lies in its ability to allow anonymous two-way communication by setting up a path through the network. An early paper by Goldschag and colleagues set out highlighted hidden services as a logical extension of the onion routing approach (Goldschlag et al. 1996). Hidden services mean a person or group can set up messaging, hosting, or other services which benefit from hiding the originating IP. Tor hidden services are configured with an onion address instead of an IP. Onion addresses do not use the web's Domain Name System (DNS) to translate a web name into an IP address. DNS servers can be compromised. The onion is the actual address of the site. Hidden services were revamped as 'onion services' in 2017 and rebranded to make them sound less sleazy and to allow for friendlier names. In my view hidden sounds good though and it is nothing to be ashamed of.

Discussing Technology and Crime Means Discussing Values

Focusing on technical threat means we miss what values are involved. Many of the technical and security challenges we face are ways of playing out political problems and disagreements. They are about power, how it operates, who has it and whether we can understand its operation at all. Much has been made about the role of dark money in politics. The issues now go beyond some of the wealthy clubbing together to make their interests appear as if they are everyone's interests. It suits some powerful operators to hide the possibility of these questions being asked at all. If it is not clear to you who owns your personal data, or who you could ask if you were inclined to, then you never know. When we are told that an aspect of digital life is impossible to regulate or to grasp then the question is abandoned before it is asked. There is an obfuscation of technical and political questions happening. Because some types of regulation are deemed to be technically infeasible they are ruled out of bounds as being politically impossible. But those are choices. We decide to give up certain common law rights to privacy when we activate a smart speaker or a smart lock on our front doors.

Technofear is often anxiety about value change. What we actually see are shifting priorities and centres of power. The political aspect means examining what kind of crimes we prioritise, investigate and punish, how they are investigated and whether some kinds of harmful behaviour are defined as crimes at all. For example, developing, hoarding and deploying zero day vulnerabilities are activities that both security agencies and cybercriminals invest a lot of time and labour in. Crime is used to signal, such as the 2017 Wannacry ransomware attack, a vastly disruptive attack that netted very little money for its creators. This looked to be an extension of North Korea's internet disruption programme. The aim is to signal the existence of their malware capacity rather than gathering up all the bitcoins.

Some technologies are promoted in order to track and trace people, to divvy their behaviour up into digestible chunks of data which can be put to good commercial use. The claims made for the big data technology that result are often overblown. In the main the most effective companies are just those who have a lot of data to work on. Therefore, what matters is who has the data, not how fancy your algorithm is. They are overblown for a reason. It allows the new economy gurus to get away with being casual about law abiding when it comes to ethical and even legal business behaviour, or to reframe the debate about data, privacy and labour rights in ways that suit their particular business model. They often start with the claim that what they do cannot, as well as should not, be regulated.

A way of doing this is to use data analysis capacity to evade authorities. The 'we're not a taxi company we are an app' taxi company Uber used software it called Greyball, which the company claims was primarily to avoid use that violated its Terms of Service (Calo and Rosenblat 2017). It allowed them to hide their operations from local authorities in locations where they were not licensed to operate. Uber could then operate in a murky grey zone. It is not the case that this is behaviour confined to companies in the new economy. It is the case that they tend to get an automatic free pass from sections of the media and politicians when it comes to such bagatelles as labour laws. Anything that appears 'heavy' or old economy is immediately defined as unworkable in relation to the flow of information bits, as if those bits do not involve people, physical infrastructure, and institutions. Let us not overdo this. Dodging taxes, playing fast and loose with the law and undermining it at every turn have long been the habits of some businesses. Nobody expects them to be nice. It is striking now because the difference between the 'don't be evil' image that these companies project and the 'see no evil' reality which sometimes appears when they actually have to do boring stuff like paying people.

That is why the resolution of these problems is political and not only technological. Discussion of cybercrime demands that we say what values we want to protect and whether we are prepared to sacrifice some in the name of security. It puts our values back in and involves thorny questions about what exactly those values are or should be and how much effort we are prepared to go to in order to preserve them. I have found when researching the darknet that these are precisely the questions users are tussling with. Cyber security is increasingly seen as essential and yet it is also as a point of contention between citizens, states, non-governmental organisations and private corporations as they grapple with existing and developing technologies. The changing salience of privacy online has recently sparked concerns about, on the one hand, the loss of privacy and autonomy in the face of state and corporate surveillance and, on the other, the creation of ungovernable spaces and the facilitation of terrorism and gendered violence.

There are a growing number of conflicts around cyber security that combine technical challenges and competing political and public agency priorities. For example, increased online surveillance might mean decreased technical security, in cases where it is proposed that encryption is weakened to facilitate surveillance. Competing demands are not necessarily reducible to a single concept of what cyber security should be nor can they be dealt with effectively on a purely technical or system level. These differences and disputes highlight the dual nature of the internet, both allowing counter-publics to emerge and also opportunities for state and private domination through control of the data infrastructure. I argue that far from being a dangerous morass, the darknet and the technologies used in it have benefits and significance for everyone online. Even if you have not interest in using them yourself, their principles of operation are useful guides to think about the way risks from crime are structured and distributed.

Governments hope to separate 'good' and 'bad' technical systems but that is not possible. One way this is done is in arguments over whether encryption should be a publicly available security good or should be artificially weakened to allow security services and law enforcement access to communications. Technical systems integrate with and develop alongside ideas of economic value, security, personal privacy and desirable secrecy. Some of the scariest systems are those that appear to embed values we do not like, such as anonymity. In technical change, the values that we hold change more slowly than how we and our actions are valued financially. The attention economy has significantly changed this. It has created a system of expectations, norms and technology that encourages sharing certain kinds of experience. Some platform camera filters smooth out skin and sharpen eyes and facial features, making a porcelain mask aesthetic. It is one example of technology embedding some values specific to a dominant culturally accepted aesthetics.

Myths of the Internet Make Digital Crime Look Strange When It Is Normal

Cybercrime is only outlandish because we hope the internet is democratic, distributive and user controlled. Well, it is not that. When we reproduce erroneous claims about what cybercrime is like we are often attaching them to some of these myths. These are often based on the self-aggrandisement of Silicon Valley evangelists, the bewildered dotcom boomers, techno-slaves and their acolytes. They are frequently repeated by half-listening politicians and an echo chamber media.

Misapprehensions exist because they are handy to think by, lazily reassuring or persist in the teeth of reality because they are useful. Some have faded rapidly in recent years, of which a major one is. .

1. The internet is free, lawless and resists state interference. It cannot be repressed, controlled, named, ranked or numbered. In fact, it can and is. In fact, the internet is perfect for states to occupy. The internet inside the Chinese firewall is doing very well, thank you. Chinese companies do not appear to suffer from the close watch maintained by their government on what they can and cannot say. Innovation goes on at a roaring pace. Authoritarianism carries on just fine.

2. It is unencumbered by geography, place, nation, borders or any solid construct of the wheezing behemoths that occupy meatspace—the anchored offline world. There was a time in its early years when the internet could be thought of as occupying an ethereal cloud inhabited by cross-national Western academics. Even at that point, it was firmly grounded in the military-smartalec complex of the US Defence Department and elite Western universities. More so now, it is defined by global regions and nation. Search results, web access, and services provided over the internet are geo-located and restricted.

3. It is a flat network. Each node in the network is as important as any other node. That flat quality makes it impenetrable by hostile actors and able to survive any attempt to censor it. In reality it is lumpy in physical and software terms with many choke points and a few off switches. Lumpiness is an inherent characteristic of networks. They quickly cluster and reinforce clustering due to network effects.

4. It is a blank canvas with no inherent characteristics other than those imposed by the user. In truth it is designed, prioritised, governed, coded to reflect the priorities and needs of the maker.

5. It is ubiquitous. In reality there are many people whose connection is costly and unreliable and who move through the digital only with difficulty. Others—often at the other end of the economic scale—deliberately avoid and resist digitisation of their social and economic lives. A related assumption is that all would be better if everyone were connected and all economies were digitally mediated.

6. It is characterised by reciprocal sharing. Humans build relationships through sharing, we need to share, and the internet can make sharing a possibility. However the so called sharing economy is less about reciprocity and more about centralising transactions in a limited set of platforms. Sharing implies a relationship of equals, but reciprocity is minimal.

7. It undermines power and promotes equality. Power does not get away that easily. Power is redistributed and reconfigured through the internet, using its platforms and the states, societies and economies in which they are grounded.

8. It is anonymous. As with the other myths, the opposite is more often the case. It is de-anonymising and with a little concerted effort the user's real world identity is not far away.

9. It will make the economy cashless—this is being pushed by financial institutions but few societies are ready or will ever be. It just involves pushing costs onto less able citizens who cannot or cannot afford to use digital services and find themselves forced on to expensive, hard to access second best cash services.

10. Technological verification can substitue for trust—the idea that problems of contract organisation and human communication can be

solved by technologies which embed trust in them—blockchains, sexual consent apps, etc. These sound great because they cut out a huge layer of administration. But they don't really work by themselves.

11. Tech rules it. This comes in two myths used to justify the direction of technological and social development around it: Because you can, you should as everything is different online and there are no consequences, and… Because you can, somebody will, so we might as well let it happen. This is often expressed as humans being at the mercy of technological development. As in, because it is technically feasible to monitor everyone, all the time, somebody will and we have no choice but to let it happen.

12. Technology diffuses from the West to the rest. In fact most innovation happens in low and middle income countries, and tech diffuses faster where this is greater need. Myths are fine to live by but they are a problem when they hold up our thinking. Some of these myths are cruft, some of the early over-the-top claims made about the internet which still stick to it. Some are reproduced by those who have an interest in claiming that one or the other is true. For example, that internet-based companies cannot be expected to pay tax or adhere to basic labour law because their jurisdiction is nowhere. That is despite the value they produced being extracted from very real people and activities. Another is that their corporate structure is fundamentally different from that of 'bricks and mortar' companies and that justifies a wholly different kind of regulation or—better yet—no regulation at all. Ask those same companies how they feel about the enforcement of intellectual property rights in Russia and China and you may find that some old boots-on-the-ground gunboat regulation is just the ticket for them, negotiated by a very real government, paid for by your taxes. The digital society is characterised by the following characteristics: we are not equal and it shows. It is not screened but felt. It is governed without rules. It appears automatic but is curated. It always looks back at you.

The function of the darknet in my analysis is to reflect many of the challenges posed by the modern internet at us, which are themselves really the challenges of modern society and economic arrangements. The darknet is of special interest to me because it exposes some of these myths, crystallises some of these problems and provides some solutions to them. The darknet provides a window into some kinds of cybercrime. It also provides lessons for how to respond to some challenges facing all internet users, of surveillance, risk, interception, loss of autonomy and changes to the deep structure of our lives in the digital world. As we will find, the darknet produces its own myths and becomes the location for some prevailing myths about digital crime that I investigate in this book.

Conclusion

The darknet is presented by detractors and fans in opposition to the open web. Fears tend to be attributed to dark systems and dark actors. However, the darknet is far from shady, and we have more to fear form actors operating in and exploiting the opaque, grey spaces of the digital world, or hiding alone among the mob. Trolls engaging in organised harassment of women are taking advantage of the power of digital to coordinate disparate individuals to create a force much more harmful than achievable by a set of uncoordinated armchair misogynists. These points are where extensive havoc and harm can be wrought by a few. Alongside that, they can be the location for supportive communities who establish norms for reasonable behaviour, assessment of harm and value, and supportive interaction.

References

Afilipoaie, A., & Shortis, P. (2018). *Crypto-market enforcement—New strategy and tactics.* Swansea: Global Drug Policy Observatory.

Alazab, M., Venkatraman, S., Watters, P., Alazab, M., & Alazab, A. (2011). Cybercrime: The case of obfuscated malware. In *Global security, safety and sustainability & e-Democracy* (pp. 204–211). Berlin: Springer.

Aldridge, J., & Décary-Hétu, D. (2014). *Not an 'e-Bay for drugs': The cryptomarket 'Silk Road' as a paradigm shifting criminal innovation.* Rochester, NY: Social Science Research Network.

Anderson, R., Barton, C., Böhme, R., Clayton, R., Van Eeten, M. J., Levi, M., et al. (2013). Measuring the cost of cybercrime. In *The economics of information security and privacy* (pp. 265–300). Berlin: Springer.

Andersson, J. (2011). The origins and impacts of the Swedish file-sharing movement: A case study. *Critical Studies in Peer Production (CSPP), 1*(1), 1–18.

Badawy, A., Ferrara, E., & Lerman, K. (2018). Analyzing the digital traces of political manipulation: The 2016 Russian interference Twitter campaign. In *2018 IEEE/ACM International Conference on Advances in Social Networks Analysis and Mining (ASONAM)* (pp. 258–265). IEEE.

Barratt, M. J., & Aldridge, J. (2016). Everything you always wanted to know about drug cryptomarkets* (*but were afraid to ask). *International Journal of Drug Policy, 35*, 1–6. https://doi.org/10.1016/j.drugpo.2016.07.005.

Beckert, J. (2009). The social order of markets. *Theory and Society, 38*(3), 245–269. https://doi.org/10.1007/s11186-008-9082-0.

Çalışkan, E., Minárik, T., & Osula, A.-M. (2015). *Technical and legal overview of the tor anonymity network*. Tallinn: NATO Cooperative Cyber Defence Centre of Excellence.

Calo, R., & Rosenblat, A. (2017). The taking economy: Uber, information, and power. *Columbia Law Review, 117*, 1623.

Cárdenas, A., Radosavac, S., Grossklags, J., Chuang, J., & Hoofnagle, C. J. (2009). *An economic map of cybercrime* (SSRN Scholarly Paper No. ID 1997795). Retrieved from Social Science Research Network website: https://papers.ssrn.com/abstract=1997795.

Clarke, R. V. G. (1980). Situational crime prevention: Theory and practice. *British Journal of Criminology, 20*, 136–147.

Décary-Hétu, D., & Dupont, B. (2013). Reputation in a dark network of online criminals. *Global Crime, 14*, 175–196. https://doi.org/10.1080/17440572.2013.801015.

Dingledine, R., Mathewson, N., & Syverson, P. (2004). *Tor: The second-generation onion router*. Retrieved from DTIC Document website: http://oai.dtic.mil/oai/oai?verb=getRecord&metadataPrefix=html&identifier=ADA465464.

Dittus, M., Wright, J., & Graham, M. (2017). *Platform criminalism: The 'last-mile' geography of the Darknet market supply chain*. ArXiv: 1712.10068 [Cs]. Retrieved from http://arxiv.org/abs/1712.10068.

Dodge, A. (2016). Digitizing rape culture: Online sexual violence and the power of the digital photograph. *Crime, Media, Culture, 12*(1), 65–82. https://doi.org/10.1177/1741659015601173.

Edgley, C., & Kiser, K. (1982). Polaroid sex: Deviant possibilities in a technological age. *The Journal of American Culture, 5*(1), 59–64.

Goldschlag, D. M., Reed, M. G., & Syverson, P. F. (1996, May 30). Hiding routing information. In *Information hiding* (pp. 137–150). Berlin, Heidelberg: Springer. https://doi.org/10.1007/3-540-61996-8_37.

Goldschlag, D., Reed, M., & Syverson, P. (1999). Onion routing. *Communications of the ACM, 42*(2), 39–41. https://doi.org/10.1145/293411.293443.

Goucher, W. (2010). Being a cybercrime victim. *Computer Fraud & Security, 2010*(10), 16–18. https://doi.org/10.1016/S1361-3723(10)70134-2.

Holt, T. J. (2013). Exploring the social organisation and structure of stolen data markets. *Global Crime, 14,* 155–174. https://doi.org/10.1080/17440572.2013.787925.

Iginio, G., Danit, G., Thiago, A., & Gabriela, M. (2015). *Countering online hate speech.* Paris: UNESCO.

Kamat, P., & Gautam, A. S. (2018). Recent trends in the era of cybercrime and the measures to control them. In *Handbook of e-business security* (pp. 243–258). New York: Auerbach Publications.

Karstedt, S., & Farrall, S. (2006). The moral economy of everyday crime markets, consumers and citizens. *British Journal of Criminology, 46,* 1011–1036. https://doi.org/10.1093/bjc/azl082.

Keegan, B., Ahmad, M. A., Williams, D., Srivastava, J., & Contractor, N. S. (2011). What can gold farmers teach us about criminal networks? *ACM Crossroads, 17*(3), 11–15.

Krebs, B. (2016a). *Source code for IoT botnet 'Mirai' released.* Retrieved 13 May 2019, from Krebs on Security website: https://krebsonsecurity.com/2016/10/source-code-for-iot-botnet-mirai-released/.

Krebs, B. (2016b). *The democratization of censorship—Krebs on security.* Retrieved 13 May 2019, from https://krebsonsecurity.com/2016/09/the-democratization-of-censorship/.

Kroneberg, C., Heintze, I., & Mehlkop, G. (2010). The interplay of moral norms and instrumental incentives in crime causation. *Criminology, 48*(1), 259–294. https://doi.org/10.1111/j.1745-9125.2010.00187.x.

Ladegaard, I. (2017). "I pray that we will find a way to carry on this dream": How a law enforcement crackdown united an online community. *Critical Sociology,* 089692051773567. https://doi.org/10.1177/0896920517735670.

MacKenzie, D., Beunza, D., Millo, Y., & Pardo-Guerra, J. P. (2012). Drilling through the Allegheny mountains. *Journal of Cultural Economy, 5*(3), 279–296. https://doi.org/10.1080/17530350.2012.674963.

MacNeill, K. (2017). Torrenting game of thrones: So wrong and yet so right. *Convergence, 23*(5), 545–562.

Martin, J. (2014a). *Drugs on the Dark Net: How cryptomarkets are transforming the global trade in illicit drugs.* London: Palgrave Macmillan.

Martin, J. (2014b). Lost on the Silk Road: Online drug distribution and the 'cryptomarket'. *Criminology and Criminal Justice, 14*(3), 351–367.

Mathews, P. W. (2017). Cam models, sex work, and job immobility in the Philippines. *Feminist Economics, 23*(3), 160–183. https://doi.org/10.1080/13545701.2017.1293835.

Mayhew, P., Clarke, R. V. G., Sturman, A., & Hough, J. M. (1976). *Crime as opportunity* (Vol. 34). London: HM Stationery Office.

Mba, G., Onaolapo, J., Stringhini, G., & Cavallaro, L. (2017). Flipping 419 cybercrime scams: Targeting the weak and the vulnerable. In *Proceedings of the 26th International Conference on World Wide Web Companion* (pp. 1301–1310). International World Wide Web Conferences Steering Committee.

Moyle, L., Childs, A., Coomber, R., & Barratt, M. J. (2019). #Drugsforsale: An exploration of the use of social media and encrypted messaging apps to supply and access drugs. *International Journal of Drug Policy, 63,* 101–110. https://doi.org/10.1016/j.drugpo.2018.08.005.

National Centre for Cyber Security. (2017). *The cyber-threat to UK business.* London: NCSC.

Powell, A., & Henry, N. (2017). *Sexual violence in a digital age.* London: Springer.

Powell, A., Stratton, G., & Cameron, R. (2018). *Digital criminology : Crime and justice in digital society.* https://doi.org/10.4324/9781315205786.

Rossow, C., Andriesse, D., Werner, T., Stone-Gross, B., Plohmann, D., Dietrich, C. J., & Bos, H. (2013). SoK: P2PWNED—Modeling and evaluating the resilience of peer-to-peer botnets. In *2013 IEEE Symposium on Security and Privacy* (pp. 97–111). https://doi.org/10.1109/SP.2013.17.

Squirrell, T. (2017). Linguistic data analysis of 3 billion Reddit comments shows the alt-right is getting stronger. *Quartz.* https://Qz.Com/1056319/What-Is-the-Alt-Righta-Linguistic-Data-Analysis-of-3-Billion-Reddit-Comments-Shows-a-Disparate-Group-Thatis-Quickly-Uniting/.

Zwick, A. (2018). Welcome to the Gig Economy: Neoliberal industrial relations and the case of Uber. *GeoJournal, 83*(4), 679–691.

2

How Cryptomarkets Work

Cryptomarkets Mimic the Form but Not the Content of Clearnet Shopping Sites

The Silk Road site, on its launch in 2011, was the first working example of what came to be known as a cryptomarket (Christin 2013). Two necessary parts of the underlying technical structure of cryptomarkets are the existence of Tor, and Bitcoin. Silk Road was followed by the spawning of many imitators whose success was not greatly dented by the closure of the original by the FBI in 2013 nor of various competitors, fakes and would-be successor sites under the joint Operation Onymous in 2014 (Kruithof et al. 2016; Van Buskirk et al. 2014, 2017). The systems, practices and norms developed for Silk Road have since been reproduced and refined by its many successor markets (Soska and Christin 2015).

Cryptomarkets use Tor onion services to host storefronts and discussion forums. Each cryptomarket appears as a web front to the user. It displays the product categories on offer, such as illicit drugs, counterfeit goods, fraud-related services and a listing for each one. The screenshot below is from Hansa market, which was for a time one of the larger and more active markets. It was taken down just after the leading market, Alphabay, went offline.

© The Author(s) 2020
A. Bancroft, *The Darknet and Smarter Crime*, Palgrave Studies
in Cybercrime and Cybersecurity, https://doi.org/10.1007/978-3-030-26512-0_2

The buyer guides themselves through the market by looking for highly rated vendors and products. The bigger ones like Hansa and Alphabay constituted the more polished, commercial end of the market. The design is fairly static, serving up most popular or 'featured' sites but not modifying itself to the user's preferences.

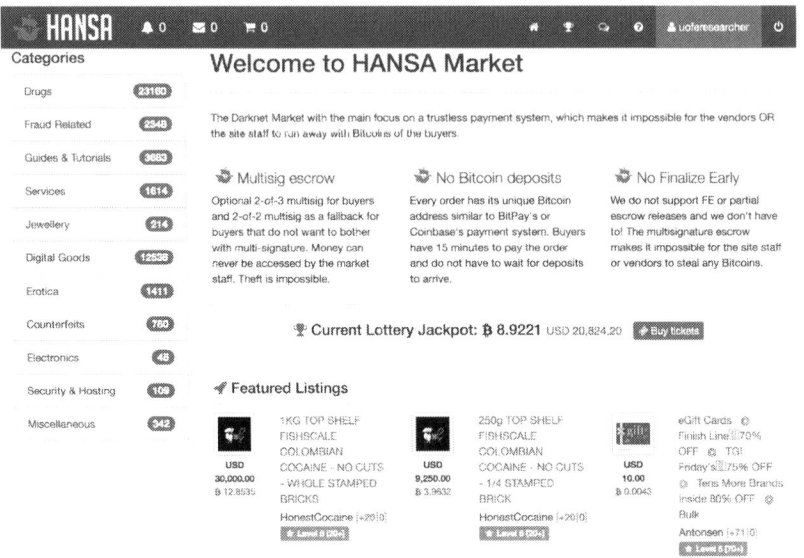

Vendors, buyers, moderators and administrators are key players. They brand themselves, make claims, buy, complain, moderate and elevate some users and ban others. There is also backstage labour that is not so apparent, coders and hosting services, without which the markets could not exist.

Some markets made a virtue of technical innovation, which was perhaps worse for them in the long run as it centralises vulnerabilities. Hansa pushed multi-sig, a particular kind of escrow that puts control over the escrow process in the bitcoin blockhain rather than the market. The lottery is for people who subscribe to it, using bitcoin hashes to generate lottery numbers. Vendors could also set up their own lotteries to attract and reward customers. Some markets also convert the price to your preferred currency in euros, American dollars or British pounds. It is a useful feature given the high volatility of the bitcoin exchange rate, which is one reason why people do not really operate in bitcoin if they can help it. Cryptomarket vendors emphasise quality and service in their listings. This example is an especially polished one.

Here is a screenshot of one vendor, dutchcandyshop. This was one of the largest vendors on the darknet with a very varied selection of drugs for sale. Most vendors specialise in one or two products but some large vendors are able to leverage the supply chain effectively, combining the resources of many suppliers into one business. Dutchcandyshop ships from different countries so is able to source its supply from various producers. The vendor page shows their history and feedback score. Feedback is given by users on their purchases. Dutchcandyshop operates across five of the major cryptomarkets. The bigger, more successful vendors are able to protect themselves against the risk of one of the markets being taken down or otherwise unavailable. The underlying infrastructure supporting these markets can be quite shaky. Their hosts might cease working or they may be subject to a distributed denial of service (DDoS) attack. Vendors can spread their risk of exposure by working in different markets. Managing risk is a critical skill for vendors.

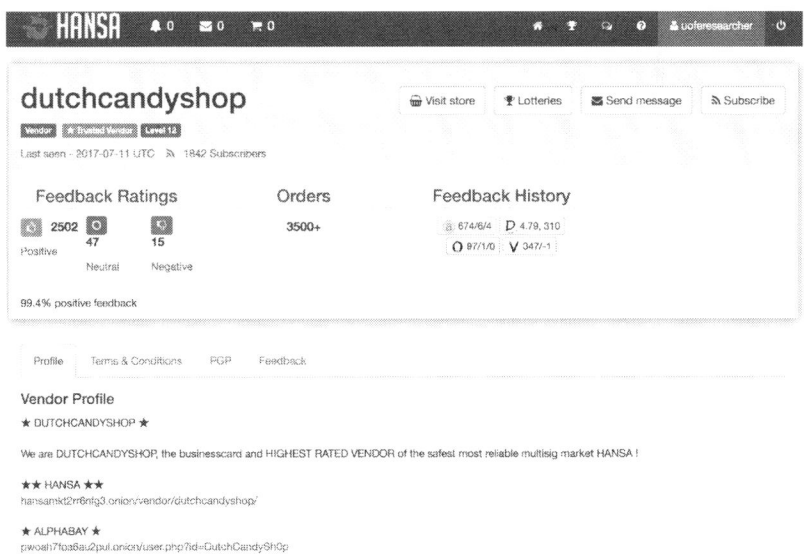

Dutchcandyshop tells interested buyers

* We ship the product within 24 hours of order placement. If your order is placed on friday/saturday/sunday, then it will be shipped on Monday.

When your package is ready for shipment you will be informed. * Estimated shipping times (in working days (monday till friday) Benelux: 2-4 days; EU: 3-10 days; Rest of the world: 5-30 days. Order process: Vacuum package; Vacuum check; Anti smell clean; Anti dog spray; Anti scan package; Stealth Package

Dutchcandyshop makes it clear that it does not have to beg for your business. The buyer must prove themselves trustworthy by already having spent a minimum amount on the markets and having no negative feedback from vendors. Negative feedback may be punished by blacklisting the buyer. Dutchcandyshop is quite happy with its market power and uses that to consolidate its already strong position.

Here is a typical listing for a drug offer, in this case for cannabis. Handily, discounts are offered for larger purchases. Notably it does not ship to the US or Australia, a common restriction based on the perceived vigilance of border security in both countries.

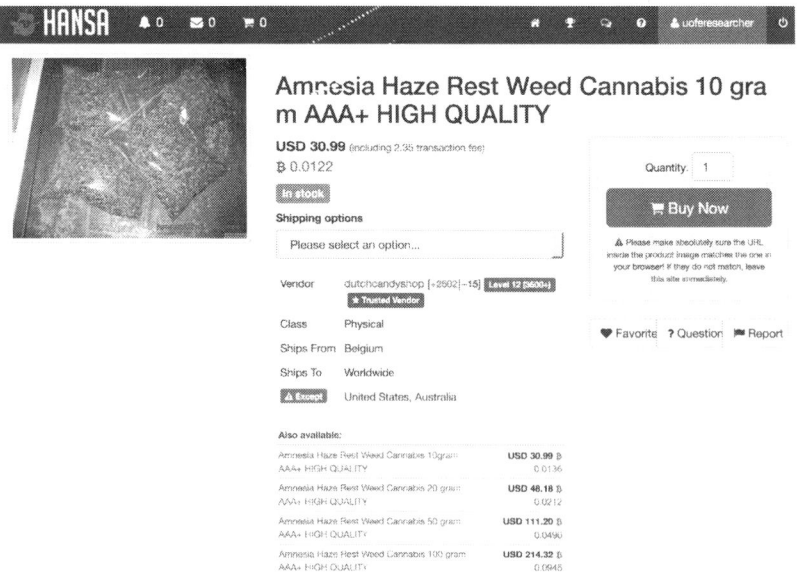

There are also many single vendor shops and combined markets and forums where the emphasis is on community first and drug exchange second.

Profit and cost-benefit analysis motivations are often emphasised in explanations of the attractions of cryptomarkets. For example, it is claimed that they must be more convenient, cheaper or provide more potent drugs. There is, however, some myth-making at work. Research shows that at the retail level they are not necessarily more potent (Rhumorbarbe et al. 2016). They are not always more convenient to obtain than in the face-to-face market. Indeed many users switch back to the face-to-face market or combine the two (Barratt et al. 2014), nor are they especially cheaper—just the opposite (van der Gouwe et al. 2017). They can allow users to obtain a more varied range of drugs and circumvent some kinds of surveillance. They are not quite the universal drug sweetie shops of critics' imaginings. Their attractions lie elsewhere, in validation and confirmation of the autonomy of users and allowing them to join a community. They also allow qualities of predictability and routinisation. Ideology is important, some spoken, some unspoken. Someone who is only in it for the money has an ideology, and much as someone who want to spread the word about the wonders of psychedelics. Both ideologies find their expression on the cryptomarkets.

New Contexts for Crime and Semi-crime

Cryptomarkets are one new context for crime. Crime is work, and value-driven work at that. To put this in perspective, the cryptomarkets are a small proportion of the drug markets overall. Lots of drug trades taking place through other digital means where the digital environment enhances existing trades. Cryptomarkets are one way of exchanging illicit goods and services online. There are many others. Plenty of drug trades take place through the open internet, by phone, using location apps such as Grindr, or via email, social media or Gumtree (Moyle et al. 2019). Cryptomarkets do offer practical benefits other exchange media do not. Cryptomarkets allow for third-party resolution of problems. Drug users can obtain much more information about what they are buying and have a range of drug types and qualities to choose from. These benefits are real. They also provide an emotional and moral attraction for vendors and buyers. Their shared hidden nature is attractive in itself. They promote a community of secret practice that users value.

Drug markets evolve with changes in technology, social media platforms and habits. Law enforcement action is one crucial part of the cryptomarket ecosystem. It acts as one evolutionary pressure among several. It drives change by destroying weaker systems or organisations (Jaros 2012). It destroys some parts of the market and creates opportunities for others, acting like a wildfire in a forest. Other changes not directly related affect the system. Changes in hosting services, changes in bitcoin value and the development of new technology all alter what cryptomarkets are.

What a market shopfront looks like to the idle viewer is very different to how they are experienced by an involved user, a vendor with a wholly different 'shop' view and an administrator with access to the backend. Cryptomarkets are one of many digital 'zones of ambiguity', spaces which allow for semi-crime to happen usually with fewer consequences (Hornsby and Hobbs 2007). Sanctioning such as it is takes place without policing in these places. Compare a seller having their account banned from e-Bay for selling counterfeits to getting arrested on the street for the same activity. e-Bay marketplaces provide the greyness needed as they can be semi-anonymous.

In terms of the technology driven perspective, the focus has often been on encryption creating an impenetrable communication layer behind which criminal activity happens. However, the example of counterfeiting shows how ambiguity can be just as effective in facilitating crime. Encryption is both a solid wall and a translucent layer. Encryption works by creating symbolic problems that are hard to answer but easy to verify. It would be no good if encryption was undecipherable. The system chosen has to ensure that an unfeasible amount of work would be involved in cracking it unless one has the key. Full-strength encryption is a technology that governments have sought to keep out of public use. Phil Zimmermann created Pretty Good Privacy in 1991. PGP allowed for secure, undecipherable electronic messaging to take place. At the time, the US Government investigated him on the grounds that making encryption at a level above 40 bits publicly available amounted to exporting munitions. The attempt was not out of character but the culmination of a long held sense that encryption was itself a secret. Zimmermann's solution was to publish the source code as a book, protected by the First Amendment to the US Constitution which guarantees publication of opinion free from government interference. The fact that many governments have sought to keep encryption to themselves is worrying. Backers of the Second Amendment which confirms the right to own firearms often argue that without guns in private hands, public tyranny would inevitably follow. They could perhaps turn to protecting encryption with the same gusto. The crypto wars revived in this century with various governments around the world in the UK, Russia and elsewhere questioning whether it should be weakened to allow for security services to monitor communications. It is doubtful nowadays that encryption could be protected on free speech grounds, given how much free speech and protest rights themselves have been eroded globally since the 1990s. What has changed is how this kind of activity is spoken of and regulated equivalent of hate speech.

Without encryption, there are no secrets. Without encryption, online commerce would be highly risky. There would be few private thoughts or experiences. Despite various government's discomfort with the technology, encryption is vital in creating and protecting the modern digital infrastructure. Cryptography also provides other benefits. It can be used to verify and sign documents, providing sender authenticity and verifiability and in the form of hidden hosting protect against cyber or physical attack. Recently a theme has emerged which places encryption and security in opposition. Many voices have hoped for a 'little less' encryption, or that devices have backdoors usable by law enforcement and security agencies when needed. However, there is no way of generating vulnerabilities that will not be exploited by malicious actors. Encryption is one of a number of security dilemmas where weakening technical protections used by terrorists, cybercriminals and other outlaws would weaken it for all. It is an example of how many political actors assume that because something is on the internet then it is fundamentally different. Sometimes it is, often it is not. Nobody proposes weakening combination locks because criminals could use those and they involve a code. Yet politicians frequently propose diluting encryption so the good guys can circumvent it.

A further requirement for digital crime is an infrastructure. The point to focus on here is not the technologies as such but how they come together in an infrastructure that is part social and part technical. Tor nodes are a key infrastructure for the darknet. They are kept alive by voluntary foundations, Universities and the secret police. The infrastructure is political. Much of the discussion on Tor focuses on the encryption, because it is exciting, and forgets about the nodes, which are dull. However, the nodes are every bit as important to the working of Tor as a securely anonymous network. Nodes are relevant because they are the backbone, and therefore who runs them, why and where they are does matter. Not least because any agency could set up some nodes and start trying traffic analysis. Tor design means the cost of this is high.

Internet representations often talk of nodes as empty points of connection but they are not. They are physical points in space that connect to other networks. They can operate in the way the Tor developers implicitly intend. Or they can be modified to track traffic and be coordinated with other nodes to trace it—a darknet within the darknet. As this is the most obvious way to crack the darknet on a large scale, there can be little doubt that it has been tried and is being tried. Plenty of people do analysis for fun and profit, some to break the darknet, and others to secure if further by pointing out weaknesses in it.

Tor exit relays present a problem for those running them. They may be held liable for illegal or otherwise harmful traffic as the relay node appears to be the origin of it. Owners have to field takedown notices and other complaints so there is some personal input required. Anyone running one in their home, which is not advised, can find their computer equipment seized. Nodes are mostly run by organisations who are concerned with privacy and want to support the Tor project. One development that has been exposed by Tor nodes being banned is the assumption behind much cyber law and security logic that an identifying IP address equates to an individual. This is not the case and decreasingly so as the number of non-individual connected devices grows.

Technology Shouldn't Lead and Criminals Should Avoid Bitcoin

One of the limitations of discussion in this area is the tendency towards technology blame. Technologies are attributed with negative or positive characteristics. Bitcoin is one where both tendencies are applied. On the one hand, techno-libertarians present it as a form of money that resists state regulation and allows users to embed voluntary agreements in the code. On the other, it is represented as the currency of drug traffickers, pimps and tax-dodgers.

Bitcoin is characterised as a distributed peer-to-peer currency. It is a shared accounting system that uses a public ledger called a blockchain to record transactions. Bitcoins are 'mined' by solving cryptographic equations which are hard to do but easy to confirm. The system has an upper limit of the number of bitcoins possible to produce. It is like digital gold with all the problems that implies. Like gold, it attracts obsessives who think that the economy should function in reality just like it is meant to in theory. Like gold, its production involves a huge amount of waste. Many miners compete to solve equations. When one is solved, the work done by the others is cast aside and they move on to work on the next equation. Like gold, nobody is sure what it is really worth, in the sense of what its final, at bottom value is. Is it worth the usefulness of having a shared and fairly robust accounting system? A payment system that can work anywhere there is an Internet connection, without creaming a percentage off the top? Or is it worth the amount of electricity used to maintain it? Questions of the value added by it and whether its deflationary logic makes it evil run around the Internet without resolution.

Bitcoin is a shared system for recording interactions. It is called a currency because we choose to call these interactions 'transactions'. A bitcoin is a virtual string with marks for every hand it has been through. Bitcoin is rather unlike money due to some of its recording qualities, allowing you to see who has spent it before you, and after. What you did with it will always be there. So there is no natural degradation of the data and therefore none of the simple obfuscatory anonymity we might have been used to up to now, e.g. 'I basically don't need to worry about various petty crimes committed in my past because it's degraded. Records have been erased, nobody could trace my cash transactions if they wanted to. Well, if I use bitcoin, all of that changes. I might use it to buy drugs, and ten years later run for office.' That exchange will always be preserved. Furthermore, related exchanges will be too. Did that transaction end up funding a terrorist network? People can be incriminated for a vast range of past associations (Maxwell et al. 2017). This bookkeeping quality of bitcoin is new and the implications if cryptocurrencies become the future of finance are far beyond its qualities as money. Users of bitcoin might have their entire sordid lives exposed. We see this with politicians exposed for various social media expressions from their past. We are no longer able to rely on the natural degradation of information to free us from our perhaps different past selves. Given the growing illiberalism in the world, this is more than a conceptual problem. Money that remembers your purchase of gay pornography might be handy to a totalitarian state.

Bitcoin is a record of community interactions that are called financial for no reason than that we choose to frame it in that way. All the other things that people hate about bitcoin—it is deflationary, volatile and attracts the worst sort of person—are because users have tried to adapt it into a financial system that has many worse qualities. It could then be see it as a sophisticated, resource-intensive communication and recording system that interacts with less informationalised monetary systems.

The distinction between the currency and the technology is relevant because lots of people 'invest' in the mining of it thinking they are investing in the technology. They are not. Some of the problems it faces arise from its strengths. It is distributed so has no institutional backing. In part that is what makes it so volatile in comparison with other currencies that have central bank backing. The collapse of one exchange can trigger panic selling. There are possible prosocial uses. Companies seek to build applications on top of it and realise some of its original promise. An immutable information record may come in handy in a world of deepfakes.

Bitcoin highlights an often missed aspect of the internet: its heaviness. The complex calculations required by Bitcoin came to demand, and drove the development of, a specific type of microchip capable of executing specialised calculations rapidly. When these chips came on stream, a significant shift in the material Bitcoin economy happened. New mining operations in China rapidly became the bulk of bitcoin processing power so the focus of discussions about the direction of Bitcoin moved there. This makes for path dependency in the coding and community of bitcoin (Maurer et al. 2013). We might like to think of the internet as a light, free environment where all code and network traffic is created equal. The history of the internet is of a distributed network slowly becoming lumpy and dominated by a small number of powerful operators. That of bitcoin is similar. As we shall see in later, one of the iron laws of the internet appears to be the march from open to locked-in, shared to monetised, flat to lumpy networks. Bitcoin is no longer decentralised. A few mining operations control most of the 'voting' processor power. As soon as it became worth much, this happened. Like many technical networks, it is in practice concentrated. A highly concentrated group of around 1000 'bitcoin whales' own 35–40% of the market, according to Aaron Brown of AQR capital management in 2018. The size of the group is notable, as is the way in which they are socially coordinated.

Bitcoin is a poor payment system because it is mainly a commodity, and like a commodity, it is controlled by a small coterie of players. The more people inflate the price because of speculation the worse it works as a currency. Nobody wants to spend it when it might double in price tomorrow. An insurmountable issue is the upper limit of bitcoin that means that its price should inflate over time, making it an inflationary exercise in benefitting those who bought in early. As ever with these controversial aspects of the financial architecture, it is a matter of opinion and position as to whether this is a bug or a feature. It exposes some of the assumed features of life in connected, developed societies: that everyone is able to use electronic payment systems, which is not true; that these systems are generally reliable and non-corrupt, also not always the case; that they have little cost, which is only true if the user is affluent. Electronic payment systems are not accessible to those with fewer resources, and when accessed at all, are often expensive and flummoxing. They can be hit with a variety of charges for what people in less straitened circumstances appears to be a free banking system. Routine activities like checking one's balance or making a payment become costly. There are few options as more and more systems require electronic payment. Bitcoin is not necessarily the solution to this but it has exposed some of the problems in the existing financial infrastructure. However, this limit is open to change. The protocol was forked in August 2017 by miners who, hoping to increase the upper coin limit, created Bitcoin Cash. Numerous other coin offerings have sprung up since. Most are desperate throws of the dice, some initially merely fun such as Dogecoin.

Bitcoin allowed for ransomware to really take off as there was a way of collecting payments without a central, traceable system. Monero is another cryptocurrency which is designed to anonymise the exchanges by using chaff, effectively every transaction is hidden among four fake ones. Monero is becoming more popular but still suffers from the inherent non-deletion problem. All someone has to do is become good at separating chaff from real activities. The tools favoured by criminals are useful for the rest of us and also rather good at highlighting some of the problems we face in terms of tracking, surveillance and deanonymisation.

Cultures of Digital Crime

There is growing recognition of the sociality of cybercrime (Leukfeldt et al. 2017). This is in opposition to the tendency to see criminal market spaces primarily as meeting points for exchanges of goods, intelligence and personnel. Crime is thought of as converging in these darker zones of cyberspace. One approach is to recognise the productive qualities that attract users and through which they reformulate their approach. Morality as a perspective in criminology has tended to look at justificatory narratives by criminals. Like the hacker, there is a range of criminal and non-criminal self-perceptions of cryptomarket users (Masson and Bancroft 2018; Steinmetz 2015). There is disagreement among users about the nature of cryptomarkets as political (Munksgaard and Demant 2016). There is a great range of skill-level engagement in cybercrime with many script kiddies and few malware masters.

Cultural change is noticeable from the days of hacking for fun to hacking for profit (Jordan and Taylor 1998). Hacking can be used to mean gaining unauthorised entry and control over a computer system and in another related sense as bicolage, re-tasking systems to make them do what they are not designed for. There is a fairly simple sense in which the combination of systems of the darknet could be seen in this way. It is the nature of hacked information that it is tradeable. Hackers got into Citibank to show they could, then one sold the secret to others for $100 and some vodka. It allowed criminals to make $10 million. The 'good hack' is an event in itself. The breach, the proof of how able they are to get into a protected systems, is the end point. What might come from that is not what they are after. However, the nature of circulating information about weaknesses and the kinds of incentives now available means this must be getting harder. You can stop a hack being used in this way by publicising it so the hole is sealed up, though that makes the hacker themselves vulnerable to being pursued and prosecuted. Secrecy has to be shared to create security.

One key point is that the cryptomarkets are composed of many different individuals with different motives. Some want a quick profit. Others provide harm reduction advice such as Doctor X, who posts advice on numerous darknet forums. Others seek to demonstrate their technical ability or provide social supply for others. So there are many different roles, some of which are designed into the cryptomarkets (such as the division of labour between administrator) and some of which arise within them (such as reviewers, harm reduction people). So motivations that might be thought of as economic (such as for better quality drugs, cheaper or more convenient) have been at the fore. However, this may not be true. Buyers tend to be loyal. A social network analysis of opioid sellers showed a low network density, and high levels of loyalty to specific vendors. Most buyers do not switch vendor very often (Duxbury and Haynie 2017). Their attractions lie elsewhere, in validation and autonomy of users. They allow for a demonstrably moral market to emerge, we suspect. The moral is part of how the market is entered, exited and made comprehensible (Masson and Bancroft 2018).

In this context, 'culture' means a comprehensible way of doing things and accounting for them (Yar 2005). Cultural criminology approaches allow us to consider various ways of making sense of criminal activity as 'professional', kinds of work such as 'craft', machine work that stabilises shared concepts, and their sense of their position in relation to 'the underworld'. Being at the heart of the underworld can give one a certain cachet but clearly draws the attention of cops and rivals. It can be better to operate a few layers away from it, or better in an environment where there is no strict centre. Position and moral distancing are crucial activities. This involves practical actions such as covering one's traces and also moral acts that involve situating one's actions within a moral frame from dark to light (Masson and Bancroft 2018). There is always something darker.

Implications of Cryptomarkets

Digital crime is not the result of system weakness. Crime has an extensive 'back office' much of which involves non-criminal activity. Cryptomarkets show how crime is changing and how much of the behaviour associated with criminal activity is not actually criminal or wrong. Crime increasingly involves a range of skills in computing, customer services and human resources which are mediated by the cryptomarket structure. Though we might assume that crime is tech-savvy and globalised, this is not quite the case. Crime is operating more like a service, with many organisations involved in reducing the cost of criminal activity. They do this by providing malware services, hosting cryptomarkets and building sites for front ends for single vendor shops for drugs and illicit pharmaceuticals. The most successful cybercriminals are not those who can hack and tunnel their way undetected into banks or the Federal Reserve. They are the middle, those who can mediate and connect legal and illegal systems and activities on and offline.

Agreeing to separate out technical and political questions looks to be one possible point of agreement but even then it is difficult to agree which are which. The nature of encryption might mean it is inherently a troublesome technology for law enforcement and government. The most pervasive background assumption is that cybercrime is only limited by the weakness and vulnerabilities in the cyber infrastructure and the capacity of criminals to exploit them. However, many of those engaged in these activities place limits on what they do. These thresholds may be more conceptual than real but they are part of how the involved view their activity and themselves.

Cryptomarkets signal several changes in the internet and in crime. They highlight that the internet is not a single object or network. It is a series of spaces which are subject to different rules and expectations. The private ownership of our digital selves is growing. As this happens, we fragment into different data proxies depending on who is asking and what data they possess about us. There is the medical proxy of wearable tech data on the body, and inferences about risk from what we post on social media. There is the security proxy whereby your risk to others is calculated by border authorities, police, private security assorts and others. These proxies fragment us into selves that are by turns saleable or suspect. The darknet is one way of taking some of this back.

Conclusion

To some, the cryptomarkets are a crime scene. To others, they are a site of power, agency and independence. To me, they are online spaces that are steadily growing closer to the offline drug dealing world they partly represent. It is best if we do not approach crime as something entirely distinct from the society in which it operates, in fact, as something that is becoming more and more embedded in current politics, power structures and the evolution of the digital away from liberty and towards securitisation.

References

Barratt, M. J., Ferris, J. A., & Winstock, A. R. (2014). Use of Silk Road, the online drug marketplace, in the United Kingdom, Australia and the United States. *Addiction, 109*(5), 774–783. https://doi.org/10.1111/add.12470.

Christin, N. (2013). Traveling the Silk Road: A measurement analysis of a large anonymous online marketplace. In *Proceedings of the 22nd International Conference on the World Wide Web* (pp. 213–224). Rio de Janeiro, Brazil: WWW 2013.

Duxbury, S. W., & Haynie, D. L. (2017). The network structure of opioid distribution on a darknet cryptomarket. *Journal of Quantitative Criminology*, 1–21. https://doi.org/10.1007/s10940-017-9359-4.

Hornsby, R., & Hobbs, D. (2007). A zone of ambiguity. *British Journal of Criminology, 47*(4), 551–571. https://doi.org/10.1093/bjc/azl089.

Jaros, D. M. (2012). Perfecting criminal markets. *Columbia Law Review, 112*, 1947–1991.

Jordan, T., & Taylor, P. (1998). A sociology of hackers. *The Sociological Review, 46*(4), 757–780. https://doi.org/10.1111/1467-954X.00139.

Kruithof, K., Aldridge, J., Décary-Hétu, D., Sim, M., Dujso, E., & Hoorens, S. (2016). *Internet-facilitated drugs trade: An analysis of the size, scope and the role of the Netherlands.* Santa Monica, CA: RAND Corporation.

Leukfeldt, E. R., Kleemans, E. R., & Stol, W. P. (2017). A typology of cyber-criminal networks: From low-tech all-rounders to high-tech specialists. *Crime, Law and Social Change, 67*(1), 21–37.

Maurer, B., Nelms, T. C., & Swartz, L. (2013). "When perhaps the real problem is money itself!": The practical materiality of bitcoin. *Social Semiotics, 23*(2), 261–277.

Masson, K., & Bancroft, A. (2018). 'Nice people doing shady things': Drugs and the morality of exchange in the darknet cryptomarkets. *International Journal of Drug Policy, 58*, 78–84.

Maxwell, D., Speed, C., & Pschetz, L. (2017). Story blocks: Reimagining narrative through the blockchain. *Convergence: The International Journal of Research into New Media Technologies, 23*(1), 79–97. https://doi.org/10.1177/1354856516675263.

Moyle, L., Childs, A., Coomber, R., & Barratt, M. J. (2019). #Drugsforsale: An exploration of the use of social media and encrypted messaging apps to supply and access drugs. *International Journal of Drug Policy, 63,* 101–110. https://doi.org/10.1016/j.drugpo.2018.08.005.

Munksgaard, R., & Demant, J. (2016). Mixing politics and crime—The prevalence and decline of political discourse on the cryptomarket. *International Journal of Drug Policy, 35,* 77–83. https://doi.org/10.1016/j.drugpo.2016.04.021.

Rhumorbarbe, D., Staehli, L., Broséus, J., Rossy, Q., & Esseiva, P. (2016). Buying drugs on a darknet market: A better deal? Studying the online illicit drug market through the analysis of digital, physical and chemical data. *Forensic Science International, 267,* 173–182.

Soska, K., & Christin, N. (2015). Measuring the longitudinal evolution of the online anonymous marketplace ecosystem. In *Proceedings of the 22nd USENIX Security Symposium.* Presented at the USENIX Security 2015, Washington, DC.

Steinmetz, K. F. (2015). Craft(y)ness an ethnographic study of hacking. *The British Journal of Criminology, 55*(1), 125–145. https://doi.org/10.1093/bjc/azu061.

Van Buskirk, J., Bruno, R., Dobbins, T., Breen, C., Burns, L., Naicker, S., & Roxburgh, A. (2017). The recovery of online drug markets following law enforcement and other disruptions. *Drug and Alcohol Dependence, 173,* 159–162.

Van Buskirk, J., Roxburgh, A., Farrell, M., & Burns, L. (2014). The closure of the Silk Road: What has this meant for online drug trading? *Addiction, 109*(4), 517–518.

van der Gouwe, D., Brunt, T. M., van Laar, M., & van der Pol, P. (2017). Purity, adulteration and price of drugs bought on-line versus off-line in the Netherlands. *Addiction, 112*(4), 640–648. https://doi.org/10.1111/add.13720.

Yar, M. (2005). The novelty of 'cybercrime': An assessment in light of routine activity theory. *European Journal of Criminology, 2*(4), 407–427. https://doi.org/10.1177/147737080556056.

3

Fracturing Research in Splintering Digital Environments

The Internet Is More Mobile, More Ingrained and also More Fractured

> … so research methods mirror that, but they also have to sew things back together again.

The paradox of digital society is that the more commonplace the Internet has become, the less whole it is (Hine 2015). The data infrastructure is presented by its boosters as creating certainty and knowability (of one's health, frenemies, verified job skills) while in fact creating a radical incompleteness in the metric performance society (Beer 2016). Nobody can measure up to the shared ideal, or know exactly where they are in relationship to it. It is a deliberate choice in the way the data infrastructure has been created. It is both privatised (the data is owned by the private platforms that constitute most of the Internet), socialised (labour is distributed and labour processes organised through work platforms) and nationalised (governments seek to make it accessible to themselves). It creates new dangers (online revenge porn, harassment, leaking of personal data) and opportunities. It is more mobile than ever. Most of the hardware through which humanity logs

© The Author(s) 2020
A. Bancroft, *The Darknet and Smarter Crime*, Palgrave Studies
in Cybercrime and Cybersecurity, https://doi.org/10.1007/978-3-030-26512-0_3

in is designed to be untethered. It is also more tied-in, more identifying, and in the case of the non-human internet, with limited human ability to control it.

Illicit drug supply is arranged using the cryptomarkets, via Facebook, Instagram, Grindr or WeChat, or through Gumtree (Barratt and Aldridge 2016; Aldridge and Askew 2017; Yang and Luo 2017). These are processes involving buyers and users in platforms with very different capabilities and risks, some of which are shared by other platform users. Platforms allow for both open information flow and constraint simultaneously (Wang and Gu 2016). They can be sites for activism, dissent and production of new knowledge. They are also new sites for new forms of surveillance and policing of citizens, and systems through which the flow of information about illicit activity can be disrupted (Ladegaard 2018).

In a similar way, platforms generate new social research capacities such as the production of near real-time metrics and rapid analysis(Horton-Eddison and Cristofaro 2017). Cryptomarkets have been the object of many research innovations such as digital trace analysis (Aldridge and Décary-Hétu 2016a). One of the hoped for benefits of the internet was its capacity to support research with hard to reach groups who wish to remain anonymous (Coomber 1997a). Surveys can be delivered remotely, and respondents should be able to register their views and experiences with minimal fuss and risk. As the data processing capacity has grown, so has the seductive abundance of the data sphere. Digital platforms allow for the rapid production of massive data and the coordination of labour efforts, producing new collaborations such as crowdsourced citizen science (Giommoni and Gundur 2018). So: more contexts to study, more data about them, better ways of conducting research and more people contributing ideas, what can the problem be? One of the challenges is that the flow of data can obscure how it comes ready-structured and partial, the illusion of data completeness leads us to think that it can be theory free and the hard work of thinking through what we are seeing gets shunted out the door.

Reshaping Expertise in Social Research

A recurring theme is that digital disruption recreates and reaffirms as much as is erodes and disrupts. The contrast between the internet as affirming and recreating existing institutional and power structures, and freeing participants from them, is explored by Barratt et al. (2013). They account for the potential of digital services for information exchange by drug users and the limits on that which come from platform providers and state authorities. Drug user forums, threads and instant messaging services can be sites for challenges to expertise and expert authority where users can develop and disseminate shared understandings of drugs and drug-use practices (Boyer et al. 2007).

Local face-to-face drug markets often have restricted information flow, though it is rare for them to be entirely without it. Users compare and share experiences and drugs from different supplies. Internet and darknet forums allow drug users to share and compare across a much greater range of substances and user-experiences (van Hout and Bingham 2014). They have emerged to address the need for drug users to have information about what they are consuming. The popular harm reduction focused forum Bluelight started from a message board for MDMA users and grew into a comprehensive discussion forum and reference point. One spinout, Pillreports, compiles user reports, drug alerts and test data on ecstasy. The sites are largely volunteer run and provide a peer harm reduction approach which is more responsive, less stigmatising and more trusted than many official sources (Bilgrei 2019).

There is however a constant threat to various sites for drug users in the form of expanding internet regulation. There is a growing body of regulatory practice that compels platforms and service providers to regulate who uses their services and what they contain. In the case of Australia, service providers can be compelled by the Australian Communications and Media Authority to block sites hosting instructions on illicit drug use. That could in theory mean users could not access harm reduction information. That has not come to pass, thought it remains a possibility. In 2018 Reddit banned its largest darknet discussion forums, telling users that the subreddits were 'banned due to a violation of Reddit's policy against transactions involving prohibited goods or services'. The subreddits r/beertrade and r/shoplifting also fell foul. Third-party regulation is now the norm. The UK Digital Economy Act 2017 compelled pornography hosting sites to introduce age verification checks for UK-based users on the grounds of protecting children from adult content. The provisions are expected to come into force in 2019. The precedent could be used in other ways, for instance to restrict who accesses places where safer injecting practice is discussed. Generally these changes make the internet more confined, increasing the demands on users to validate who they are. Requiring personal identification is also a barrier to access because it can make users reluctant to identify themselves. It also contributes to the digital divide by only permitting those who have verifiable ID to make use of some sites (Gangadharan 2017).

The internet is personalised, customised and responsive, which gives the impression of something completely fluid, especially in the urban West where many users are used to unlimited bandwidth. Underlying it is hardware, and the obdurate fact that it is all is happening on someone else's computer. Virtual private networks and Tor routers all exist in real space. In the developing world, mobile airtime is often the only way to get online and is costly and narrow. Internet space is bumpy, lumpy and corrugated ground. In part it is a digital extension of other institutions such as the mass media, states, corporations, education systems and others, looping from the open web to the internet of things (Sadowski and Pasquale 2015). There is a range of technologies, social systems and cultural patterns that work through infrastructures and platforms that are sometimes shared and sometimes distinct or incompatible. Citizens around the world can have access to parts of the 'splinternet' and to various services blocked or redirected by private or state geo-locking (Ananthaswamy 2011). The fractured internet creates and distributes visibility and invisibility (Bucher 2012), and varied accessibility. Platformisation affects criminal activity in the same way. Drugs flow through platforms, as much as markets (Dittus et al. 2017) meaning a more rapid responsiveness to consumer signals, and innovation in drug types and forms (Gilbert and Dasgupta 2017).

In China much online communication and commerce takes place through the WeChat platform, easily exposing drug users to police surveillance (Qiang 2019). Responding to the enforced lack of privacy of the modern internet are new privacy-focused communities and philosophies

(Lewis 2017). Technological solutions will not be supportable by themselves. They require meaningful communities of practice to support them (Dodd 2018). There were expectations that the Tor darknet would mean the emergence of sites unreachable by government censorship. These sites are often impermanent due to shaky hosting infrastructure and fractious relationships between administrators and rivals (Bancroft and Scott Reid 2017). Drug users have to reformulate and recreate communities when the underlying infrastructure provides to be impermanent, as when Reddit threads are closed or darknet discussion forums collapse.

As well as digital environments being a location for data collection and recruitment, they constitute a set of spaces that produce and reinforce subject and researcher sensibilities. There are three ways this works. In ontological terms, digital methods integrate user, dealer and researcher identities into a machine assemblage (Fox and Alldred 2015). Human agency is shaped and constructed by software, hardware, communication platforms, data commodification, algorithmic assessments of individuals and internet regulation and oversight (Noble 2018). In epistemological terms, there are extensive hidden process and effects. For example, web scraping is now a widespread method used by researchers, marketers and law enforcement agencies, which can collect very large amounts of near real-time data (Marres and Weltevrede 2013). It can give the appearance of completeness rather than the reality. Twitter's public APIs deliver up 1% of the Twitter stream unless the researcher has access to the main 'firehose' which usually has to be paid for and conducted under the governance of Twitter (Morstatter et al. 2013). Which 1% the researcher sees is up to the platform algorithms. A complete dataset is also often unmanageable, requiring excessive amounts of human and computational labour to process (Smith et al. 2017). On the one hand, digital methods allow a much greater scale and reach of method. On the other, researchers fear drowning in the theory-less big data swamp. Yet, alongside these methodological and theoretical challenges, researchers have developed methods that tell us much more about drug use than would be possible otherwise, and build new research norms around open participation where drug users and others take a role in defining what is said for and about them (Barratt and Lenton 2010). Finally, the location of expertise is changed. Social scientists have always researched users who are experts in their lives and are experts in the significance of what they are doing. Increasingly users are also able to take on the role of public expert, influencing scientifc and public discussions about drug use and drug markets.

Questioning Scientific Hierarchies

The production of massive sets of naturally occurring data, and the growing informational savvy of drug user communities lead us to question the classical hierarchies of social science. One is the value of particular kinds of data, the other is who is producing and declaiming on knowledge. To take the first, Barratt et al. (2017) assess the automatic assignment of non-probability survey research to a lower place in the social science pecking order and the valorisation of randomness in the sample. They use the example of the Global Drug Survey (GDS), an annual global online distributed non-probability survey (Winstock et al. 2018). It is particularly oriented to non-treatment drug users. It provides relatively fast results which are of use to the drug using population. There is a high degree of buy-in from drug using populations which makes GDS something of an annual event. Population surveys have biases stemming from low response rates and invisible self-selection, which it takes effort to correct, if at all possible. There is a declining response to traditional methods, which challenges how meaningful and representative population datasets are (Czajka and Beyler 2016).

The Global Drug Survey has shown the efficiency of contemporary drug delivery. 58.7% of 15,000 cocaine using respondents had cocaine delivered to them, 30.3% of those within 30 minutes—faster than most pizza deliveries. Surveys like this can vastly expand the numbers and range of people taking part and engage otherwise invisible research subjects. It allows methods to be highly responsive, asking about new drugs and new ways of obtaining them. It provides new modes of dissemination, through its media and social partnerships.

The online survey works well when it both addresses and affirms a public of interested research users as much as a population. The Global Cannabis Cultivation Research Consortium's survey of domestic cannabis growers worked in this way. Researchers made themselves available to potential respondents on drug-related forums, answering questions about anonymity, the purpose of the study, and its potential uses in relation to prohibition reform (Barratt et al. 2017). Potential participants had varied responses, some sceptical, some positive about the need for reliable knowledge about cannabis growing. The researchers noted the value of a proven track record of past research to point to in order to themselves as independent.

The second issue is the politics of knowledge production. Online methods can give us a model for democratic ownership of the research process and findings. But it also means we have to consider whether we should operate with a gold standard of research and what that might be. Basing informed consent in a discussion about the purpose of the research widens the conversation about research and expertise, where the research population is invited to be part of a dialogue about their experiences and practices (Decorte et al. 2019). One aspect is practical. Many online research projects can be conducted at a lower cost than household surveys so can be relatively independent of governments and state funding bodies. They then do not have to make the same performative claims about 'the problem'. This is useful when dealing with a politically controversial or stigmatised topic where the temptation for political interference is irresistible and where research becomes part of a policy political economy (Stevens 2011). Originally, population surveys were derived from a governing idea that the human population needs to be marshalled and managed, and an epidemiological idea about contagion and disease spread (Curtis 2002). Online methods can allow for egalitarian understandings of expertise and knowledge to be developed.

There is still a baseline assumption about what a normal population looks like which is static and this is becoming dated in a world of high immigration, precarious employment and mobility. It also means we have a built in assumption about what normality is, usually settled and middle class. This is particularly a problem with drug users where there are large hidden populations. On the other hand, online methods are biased towards those who are able and wiling to participate in the digital environment. There is then a continued role for traditional survey and other face-to-face methods due to the digital divide which limits the participation of many groups in the population, and the way in which digital platforms produce, distort and select data to their own or their owners' ends.

New Data Types and Combinations

One of the opportunities digital methods make easier is the way that different data types can be usefully correlated and triangulated. Forensic methods can be correlated with cryptomarket data using chemical testing of a sample of products (Caudevilla et al. 2016; Rhumorbarbe et al. 2016). It allows researchers to assess whether claims made about drug quality are accurate and whether vendors and buyers have a good sense of what they are exchanging. Doing so punctures some myths held with equal fervour by buyers, sellers and the public (Coomber 1997b). Researchers can use the data infrastructure to combine objective and interpretive data. In many of these environments, users are doing the exact same thing, testing products and posting their findings for others to read and also discussing ontological questions about the boundaries of different drug categories (Orsolini et al. 2015).

A question posed by the use of digital methods is whether different forms of digital data map onto or challenge traditional social science taxonomies and concepts of what constitutes data. Drug user discussions that take place online can be modelled using automated natural language processing (Cameron et al. 2013). However, data can be highly idiomatic as in the use of emojis to represent drugs by dealers who use apps (Moyle et al. 2019). Apps allow for 'visual' dealing and displays of quality, whereas researchers may be used to textual or numerical analysis and the tools used are adapted to that. Even there we cannot assume a fixed meaning to textual data. Language changes quickly and online groups may develop fast changing insider terminologies.

Naturally occurring taxonomies may be handy, or they may be misleading. Mobile apps have clear attractions for drug users and dealers, being immediately available in communication platforms that users will be using anyway (Thanki and Frederick 2016). They do not have the technical barriers of cryptomarkets nor the risks and learning curve required when using cryptocurrencies. App use is a case where the platform invites new behaviours. Apps like Snapchat allow dealers to spamvertise products by searching for threads discussing drugs and posting in them. As in other settings, the platform my be designed to inflate numbers regarding usage and throughput. Extensive effort must be put into de-duplication and data cleaning (Boyd and Crawford 2011). Data inflation is not just data noise, it tells us about the motives of platform designers and administrators and the problems encountered by users who like us are trying to identify signal from noise.

Aldridge and Décary-Hétu (2014, 2016b) examined the language Silk Road cryptomarket vendors were using and noted their presentation and pricing was characteristic of people expecting to sell in large quantities to other dealers. They note that drugs sold tend to be the 'recreational' ones (cannabis, psychedelics and ecstasy) rather than the 'chaotic' ones (heroin, methamphetamine, crack cocaine) and posit some reasons why that might be. One is that Silk Road evolved from a skilled, recreational, retail market and did not pick up these buyers. Another is that many vendors of crack cocaine and methamphetamine are also producers so they may buy precursors such as powder cocaine online to cook up into their final product. By studying the amounts typically sold in each transaction, the authors were able to make claims about is closely the length of the supply chain. Synthetic drugs and cannabis, which can be usually manufactured locally, were those most likely to be available wholesale. Cocaine and opiate derived drugs have longer supply chains with more steps in manufacture. Cryptomarkets cannot support the lab/hydroponic garden to dealer supply chain represented by the ecstasy/cannabis supply chain and so were sold in smaller quantities. This indicated that the cryptomarket was being used by middle level drug dealers to supply opiate consumers.

The analysis is effective because infers the relationship rather than assumes that bulk sales exist beyond a particular threshold. Dealers are going to be asking about specifics and vendors will present their listings in ways that reflect the needs of dealers. In addition there was a large drug precursor market on Silk Road. They noted that many bulk listings were likely to be private listings so not available to them so there is an incalculable dark figure that cannot be assessed just from the public data. The categories set by the market administrators and understood by the vendors might not be the ones we want to use and we do not want to rely on their decision-making nous either. However as data, indigenous categories can signify a great deal. Some drugs are sold in terms of 'doses' while others such as the artificial opiate fentanyl can be and are sold to be re-dosed. Fentanyl is potent so a 'bulk' purchase might be relatively small.

In data scraping, there is a standard technical structure (what, how often, how much, how extensive) and a theoretical structure (does it match the platform's structure or our analytical structure?). It leads to technical and epistemological questions such as whether we use site metadata our impose our own metadata structuring using timestamps, location data, and other meta data markers. Making sense of the large amounts of data involved need us to make scalable tools to interpret it and those involve design choices.

Ethics and Politics in the Data Infrastructure

It is possible to obtain a lot of data from social media and other internet sites without quite knowing why it says what it says. A social media aggregator may produce metadata whose source is opaque. For example, when it says that one user is based in the UK, is that inferred from geolocation information, from behavioural information (they put the kettle on at 5 pm), or associational logic (they studiously avoid talking about anything rancorous)? Choices made in the design of discussion forums might seem inconsequential but make an impact on how people interact. For example, if a discussion forum simply presents the most recent post first, or the most popular post at the top, that shapes discussion and who is promoted as an expert in that setting. In the case of Facebook it now seeks to promote the highest quality posts over others—a contentious assessment to be applied to information with great political relevance. There has been a decline of 'the search engine' as the source of information. More and more sites are only internally searchable, and users browse through surfacing rather than searching. Information may be equally available to all, but it is not equally accessible.

Illicit drug research faces boundaries of politics and legality (Sandberg and Copes 2013). Some methods such as collecting forensic and market data are only possible in jurisdictions which allow for research exemptions to drug prohibition. There are other changes that have happened in the politics online research such as the fall and rise of the gatekeepers. Given the amount of public data, researchers involve user communities much more easily without needing the nod from trusted insiders. Instead we have the invisible gatekeepers, Twitter editors, algorithms, forum moderators and reCaptchas that inhibit scraping. It is an interdependent research infrastructure. We are pulling at the same algorithmically constituted threads, hence the need for some research that is wholly independent of the platforms being studied. More positively there are many non-academic researchers who produce and share a vast amount of data and insight (Branwen 2015; Lewis 2017), part of a process where social science is less and less the property of a professional class.

There is a growing problem of access. One of the benefits of online methods is that we can research anonymously and that respondents have a greater capacity to set the terms of their engagement in research. People seek anonymity to protect from stigmatisation and criminalisation, but on the other hand anonymity may not be as secure as they think. Barratt (2011) makes a distinction between technical and social anonymity, which will be explored later. The former is less secure than assumed due to the qualities of social media platforms, the Bitcoin blockchain, and the growing capacity of analysts to fingerprint and link individuals.

The ability to gather data unobtrusively is a benefit and a temptation. Researchers may be working with dichotomies of public and private, identifiable and anonymous, consent and refusal that do not transfer well to in digital settings (Chiauzzi and Wicks 2019). It might mean taking advantage of users' assumptions about the kind of protection the digital infrastructure offers their privacy, which is in practice very little. Social media data may be accessible, but that does not mean users think of it as public property for researchers to mine at will (Williams et al. 2017). De-anonymising is easily done, deliberately or accidentally. A range of stakeholders have to be considered, from big platforms to small community groupings and private site owners. Meaningful involvement takes time for the researchers to become known and accepted. Some steps can be taken protect people who participate in online forums from identification through searches, paraphrasing the quotes from them at the risk of losing some felicity (Aldridge and Askew 2017). The principle is that the users' pseudonymous identities should be protected along with their real ones.

This brings us to a new concept of what subject identity is and what should be protected. This might include pseudonymous online profiles, which are also of value and meaning to them. It also leads me to question some of the normative assumptions about who and what constitutes the research subject. For example, when collecting data through interviews we assume that people are primarily interacting in a conversational, question and answer world, or see that as the primary mode of interacting. In digital environments, people may interact sporadically over a longer period of time but see it as part of the same conversation, while they conduct many other interactions with others. Conversations can last days, with long breaks as the interviewee engages in other activity (Barratt 2012). The baseline assumption in social research about continuous person-to-person interaction as the defining mode of interaction does not necessarily hold, particularly when many digital interactions are person to machine, or machine to machine. Much internet traffic is non-human, to the point where it is the human which stands out as suspicious (Read 2018).

End of the Online

The once hoped for model of cyberspace as a separate entity governed by its own democratically decided rules is now looked back on as hopelessly naïve (Thomas 2006). There is sometimes little point making a direct distinction between on and offline. Mobile apps facilitate digitally mediated local markets and so alert us to the fact that the online and offline are indistinct. In those cases, dealer and buyer still mostly need to meet in person to exchange. Cryptomarkets mediate rather than replace offline supply chains (Aldridge and Décary-Hétu 2016b). Existing open-air markets are facilitated by the exchange of information via mobile devices, messaging services which use the internet. There is little distinction to users between using a messaging app and texting, though each may use a different infrastructure. For the most part, people are rarely offline, and even when they are not directly connected are still held within a lattice of digitally enabled, connected devices and platforms. The digital can be the site of effective, knowledge producing, information sharing, harm reducing communities (Davey et al. 2012). For most users, however, the importance of digital life is how it reconfigures the relationships between those involved in drug communities and markets and the means through which they interact, share, and evaluate (Tzanetakis et al. 2016).

In addition to the digital not being a distinct sphere, it is also not everywhere in the same way. In the developing word, the ubiquitous mobile internet does not fully substitute for the absence or patchy availability of a fixed service. The physical availability of good fibre optic cable and short range wifi makes for a more reliable, effective and cheaper internet. In many parts of the world people have to rely on limited and costly cellular broadband. Infrastructure is important in how people interact with digital services and spaces. Increasingly people have no choice but to interact with these services and conduct their work and finances through them, so the digital reproduces unbalanced power relations. In part that explains why the cryptomarkets are relatively localised to Western countries. Drug producers in South America, Afghanistan and other places cannot replicate the supply chain through the internet and have little incentive to when there are well established trafficking systems.

The digital also produces new ambiguities, such as between legal and illegal, and between healthy and unhealthy. Users of study drugs in Western countries rely on semi-legal websites to buy modafinil, ritalin, adderall and other psychostimulant pharmaceuticals, following at the pattern established by the earlier availability legal highs (Bruneel et al. 2014). The site owners rely on deliberate ambiguity about the legality of making regulated drugs available in this way. Contributors to internet forums challenge the idea that drug use is automatically incompatible with good health. In both instances, users are moving beyond the binary oppositions that have in the past informed research and governance. Digital life facilities this, both practically and conceptually. This is a challenge for drug research and for sociology more widely. There is little of social life that is not digitally mediated, and many previously unmediated aspects of social life have moved into the digital sphere, making their processes sometimes invisible to previously effective methods.

The Network and the Limits of Metaphor

In research, metaphors are good to think with. Society as organism, or pressure cooker; interaction as script, or game. A common one is the 'network', which serves as metaphor, normative statement (networks are good!), as a claim about inherent qualities of the unit of analysis, analytical frame and methodological approach. Networks are generally defined by the density, quality and distribution of their social ties, which are thought to be loose, reformable, impermanent and in contrast to hierarchal organisations. The nature of the network is that it is a relationship independent of the individuals and whatever is being transferred through it. One cannot substitute 'love' easily but one can substitute a network position for another person. The characteristic of a network is whether you can substitute within it and whether it is person or node independent. Any network relying on a specific node or individual is not really a network. This means that increasing parts of the internet are not networks. However, offline trafficking groups often have ethnic homogeneity for practical reasons. Online groups might display greater heterogeneity as they are less place-dependent.

Metaphors mislead as they illustrate, as it becomes easy to frame everything in terms of a network. To temper default network-thinking there is criticism of the de-territorial, networked, battlespace drone warfare love of networks as a metaphor (Coward 2017). The 'network' justifies a lot and disguises much. The Facebook attention network grabs and holds attention with anything. It justifies not discussing values. Information integrity, impartial reporting and such are ruled out of the discussion because they have no network value. They are nice things to have, sure, but effectively do not exist in relation to network metrics. Network systems instead promote in-referencing and confirmation bias. Partly, the network image is just wrong. Networks are characterised as lacking geographic boundaries, not being hierarchal and being resilient and adaptable. Are they inherently those things? Those that survive by definition are going to be resilient but that might not be because they have those other qualities.

Network love is a good example of how we end up mixing methods and metaphors. Things appear networked so we do network analysis and then proclaim the fine, resilient and adaptable qualities that these networks have. Then we do more network analysis on the assumption that the objects of our study actually are networks. Perhaps they are best approached as dyadic interactions, or organisations, or territories. Researchers are arguably a bit guilty of using the network to substitute for theorising interaction. Even predatory criminals like to have repeat relationships with their victims. They know the difficulty of finding a new 'customer' versus the easy of keeping an old one. The ransomware supply chain relies on this. It needs trust between criminal and victim. The victim must trust that paying the money will get their files back (Cusack and Ward 2018). The criminal must trust that the victim has the ability to use the payment system they have set up.

Phrenology was the first big data-based crime study. The data world means that that ere is a constant stream of data, and people are dealt with as collections of data points rather than individual subjects. Social media is just one of the more tangible data collation infrastructures that define us, but there is a far more intricate infrastructure of censoring objects, inbuilt monitors, connected pacemakers, breathalysers and the like (French and Smith 2016). There are interrelated developments that shape the data assemblage. Insights from neuroscience show that the mind is a material entity and that interpretive, cognitive activity is spread throughout the body. The eye 'thinks', the stomach 'feels'. Artificial intelligence transfers decision-making functions to machine algorithms, drawing on datafied sensory input. Non-human systems make decisions. There is a growing range of automatic crime using non-human systems—botnets, bots and so on. A troll using bots to flood a target's social media account with abuse is extending his or her capacity for harm by using the data infrastructure.

This matters because of interception, detection, sanctioning increasingly bypass due process and criminal justice methods. Remotely taking down a botnet is done without any warrant or process, which would in any case not be feasible. An assemblage could be a drone-computer-operator weapons system, territory the legal and technologically bounded area over which it has an effect Much regulation is private, through Twitter or the payment infrastructure, which happily throws off people and organisations to protect the brand. The power vested in private hands is significant. Twitter gets to decide what is hate speech and bans people on that basis.

How This Changes What We Study

What do we mean by big data? Big data has qualities of connected-ness and identification that large volumes of data do not. True big data produce data profiles of individuals which can be used to predict their preferences and identify connections between individuals (Smith et al. 2017). Some people are data poor and unable to get credit or sign a contract because of it, so the relentless datafication of society is not all bad. It just allows power to work again through a turbo-charged data system. The social credit score being developed in China sounds totalitarian but the credit score that exists in the USA is similarly configured. These systems are seldom wholly novel.

The concept of culture in relation to illicit drug use has often been used to talk about subcultures or youth cultures as in popular culture, dance culture, grime culture, or that of non-western indigenous groups. Culture in that sense means something apart from the rest of society, whereas I want to use it to understand how culture suffuses society and the illicit, from the digital to the economic, and from the illicit to the normal. I argue that intoxication is designed into drugs and drug-use places which increasingly are shared with and draw on licit leisure, treatment and work cultures. The way I frame this is as intoxication as an assemblage of algorithmic culture.

An algorithm is a set of instructions which respond to inputs and reach an outcome. Globally, societies are increasingly algorithmic, governed by digital and paper instructions, increasingly opaque and impenetrable (Dourish 2016). In considering how we can understand illicit intoxications in the algorithmic age, I consider how many of their cultural functions are embedded in algorithms, in software or hardware. Intoxicants are analogue algorithms, a set of chemical instructions for body and self, the hardware and software of intoxication. They operate in the same sense that camera film is an algorithm. The chemistry is set to respond to certain kinds of inputs in designed in ways, responding differently to light and shade, skin tones and colours. Drugs have these designed in qualities, designed for particular bodies or averages of bodies, or psyches. Drugs embed expectations about pleasure, pain, risk and enhancement. Like algorithms, they interpret and produce knowledge.

As with digital algorithms, they are complex and not pre-determined, and in a similar way intoxication is produced but not determined by culture. They are intricate, rich lattices of objects, habits and sensory experiences out of and into which humans weave our symbolic, cultural, economic and social lives. For their ability to meld the physical, the social, the cultural and the psychological into one simple package, intoxicants have a special place in this. They are chemical substances to which the ability to change the relationship between self and environment are attributed. They are powerful mediators of social life. Among its algorithmic effects, intoxication changes or stabilises the relationship between world and self (Hunt and Frank 2016). It does so in ways that are symbolic, cultural, psychological and material (Duff 2014).

The illicit is a structural factor which looms large in all these aspects, part of what Duff (2011) called its 'enabling place'. The illicit is part of the place of intoxication, in prisons, in courtrooms, in pubs, clubs, underpasses, streets and private homes, criminalising intoxication but also enabling it, producing the place for it. The illicit is present in the difference between prescribed, legitimised diamorphine and illicit heroin. The illicit is often presented in binary terms. There are illicit drugs and then there is everything else. What there is in practice is an overlapping set of regulations and controls which criminalise some intoxication contexts and legitimate others. Law itself is algorithmic, a set of conditions and instructions that define rather than solve problems. Cannabis is legal in Uruguay and Canada, but possession will incur severe legal and social penalties in Sweden and China. The African drug crop is dominated by khat which is sometimes legal but always dubious social status along with cannabis which is everywhere illegal but is ubiquitous and quasi-legal (Carrier and Klantschnig 2017).

As well as more variety in legal controls of drugs, and the grey zone of quasi-legality, regulation of the illicit is more and more a hybrid between public and private, criminal and regulatory, and punitive and reformatory. Schools, employers and universities run drug tests and produce both sanctions and data to be fed into systems governed by other algorithms. So there is a burgeoning set of regulatory modes governing intoxication that might technically be illicit but are not directly criminalised. A growing trend is towards non-human governance, as in the Chinese social credit system.

Research for This Book

This book draws on interrelated projects involving qualitative and quantitative analysis of cryptomarket users' views and experiences, and data on market resilience and failure. Data were collected through scraping discussion forums, interviews with market users, and collection of market information on products sold, prices and branding. I supplemented this with interviews with darknet users and diaries from people who used drugs, conducted by myself and Peter Scott Reid. I am very grateful to Peter for his work and insight.

One of the problems researchers have found is identifying who knows what. A simple but incomplete answer is to ask those involved. However, what market organisers and dealers say about themselves is often incomplete. They will usually have good day-to-day intelligence about their operations. Coomber's (1997b) work showed how drug dealers were not the final experts on what they sold, or the markets they were a part of. One dealer cut drugs (badly) because he thought that was what you did; he didn't particularly want to. Thus criminals do not necessarily give superior insider accounts, because they often do not know what is going on.

Interviewing people who used the cryptomarkets, I found they shared an interest in the research agenda and often saw themselves as contributing to and shaping it. They are knowledgable participants. One had compiled a far more extensive library than I had covering pharmacology, ethics and sociology. Others sought to understand the dynamics of the cryptomarkets and how new drugs filtered onto them from the offline market. There was a keen awareness of the different contexts which shaped the markets: drug prohibition, the capacity of law enforcement, competition between markets and financial incentives, and the operation of power in the internet.

People are not dumb and they know what the well-meaning researcher wants them to say about their lives: that we are all basically good people and that some of us end up in bad situations. That story is not invalid but it is not the whole story at all. People in these circumstances are the authors of their own lives, though their circumstances are constrained by factors they cannot control. One of the advantages of ethnography when it is well conducted is that it cuts through that public story. The public story is not in itself untrue but separated from the context of people's lives it becomes misleading.

Conclusion

Drug users and dealers took to the digital rather faster than researchers did, and are also more aware of the limits of new digital platforms. In past decades, deals were conducted by Internet Relay Chat (as they still are), pager, then mobile phones, and now through mobile apps and darknet cryptomarkets. In the process, there is a growing ecosystem of drug dealing and information production happening on or through digital devices and platforms. The role of researchers is more than being bystanders that tap into that datastream as and when they like. Researchers who work with the digital are also working with and responding to emerging and maturing digital communities. Increasingly, research priorities are set in conjunction with them. These communities inhabit various digital spaces, whether a relatively fleeting and pared down Grindr or Tinder account, or a richer and more developed cryptomarket forum. They have varying degrees of entanglement with the material world. Increasingly our methods will reflect and recreate that entanglement as the space in which drug users and dealers inhabit.

References

Aldridge, J., & Askew, R. (2017). Delivery dilemmas: How drug cryptomarket users identify and seek to reduce their risk of detection by law enforcement. *International Journal of Drug Policy, 41*(Suppl. C), 101–109. https://doi.org/10.1016/j.drugpo.2016.10.010.

Aldridge, J., & Décary-Hétu, D. (2014). *Not an 'e-Bay for drugs': The cryptomarket 'Silk Road' as a paradigm shifting criminal innovation.* Rochester, NY: Social Science Research Network.

Aldridge, J., & Décary-Hétu, D. (2016a). Hidden wholesale: The drug diffusing capacity of online drug cryptomarkets. *International Journal of Drug Policy, 35,* 7–15. https://doi.org/10.1016/j.drugpo.2016.04.020.

Aldridge, J., & Décary-Hétu, D. (2016b). Cryptomarkets and the future of illicit drug markets. In *Internet and drug markets, EMCDDA insights* (pp. 23–30). Luxembourg: Publications Office of the European Union.

Ananthaswamy, A. (2011). Age of the splinternet. *New Scientist, 211*(2821), 42–45.

Bancroft, A., & Scott Reid, P. (2017). Challenging the techno-politics of anonymity: The case of cryptomarket users. *Information, Communication & Society, 20*(4), 497–512. https://doi.org/10.1080/1369118X.2016.1187643.

Barratt, M. J. (2011). Discussing illicit drugs in public internet forums: Visibility, stigma, and pseudonymity. In *Proceedings of the 5th International Conference on Communities and Technologies* (pp. 159–168). https://doi.org/10.1145/2103354.2103376.

Barratt, M. J. (2012). The efficacy of interviewing young drug users through online chat. *Drug and Alcohol Review, 31*(4), 566–572.

Barratt, M. J., & Aldridge, J. (2016). Everything you always wanted to know about drug cryptomarkets* (*but were afraid to ask). *International Journal of Drug Policy, 35,* 1–6. https://doi.org/10.1016/j.drugpo.2016.07.005.

Barratt, M. J., Ferris, J. A., Zahnow, R., Palamar, J. J., Maier, L. J., & Winstock, A. R. (2017). Moving on from representativeness: Testing the utility of the global drug survey. *Substance Abuse: Research and Treatment, 11.* https://doi.org/10.1177/1178221817716391.

Barratt, M. J., & Lenton, S. (2010). Beyond recruitment? Participatory online research with people who use drugs. *International Journal of Internet Research Ethics, 3*(1), 69–86.

Barratt, M. J., Lenton, S., & Allen, M. (2013). Internet content regulation, public drug websites and the growth in hidden internet services. *Drugs: Education, Prevention and Policy, 20*(3), 195–202. https://doi.org/10.3109/09687637.2012.745828.

Beer, D. (2016). *Metric power.* London: Palgrave Macmillan.

Bilgrei, O. R. (2019). Community-consumerism: Negotiating risk in online drug communities. *Sociology of Health & Illness, 41*(5), 852–866.

Boyd, D., & Crawford, K. (2011). Six provocations for big data. In *A Decade in Internet Time: Symposium on the Dynamics of the Internet and Society* (Vol. 21). Oxford, UK: Oxford Internet Institute.

Boyer, E. W., Lapen, P. T., Macalino, G., & Hibberd, P. L. (2007). Dissemination of psychoactive substance information by innovative drug users. *CyberPsychology & Behavior, 10*(1), 1–6. https://doi.org/10.1089/cpb.2006.9999.

Branwen, G. (2015). *Silk Road: Theory & practice.* Retrieved from http://www.gwern.net/Silk%20Road.

Bruneel, C.-A., Lakhdar, C. B., & Vaillant, N. G. (2014). Are "legal highs" users satisfied? Evidence from online customer comments. *Substance Use and Misuse, 49*(4), 364–373. https://doi.org/10.3109/10826084.2013.841243.

Bucher, T. (2012). Want to be on the top? Algorithmic power and the threat of invisibility on Facebook. *New Media & Society, 14*(7), 1164–1180. https://doi.org/10.1177/1461444812440159.

Cameron, D., Smith, G. A., Daniulaityte, R., Sheth, A. P., Dave, D., Chen, L., et al. (2013). PREDOSE: A semantic web platform for drug abuse epidemiology using social media. *Journal of Biomedical Informatics, 46*(6), 985–997. https://doi.org/10.1016/j.jbi.2013.07.007.

Carrier, N., & Klantschnig, G. (2017). Quasilegality: Khat, cannabis and Africa's drug laws. *Third World Quarterly, 39*(2), 1–16. https://doi.org/10.1080/01436597.2017.1368383.

Caudevilla, F., Ventura, M., Fornís, I., Barratt, M. J., Vidal, C., lladanosa, C. G., et al. (2016). Results of an international drug testing service for cryptomarket users. *International Journal of Drug Policy.* http://dx.doi.org/10.1016/j.drugpo.2016.04.017.

Chiauzzi, E., & Wicks, P. (2019). Digital trespass: Ethical and terms-of-use violations by researchers accessing data from an online patient community. *Journal of Medical Internet Research, 21*(2), e11985. https://doi.org/10.2196/11985.

Coomber, R. (1997a). Dangerous drug adulteration—An international survey of drug dealers using the internet and the World Wide Web (WWW). *International Journal on Drug Policy, 8,* 71–81.

Coomber, R. (1997b). The adulteration of drugs: What dealers do to illicit drugs, and what they think is done to them. *Addiction Research and Theory, 5*(4), 297–306.

Coward, M. (2017). Against network thinking: A critique of pathological sovereignty. *European Journal of International Relations.* https://doi.org/10.1177/1354066117705704.

Curtis, B. (2002). *The politics of population: State formation, statistics, and the census of Canada, 1840–1875.* Toronto: University of Toronto Press.

Cusack, B., & Ward, G. (2018). *Points of failure in the ransomware electronic business model.* Twenty-fourth Americas Conference on Information Systems. New Orleans.

Czajka, J. L., & Beyler, A. (2016). *Declining response rates in federal surveys: Trends and implications (background paper)* (Mathematica Policy Research).

Davey, Z., Schifano, F., Corazza, O., Deluca, P., & Psychonaut Web Mapping Group. (2012). e-Psychonauts: Conducting research in online drug forum communities. *Journal of Mental Health, 21*(4), 386–394. https://doi.org/10.3109/09638237.2012.682265.

Decorte, T., Malm, A., Sznitman, S. R., Hakkarainen, P., Barratt, M. J., Potter, G. R., et al. (2019). The challenges and benefits of analyzing feedback comments in surveys: Lessons from a cross-national online survey of small-scale cannabis growers. *Methodological Innovations, 12*(1). https://doi.org/10.1177/2059799119825606.

Dittus, M., Wright, J., & Graham, M. (2017). *Platform criminalism: The 'last-mile' geography of the darknet market supply chain.* ArXiv: 1712.10068 [Cs]. Retrieved from http://arxiv.org/abs/1712.10068.

Dodd, N. (2018). The social life of bitcoin. *Theory, Culture & Society, 35*(3), 35–56. https://doi.org/10.1177/0263276417746464.

Dourish, P. (2016). Algorithms and their others: Algorithmic culture in context. *Big Data & Society, 3*(2). https://doi.org/10.1177/2053951716665128.

Duff, C. (2011). Networks, resources and agencies: On the character and production of enabling places. *Health & Place, 17*(1), 149–156. https://doi.org/10.1016/j.healthplace.2010.09.012.

Duff, C. (2014). The place and time of drugs. *International Journal of Drug Policy, 25*(3), 633–639. https://doi.org/10.1016/j.drugpo.2013.10.014.

Fox, N. J., & Alldred, P. (2015). Inside the research-assemblage: New materialism and the micropolitics of social inquiry. *Sociological Research Online, 20*(2), 1–19. https://doi.org/10.5153/sro.3578.

French, M., & Smith, G. J. (2016). Surveillance and embodiment: Dispositifs of capture. *Body & Society, 22,* 3–27. https://doi.org/10.1177/1357034x16643169.

Gangadharan, S. P. (2017). The downside of digital inclusion: Expectations and experiences of privacy and surveillance among marginal internet users. *New Media & Society, 19*(4), 597–615. https://doi.org/10.1177/1461444815614053.

Gilbert, M., & Dasgupta, N. (2017). Silicon to syringe: Cryptomarkets and disruptive innovation in opioid supply chains. *International Journal of Drug Policy, 46,* 160–167. https://doi.org/10.1016/j.drugpo.2017.05.052.

Giommoni, L., & Gundur, R. V. (2018). An analysis of the United Kingdom's cannabis market using crowdsourced data. *Global Crime, 19*(2), 85–106. https://doi.org/10.1080/17440572.2018.1460071.

Hine, C. (2015). *Ethnography for the internet: Embedded, embodied and everyday.* London: Bloomsbury Academic.

Horton-Eddison, M., & Cristofaro, M. D. (2017). *Hard interventions and innovation in crypto-drug markets: The escrow example.* Swansea: Global Drug Policy Observatory.

Hunt, G., & Frank, V. A. (2016). Reflecting on intoxication. In T. Kolind, B. Thom, & G. Hunt (Eds.), *The SAGE handbook of drug and alcohol studies.* London: Sage.

Ladegaard, I. (2018). We know where you are, what you are doing and we will catch you: Testing deterrence theory in digital drug markets. *The British Journal of Criminology, 58*(2), 414–433. https://doi.org/10.1093/bjc/azx021.

Lewis, S. J. (Ed.). (2017). *Queer privacy: Essays from the margins of society.* http://leanpub.com/queerprivacy.

Marres, N., & Weltevrede, E. (2013). Scraping the social? *Journal of Cultural Economy, 6*(3), 313–335. https://doi.org/10.1080/17530350.2013.772070.

Morstatter, F., Pfeffer, J., Liu, H., & Carley. K. M. (2013). Is the sample good enough? Comparing data from Twitter's streaming API with Twitter's firehose. In *Seventh International AAAI Conference on Weblogs and Social Media.*

Moyle, L., Childs, A., Coomber, R., & Barratt, M. J. (2019). #Drugsforsale: An exploration of the use of social media and encrypted messaging apps to supply and access drugs. *International Journal of Drug Policy, 63,* 101–110. https://doi.org/10.1016/j.drugpo.2018.08.005.

Noble, S. U. (2018). *Algorithms of oppression: How search engines reinforce racism.* New York: New York University Press.

Orsolini, L., Papanti, G., Francesconi, G., & Professor Schifano, F. (2015). 'Navigating in the virtual mind of the web': The E-psychonauts' profiling. *European Psychiatry, 30,* 1045. https://doi.org/10.1016/S0924-9338(15)30822-1.

Qiang, X. (2019). The road to digital unfreedom: President Xi's surveillance state. *Journal of Democracy, 30*(1), 53–67. https://doi.org/10.1353/jod.2019.0004.

Read, M. (2018). How much of the internet is fake? *Intelligencer.* Retrieved 7 January 2019, from http://nymag.com/intelligencer/2018/12/how-much-of-the-internet-isfake.html.

Rhumorbarbe, D., Staehli, L., Broséus, J., Rossy, Q., & Esseiva, P. (2016). Buying drugs on a darknet market: A better deal? Studying the online illicit drug market through the analysis of digital, physical and chemical data. *Forensic Science International, 267,* 173–182.

Sadowski, J., & Pasquale, F. A. (2015). *The Spectrum of control: A social theory of the smart city* (SSRN Scholarly Paper No. ID 2653860). Retrieved from Social Science Research Network website: https://papers.ssrn.com/abstract= 2653860.

Sandberg, S., & Copes, H. (2013). Speaking with ethnographers: The challenges of researching drug dealers and offenders. *Journal of Drug Issues, 43*(2), 176–197.

Smith, G. J. D., Bennett Moses, L., & Chan, J. (2017). The challenges of doing criminology in the big data era: Towards a digital and data-driven approach. *The British Journal of Criminology, 57*(2), 259–274. https://doi.org/10.1093/bjc/azw096.

Stevens, A. (2011). *Drugs, crime and public health: The political economy of drug policy*. Abingdon: Routledge.

Thanki, D., & Frederick, B. J. (2016). Social media and drug markets. In *Internet and drug markets* (pp. 115–123). Luxembourg: Publications Office of the European Union.

Thomas, S. (2006). The end of cyberspace and other surprises. *Convergence, 12*(4), 383–391. https://doi.org/10.1177/1354856506068316.

Tzanetakis, M., Kamphausen, G., Werse, B., & von Laufenberg, R. (2016). The transparency paradox: Building trust, resolving disputes and optimising logistics on conventional and online drugs markets. *International Journal of Drug Policy, 35*, 58–68. https://doi.org/10.1016/j.drugpo.2015.12.010.

Van Hout, M. C., & Bingham, T. (2014). Responsible vendors, intelligent consumers: Silk Road, the online revolution in drug trading. *International Journal of Drug Policy, 25*(2), 183–189. https://doi.org/10.1016/j.drugpo.2013.10.009.

Wang, X., & Gu, B. (2016). The communication design of WeChat: Ideological as well as technical aspects of social media. *Communication Design Quarterly Review, 4*(1), 23–35. https://doi.org/10.1145/2875501.2875503.

Williams, M. L., Burnap, P., & Sloan, L. (2017). Towards an ethical framework for publishing Twitter data in social research: Taking into account users' views. *Online Context and Algorithmic Estimation, Sociology, 51*(6), 1149–1168. https://doi.org/10.1177/0038038517708140.

Winstock, A., Barratt, M. J., Maier, L. J., & Ferris, J. A. (2018). *Global drug survey 2018: Key findings report*. London: Global Drug Survey.

Yang, X., & Luo, J. (2017). Tracking illicit drug dealing and abuse on Instagram using multimodal analysis. *ACM Transactions on Intelligent Systems and Technology, 8*(4), 1–58, 15. https://doi.org/10.1145/3011871.

4

Illicit Trades Are Political Economies

Security and Insecurity Are Distributed by the Nation State and Global Economy

The cybercrime economy is an entangled political economy, closely linked with other economies such as sex work, human trafficking, and regulatory corruption, which are themselves embedded in regimes of migration control, welfare and labour management (Kshetri 2010). It is natural that where there is money and power, there is corruption, whether it is a city council in a Scandinavian country or a border across one of the major global trafficking routes. Global, digital crime is part of an illegal political economy that could not happen without the involvement or tacit agreement of licit industries, political control over the means of violence in nation-state territories, the acquiescence of political actors and law enforcement or other regulatory forces, and the cultural validation of key players. High taxes in the UK on tobacco represent a lucrative source of criminal profits alongside low penalties and a cultural acceptance of smuggling as a service (Antonopoulos and Hall 2016). Among interviewed people who bought smuggled tobacco, users framed their decision as a partly political one in response to the power of the government to increase taxes on their

© The Author(s) 2020
A. Bancroft, *The Darknet and Smarter Crime*, Palgrave Studies
in Cybercrime and Cybersecurity, https://doi.org/10.1007/978-3-030-26512-0_4

habit in a way that the state would never have dared raise taxes on a more powerful group of consumers.

Crime is developing as a response to a fracturing national and international socio-economic order. Some of the changes that happened were not really avoidable. These changes are: a shift to a consumption-led, debt-fuelled, deindustrialised economy; a hollowing out of local, independent power centres and solidarities such as trade unions, associations and professions; and deregulation of certain approved power centres, mainly social media companies but also parts of a newly private security state (Davis 2011).

Various aspects of the global economy have fuelled digital crime. For example, Jamaican lotto scammers phone vulnerable or easily induced people typically in the USA with what is a common script in phone and email scams: 'you have won millions, we just need a fee from you to clear the amount into your bank account' (Newmeyer 2014). It nets a large amount of funds for criminal gangs on the island and feeds into other crime. Partly the rise of this scam was driven by growing successful targeting of the illicit drug trade. As drug gangs came under pressure from law enforcement, they sought safer havens for their money and resources. Scams are lower risk, and easily executed. The Jamaican scam industry is also an outgrowth of the call centres that cluster in Montego bay. Scams are not trouble free and rival scammers inflict violence on each other and on their victims who become ensnared with them (Hamilton 2017). Successful scammers pay attention to the existing cultural norms of what is means to be a top criminal and adopt a gangsta lifestyle (Blake 2018).

Social Trauma and Harm Geography

There is a geography of harm which affects people's resilience in the face of crime and other threats. Left-behind locales in the West and the developing world are emptied of core leadership, resource bearing, social capital rich people as those move outward and upward. There is a greater geographic sorting of human capital and problems tend to be more concentrated in some neighbourhoods. This could be seen as nasty old hyper-capitalism, or social meritocracy in action. Efforts to get the best and brightest from all shores mean the creation of pockets of those left out, this can be seen as a human capital problem where locales are denuded of their best for brighter vistas. There is also a significant cultural effect, as the development of world cities creates cultural blight spots where the full force of elite indiffence can be felt. Social trauma due to violence and atomisation of once viable communities lasts across generations. Those left standing end up with a dislike of collectivities or social obligations, and a preference for criminal activity among some (Hall et al. 2013). They embody that dreamy future of becoming a star or having 'respect' without any concrete plan to reach it, other than making other people's lives difficult (Bourgois 2003). People cannot just be called 'excluded'. There are people who entirely endorse an almost caricature of capitalist success from the outside and seek to realise its most bling manifestations through petty theft, drug dealing, low level cyber crime and the rest. On the other hand, many describe a trauma biography that shows how place and harm can be shared as in this market participant:

So anyway, things were going great, I was just out of high school and I was living the dream. After about 5 years, I had to leave the city I loved, and in leaving the city I left behind my connect to an endless supply of perc 10's i got for $5 each, among other lovers and friends. I moved back to my home town, and nobody there had any use for percs. They needed drugs more powerful, because, as I found out then, most opiate addicts don't take small amounts of opiates to feel great, they take large amounts to get fucked up and feel numb. So all I could find then was opana, the champagne of opiates. Holy shit, oxymorphone is a hell of a drug. I shaved off tiny little lines and it still fucked me up. That is how I started to get addicted to opiates, fucking opana.

This is one participant in a major, now closed market, discussing the intimate connection between a declining flyover town and the growing opioid crisis. Permanent recession in some areas has undermined social stability and resilience. There is a change from poor, socially integrated areas dominated by a small number of skilled criminals to a mass of low-skilled, mainly male but some female criminals, involved in low level violence and chaos.

Heroin makes its appearance along with other opioids as medicine for psychic pain (Carnwath and Smith 2002).

> I am sure you can see where this is going, typical story. Soon, oxymorphone disappeared from the streets too, so heroin became my only option. I refused to IV, and would only snort, and it was great. I didnt suffer withdrawal symptoms like I did from opana, and I just loved the idea that I was using heroin, not sure why, can't explain it, I just thought it was cool. Then, after snorting heroin for a few months, I let my friends talk me into shooting up on the 4th of july a couple years ago. The song that was playing the first time I shot up was "Crazy" by Gnarles Barkley, and it was a perfect song for what was going on inside me as I stuck that needle in my arm. "This is fucking crazy", I thought. I was fucking shooting up heroin. I remember I felt the rush, which lasted no more than 30 seconds, and then I just felt ok. "Thats it?" I thought. I didnt think there was anything too special or worthwhile about shooting up heroin. I needed less when I was snorting it, I could get 2--3 hits out of stamp bag instead of 1, the warm hugging feeling inside wasn't as intense as the rush from IV, or as instant, but it sure as hell lasted longer, and in a way felt better, so why would anyone IV when they could save money, dope, and their brain by snorting? Of course, after that, I never snorted heroin again, I always shot up. So anyone out there who wants to try shooting, try if you want to, but remember my story.

This story from the same market recounts the attraction of heroin and the push towards injecting heroin use because it makes economic sense.

There are two developments here. We can be animated by this product of conformist, consumerist ideals and transgressive means and the tendency of liberal-anarchic criminology to see the state as the source of all problems and drug dealers as a kind of rebellious counterculture when they are largely parasitical outlaws. So we are returning to 'crime as thing', not crime as rebellion or social pressure, alienation etc. Social hostility and parasitism are produced by identifiable causes in the driving ideology of capitalism and the global economic structure. The other development is the systematised use of opioids, crack and other drugs in response to structural failure (Netherland and Hansen 2016).

Extent and Growth of the Illicit Economy

The illicit market ecosystem consists of several different economies: illegal drugs, smuggled tobacco, stolen and counterfeit goods, malware products and others that loosely interrelate. There is some circulation with the formal economy as well. Otherwise legal tobacco companies became embroiled in the illegal trade for a period in the late twentieth century (Joossens and Raw 2012). The cryptomarkets are a small part of the whole. One of the problems throughout analysing the size of the illegal economy is tying down the numbers. In the cryptomarkets, there is a lot of duplication and a 'long tail' of vendors selling little. Data can be verified through analysis of blockchain and cashing out services, though that gives a partial impression as well.

While societal attention is often transfixed in the crimes of infuriation such as various phishing efforts, the illicit economy is quite a traditional affair even when high tech. Anderson et al. (2013) assess costs between 'traditional crimes gone digital' e.g. drug dealing, tax fraud, transitional crimes that have been changed by the online such as credit card fraud, new categories of crime like spam and platform crimes (botnets and the like). The crimes are of decreasing orders of magnitude in costs, with 'old' crimes costing a thousand times more for victims than the entirely new ones. However, this is in part because it is easier to measure direct costs with traditional crimes. The indirect and defence/security costs of new crimes are much greater. The 'cost' of tax fraud is about what the criminal gets in return; however, the cost of botnets, ransomware and other mass attacks far exceeds the return the criminal earns. There is a much higher level of secondary harm, lost productivity, harm to people unable to get timely medical care because their files were on an infected computer. There is a striking gap between the benefits and costs. Spam earns relatively little for its progenitors compared with the vast costs of spam protection (in the billions). This kind of cybercrime has high external costs unlike, for example, carjacking which is local and imposes few other costs. Anderson et al.'s conclusion is that prevention is the wrong priority. Simply finding and imprisoning cybercriminals is a more cost-effective approach, but one hampered by the global nature of the activity and the non-cooperation of many source countries. They argue that this is possible because there is an over reporting of the numbers involve where in fact there are a small number of gangs involved. The sense of the problems as too big and diffuse means the approach from 'guardians' tends to be 'protect yourself' rather than 'investigate and prosecute'.

Seizure data are limited in recording the size of an illegal market as it tends to reflect the priorities and targeting of law enforcement and illicit trades will not be recorded in the economic data. Estimates exist but can be self-serving and inflated. Population survey data can be more accurate as it does not involved opaque reporting mechanisms. One study showed illicit tobacco consumption in Brazil moving from 16.6% of the total in 2008 to 31.1% in 2013 (Iglesias et al. 2017). Illicit consumption increased alongside general decrease in tobacco use. The data might suggest that illegal sectors of otherwise legal markets are larger than wholly illicit trades such as the drug trade.

Tobacco corporations and alcohol companies use smuggling as a resource, either by participating in it, or arguing that the existence of smuggling means that taxes are too high. Tobacco companies also can use it to pump up product demand. They call it 'systemic synergy' (Passas 2003) between the licit and the illicit trades. Credit is unusual except at the higher levels as it is a pointless risk, as they point out—it is intrinsic to the illicit drug market perhaps because of the need to establish longer-term relationships. Credit is a social relationship. Credit is possible at the lowest levels because there is an established relationship between dealer and user or dealers at adjacent levels in the supply chain—so it's a risk that's worth taking as it binds the lower level operative further into the chain (Moeller and Sandberg 2017). One of the points Antonopoulus and Hall make is that counterfeit smuggling is very profitable indeed (£3 million for one factory in Grimsby, 75% profit on investment). Demand is very high. It is perhaps a feature of these kind if illegal-legal markets that the potential demand is going to be more than supply, unlike illicit drugs, which are in some ways self-limiting.

Costs are not purely negative. Criminal revenue may contribute to national gross domestic product, such as when paying for hosting costs for sites engaged in illegal activity. The Netherlands showed a net gain from pirating music, as customers involved in pirating gained more than the music companies lost.

Some costs are incurred by criminals as a result of their business model. Criminal advertising as an activity which is unusual—either using ads as a vector for malware, or directly advertising illicit products such as counterfeit pharmaceuticals through Twitter, Instagram and so on. The success and reliability of operatons can be indicated by the level of return custom the sellers get.

There is an indirect service and promotion structure. Anderson et al. note the use of affiliate programs. Advertisers channel customers to counterfeit pharma operations and get a cut of business in return. Changes in the software market affect profits. Free cloud software services and the lower price of office software has cut into the profits of cracked software sellers, and those who sell cracking tools.

In terms of growth, the logic of the economy and institutional development means expanded criminogenic opportunities as more and more systems and activities are mediated online. Welfare payments go online so fraud will too (Anderson et al. 2013). There are further costs: the reputation cost, the micro-costs of time spent complying with new requirements, or dealing with broken credit histories. Criminal market opportunities are generated by a range of processes—going 'cyber' so moving systems online, criminals engaging in arbitrage such as between generic and branded pharmaceuticals, and exploiting the existence of global production systems and companies' attempts to geoblock their markets.

Illicit drug markets operate on different dynamics but are shaped by some of the same forces such as globalisation, technological change, product development, aspirational identities and the emergence of niche markets (Ruggiero and South 1997). Illicit flows tend to follow licit ones and the diversified Colombian heroin trade in the USA grew with the North American Free Trade Agreement. The image of illicit drug markets in deprived areas is one of open-air selling and using, with frequent violence as deals go sour. A study in England and Wales indicated the advent of mobile technology and response to surveillance has migrated much drug selling away from open-air settings (May and Hough 2004). Violence and stigma add to the stress of deprivation for those living in the neighbourhood whether they are directly involved or not. Spatial analysis shows that while violence may cluster around some drug markets there is no certain relationship, with factors such as law enforcement activity, competition and the type of drug for sale being more influential (Lum 2008).

Crime can be economic and rational but not necessarily in terms of the immediate outcome. Just as freelance workers in gig economy platforms may trade temporary loss or lower earnings for the prospect of moving onto brighter things so criminals may engage in low profit crime as a stepping stone to moving up in the criminal world. The criminal trajectory matters and differentiates immediate survival crimes from those that are part of a longer-term plan. In the latter case, criminals may engage in specific high-risk crimes in order to build reputation capital and contacts which can then be used to take charge of larger assets and opportunities.

Illicit drugs are often very useful stores of value, in economics with unreliable or non-existent cash or electronic monetary systems. In one part of Kyrgystan, cannabis substituted for cash as an monetary medium and a useful source of informal credit (Botoeva 2014) drawing farmers into the cannabis production business and legitimating production of it. In Afghanistan, opium works in a similar fashion (Mansfield 2002). The drugs' qualities of portability, convertibility and reliability give them a deep purchase in Afghan rural life. It is not simply a useful cash crop, and indeed farmers may get themselves into deep debt cultivating it. It structures the agricultural cycle, the labour market and family relationships, as women can be coerced into marriage to service an opium debt. Opium becomes a frozen obligation through which the rich can wreak havoc on poorer families.

Legitimate Illicit Business

Somali pirates and other professional kidnappers have to be reliable to expect payment, so a infrastructure and reputation is needed. Kidnapping insurance developed to manage the problem. The public focus is usually on high profile Western victims. Most victims continue to be local, and not especially affluent. Like other criminal activity, piracy generates stabilities through a process of implicit legitimation. The ransom tends to stabilise at a payable, if not affordable, amount. Anti-terror policies de-stabilise, since monies cannot be paid to terror groups without the payer also criminalising themselves—but they can be paid to 'criminal' piracy groups—which is which? So ransom 'prices' are agreed between kidnapper and victims' representatives, around an expected amount.

Price is not profit though. Like the alcohol industry, the majority of profits in the illegal drug industry come from a small number of high volume consumers. If everyone was 'average', the industry would collapse overnight. High taxes in the UK on tobacco represent a lucrative source of criminal profits along with low penalties and a cultural acceptance of smuggling as a service. Antonopoulos and Hall (2016) account for the range of smuggling business operations. The large, hierarchal groups are not common. There are opportunistic smugglers such as long distance lorry drivers or students who travel to continental Europe frequently and come back with more than the legal maximum. Then there are investor-led groupings who make use of multiple mules who are transporting the 'personal use' amount. One person uses his contacts to coordinate multiple small buys and pays for the trip plus an extra. Scaling up needs networks that can get hold of big infrastructure such as shipping containers full of tobacco products. Financial management is needed: capital is the first requirement. Investors may know each other through legal business or part of social networks, though marriage and so non-blood ties are also important here.

Money to invest can come from illegal profits in legal business e.g. where tax has been avoided, so the money has to be kept in the illegal economy or cashed out undetectably. Capital also comes from other illegal activities, unsurprisingly, such as drugs, illegal gambling and fighting. However, not all business deals involve trust and consent. Some use threats to muscle in on lucrative operations. They distinguish trust as largely being about functional dependence and discretion rather than something longer lasting—most exchanges are in cash because of that. Expenses have to be paid for 'runners' if it's a small-scale operation, and the significant costs of transport if it's a larger one. One of the reasons for on-shoring illicit manufacture of cigarettes in the UK identified by Antonopoulos and Hall was these greater costs. Illegal factories can be set up without much fuss: rent a warehouse and buy a cigarette rolling machine. Here there is a clear link with legal manufacturers who supply papers and packaging. Other expenses include 'cover loads', cheap goods that provide a plausible reason for transport. Labour costs have to account for runners, brokers, couriers/transporters, sellers. Costs depend on how replaceable they are. Additional costs for bribes, insurance, extortion and decoys. money was 'laundered' simply by establishing legal businesses. Drug cartels operate a more hermetic business which illegal proceeds cycle through the illegal economy.

There are a range of business types present in the cryptomarkets that combine technical and organisational systems in different ways (Moeller 2012). They can be differentiated by size and also internal structure, their trajectory and how they link with other criminal operations and supporting services such as couriers and bagmen. Greater predictability in their operations means skills of capital management, stock control, customer responsiveness come to the fore. A vendor's market strategy is constrained or enabled by financial factors such as their access to startup capital, their ability to secure product through the drug distribution chain, and proximity to distribution systems. A simple way of categorising market relations is to look at the internal structure of vendor businesses. Common business types were single vendors with one person in charge of product sourcing or production and distribution, extended organisations with sourcing and distribution separate, and franchises or secondary distribution systems. Franchising allowed a vendor to maintain their market position while limiting the size of their operation and manage risk by minimising cross-border traffic.

Related to the business strategy is the vendor's concept of the life-cycle or trajectory of their own business. Some vendors have a growth trajectory and an end point in mind, and some plan an open-ended trajectory that responds to market demand. These are not fully separate as vendors change their approach depending on changes in the supply chain, perceived risk of law enforcement interception, and changes in the cryptomarket itself. I divided trajectories into the end point the vendor is aiming for: long-term stability, scam, pump and dump (trying for low-quality rapid sales followed by a swift market exit), and going private or off-market, meaning selling to a restricted, vetted client base. Vendors' network position helped maintain their trajectory. Lone vendors could be quite successful economically but did not exist in a network of supportive sellers while others have more complex business models with separate departments for production, distribution and shipping involving numerous ancillary staff (Reuter and Mark 1986). Separating out distribution can have benefits in allowing the vendor to concentrate on customer service and operational planning but it also creates human resources problems as described in relation to this cryptomarket vendor:

> CaptainBeard had someone doing his drops for him and that person was not a good choice for him and the first package never arrived. CaptainBeard had some problems with that guy and got rid of him. So now shipping has been rectified. CaptainBeard send out another package, this one FedEx next day and it arrive AOK for my drop situation. Buyer 'Alscarpets'

Some have clearly expressed longer-term visions for their business which balance the benefits of higher turnover versus the risks it represents such as lower profit margins, greater business complexity and attracting the attention of law enforcement and rivals. For those reasons, they can seek to stay small and focused on retail level customer orders. Others have a plan to move from retail to bulk orders over time. These vendors that are trying to break into the bulk sales market seek to develop a close relationship with a selected client base.

A network strategy allowed vendors to leverage network effects by identifying 'super-reviewers', forum members who are particularly active and trusted by other users in the market who can be targeted with free samples and discounts. They are a kind of key reputation actor common in online criminal networks (Dupont et al. 2016). They are identified and acted on by the vendors in order to maximise reputation and sales for example by using free samples, a good way of building a reputation and are an effective entry strategy for new players (Coomber 2003). Reputation capital in the cryptomarkets is mediated through the reputation systems and forums. However, as many users noted, it is hard to differentiate between the many vendors who have almost the same highest possible score. They then turn to super-reviewers for judgement. Super-reviewers play a significant role in mediating a vendor's transition from small to bulk sales, and from being on the public market to taking their business private. Their role is akin to 'power reviewers' on licit platforms, a role that is deliberately created and rewarded by the platform designers. They have many weak ties to other market participants so act as diffusers of reliable knowledge.

The theory of weak ties explains much about the structure of network opportunities in the cryptomarkets as a whole (Granovetter 1973). Innovation in products, customers services, and site structure have spread rapidly and the market as a whole has been little impeded by law enforcement interventions. One study examined 88 valid markets, excluding markets that were set up as fakes or were never active (Branwen 2016). Of those, 7 were closed due to law enforcement action, 35 were closed as the result of scams, 24 voluntarily shut down and 11 hacked (others unknown). The market owner or principal administrator was arrested in five cases. A possibility is that law enforcement intervention has been predicated on the strong ties model, which assumes that each market is a dense network that can be disrupted on a long-term basis by the arrest of key players and the closure of its servers. The weak ties present on the cryptomarkets provide a high degree of resilience across markets. Law enforcement actions effectively function as a competitive pressure, weeding out less skilled or less committed players (Cubrilovic 2014). We see with the cryptomarkets an extension of the strength of weak ties in supporting criminal innovation (Granovetter 1983). Granovetter's (1973) theory that weaker ties are crucially important for diffusing innovation is relevant to cybercrime. He argues that innovations at the margins of networks diffuse more quickly due to the fecundity of weak ties. Silk Road and Bitcoin were innovations at the margins of the criminal underworld and financial systems. It is likely that marginal innovations will continue to be important in the development of cybercriminal operations and may be a key focus for law enforcement in future as the illicit economy continues to be transformed by online activity. Various factors affected whether they could follow their planned trajectory. A threat to vendors was becoming overextended and not having the staff to maintain throughput, and access to capital and the restrictions of the market feedback system which mean it was a risky investment. Capital could disappear quickly as this vendor describes:

> I'm waiting for more good reviews before I start selling in larger weights. If official tests are positive then I'll move into bulk. This takes time. The purest coke costs more and sells quickly compared to my standard product.

The standard coke takes up most of my capital. The connoisseur market is tempting but I'm not ready for it yet. Vendor, Hazmates.

Although the driving factor for some was making large profits as quickly as they could, many were self-limiting, seeing a distinct cut off point in their business trajectory, and for others there were inbuilt limitations of capital or ability to manage their customers and the rating system (Hammersvik et al. 2012). They could limit their business size to avoid the risks of having other employees, or having to commercialise. A final point in some vendors' trajectories is closing or passing the business on. Some have a set aim in mind and leave the market having achieved a desired level of profit. A good business can be sold to another vendor which allows the vendor to depart with minimal disruption to their client base.

Underpinning their market strategies were business practices that manage customer demand (Martin 2014). I have divided these into demand facing and market-oriented practices. Demand facing business practices sought to manage the business identity and the customer base, such as through branding, pricing strategies and product quality management. Market-oriented business practices involved managing challenges arising from the market infrastructure. They included practices of hedging against bitcoin fluctuation and extended to strategies to damage rivals' businesses through distributing negative reviews and all the way to cyber attacks on rival markets.

To some extent their practices were a function of market position in the sense of the relationship to the market overall rather than the size of the business. Positioning could be seen as a function of the business type but there were more complex factors at work in terms of the dynamics involving others in the market. Market position was therefore partly out of the control of vendors and was sometimes a function of business type and in other cases was due to the opportunities that came up and their ability to exploit them. Many vendors moved from retail to bulk operations as they were able to access larger quantities in the supply chain or as their customers changed their requirements. A different approach was the vendor developing their ability to control different steps in the supply chain. Some were able to take charge of most or all of the supply chain from production to retail distribution. This was the exception. Most vendors represented different steps in the chain, including the cryptomarket service industry. They provided precursor chemicals, or took other roles in the supply chain, or provided hosting or ancillary services such as bitcoin tumbling services that launder bitcoin.

Legitimate Violence

If you really are the LEET hacker and pentester you say you are, and you are actually coordinating these DOS attacks, I do hope a market(s) hires you as a pentester or that you may offer your services with a bit of charity and generosity in your heart towards the DNM community (which it seems you have, i heeded your warnings and withdrew all my btc). with power comes responsibility. Just know that the money you may be stealing might be helping a family stay off the street, or helping someone through college, or a baby get fed. some people rely heavily on these markets to survive (i was last year). You never know. That being said, lack of proper OPSEC will always result in a siezure or hacking so the only thing to do is support markets that employ the finest OPSEC and business tactics. to everyone, read up and stay safe out here. Everyday I spend a few hours beefing up my own personal opsec. we should all be doing the same. I did quite like Agora and bitcoinfog so i hope they can refurbish all their security and come back strong. : /i just want everyone to be safe and warm and happy and high omg. Cryptomarket user.

Coercion is present in the cryptomarkets. For want of a better term, it is digital violence. Attempting to destroy someone's digital life, or making their business inoperable, is digital violence. The question then is whether it is a legitimate use of force or not. The quote above references a hacker coordinating DDoS attacks against one market, lamenting that the skills would be much better directed supporting the market's technical resilience than attempting to extort it. Some markets use cyber attacks against competitors so violence is also part of the expected competition within the markets.

The illicit political economy is the confluence of crime and legitimate violence. To the extent that criminals suborn or act as the enforcers of the legally established political order then there is a political economy that trades in favours, bribes, and opportunities. A political economy analysis shows how criminal activity is customary, ordered, institutionalised and indirectly governed, and the value in the criminal economy is produced by labour and resource distribution. It is most straightforward to apply this to the illicit drug economy where there are established and well documented patterns of corruption and political complicity. The emerging digital crime economy takes up some elements of that, though in some ways makes it more difficult to apply in practice. Drugs bought and sold over the cryptomarkets do not in themselves need payoffs of local police or border agents. However when seen as part of the broader ecosystem these needs still apply.

There is however awareness of what the markets need to function. They need an ecosystem that includes other markets. Cyber attacks harm this, as one commentator observes:

> Attacks like this decrease market diversity. Decreased diversity is BAD for the darknet. Even if a perfect market does exist (and it does not. I despise TMP because I2P totally fucks with my computer and I do not like its interface at all.) Having a single target is a bad bad thing. The less competition between sites the easier a target we have. So no one who actually cared about darknet would do it. If they did have evidence agora security was poor they might expose that information publicly. They would definitely avoid doing business with the network itself. But they would not engage in an action that actually defeats their purpose entirely. Your reasoning for doing this is purely a bruised ego? Really? Grow a pair of balls and grow the fuck up. Your actions do not hurt merely the market they hurt vendors and customers. Your rationale for this is that you know better. Well you have no RIGHT to tell me you know better where I should be doing business. At least that is what I would say if I believed your purported reason. But in light of the fact that your attack actually makes no rational sense whatsoever.

The above account shows an obligation to the cryptomarket system as a whole, beyond any one market. Like the rest of the internet, cryptomarkets are vulnerable to a malicious actor parlaying their hurt ego into havoc for the rest of the digital sphere.

Markets Regulate Crime

The hybrid nature of the cryptomarkets was reflected in the way they combined formal and informal regulatory processes. Formally, the decisions of market administrators and the operation of trust mechanisms such as vendor bonds ensured trust. Informally, trust emerged from a combination of these systems and hierarchal structures, with lateral mutual surveillance by vendors and buyers. Vendor bonds are paid by the vendor when they sign up for the market. They are a cost of entry which excludes smaller or more temporary players and also provides a measure of trust as the vendor will lose the bond if they attempt an exit scam. Established vendors often have their bond waived by the market administrator. Along with other administrator actions such as importing vendors' rating from other markets it functions to consolidate existing players. Bonds are usually small amounts from US$100 to $2000 equivalent, which are little in comparison with potential income but do present a cost to a scammer seeking to create multiple fake accounts. Reputation costs in being banned means it can be a major sanction for more established vendors but a minor issues for those who are not established who don't have a reputation to lose.

An example of lateral surveillance was the ever vigilant watch for scam vendors. It was thought that scam vendors would employ their associates to puff their reputation on both the feedback system and forum. Users sought ways to evaluate whether this was happening, watching out for suspicious activity such as very positive contributions by newly registered users and sudden spikes in positive feedback for specific vendors. Negative image work could also be employed. Personal antagonisms were frequently expressed. There was a long discussion on one market's heroin thread of one vendor and whether people are trying to defame his reputation. Lists of scam vendors were posted, leading to suggestions of some vendors 'negging' others in the forum, spreading misinformation to undermine them. Vendors worried about rival vendors buying small amounts in order to post negative feedback, and law enforcement using de-anonymising attacks using multiple user accounts to undermine the trustworthiness of the market as a whole. A vendor comments:

> Guys, your support is worth a million. The feedback system is rubbish as it can spammed. It would take me a short time to create buyer accounts and get my feedback up to five starts. Reputation is what matters and is all we have to go on. Vendor, 'Elcaptynkirk'

Discussions among buyers show a number of problems in maintaining customer loyalty across markets. Buyers used to dealing with one seller on another site, now closed down, can use the seller's PGP encryption key to tell if a seller with the same name is the same person. However many do not maintain the same key since they sometimes have to 'burn' previous operations. To confirm their identity they need intelligence from other sources, a case presented by this vendor.

> Beginning on the original Silk Road and moving after to Silk Road 2 there have been the same people I use for sound insight. They agree that [vendor] twilight is the real deal, has the FIRE, and you can rely on him. These folks have shown the way to where the best heroin is. They have been sent cut skag, scammed, and seen everything is so their word is solid. Vendor, 'Pharmafarmer'

Successful vendors employed a reputation management strategy, intervening in forums and relying on contributions by forum users who had a good reputation. Super-reviewers moderated threads, and calibrated feedback. Many vendors had exceptionally positive feedback and one function super-reviewers had was to differentiate between them. Some produced lists of reliable vendors. In some cases, vendors asked not to be put on public lists of good vendors as their business had too much throughput of orders and they wanted to control the volume and type of sales. Vendors would also package the drugs in a form that was convenient to the user, for example selling cocaine in 'ready to snort' form. In this way the cryptomarkets have changed the form and presentation of the drugs sold.

Conclusion

Although cryptomarkets are often reckoned to be discrete from the wider drug market, they are embedded within it. They are increasingly national and regional in focus and are directly affected by events outside them. As they have evolved they have become more finely associated with different national and linguistic cultures. Cryptomarkets have emerged to service Scandinavia, Finland, Italy, Russia and other countries and have been places where national criminal cultures have been represented. Existing criminal cultures worked through them, so for example Russian markets tended to have much less of the social and political discussions typical of English language markets. In this way illicit digital markets are entangled is in the politics and regulation of nation states as political economies.

References

Anderson, R., Barton, C., Böhme, R., Clayton, R., Van Eeten, M. J., Levi, M., et al. (2013). Measuring the cost of cybercrime. In *The economics of information security and privacy* (pp. 265–300). Berlin: Springer.

Antonopoulos, G. A., & Hall, A. (2016). The financial management of the illicit tobacco trade in the United Kingdom. *British Journal of Criminology, 56*(4), 709–728. https://doi.org/10.1093/bjc/azv062.

Blake, D. (2018). How lotto scammers defraud elderly Americans and fuel gang wars in Jamaica. *The Conversation.* Retrieved from http://theconversation.com/how-lotto-scammers-defraud-elderly-americans-and-fuel-gang-wars-in-jamaica-90676.

Botoeva, G. (2014). Hashish as cash in a post-Soviet Kyrgyz village. *International Journal of Drug Policy, 25*(6), 1227–1234. https://doi.org/10.1016/j.drugpo.2014.01.016.

Bourgois, P. (2003). Crack and the political economy of social suffering. *Addiction Research & Theory, 11*(1), 31–37. https://doi.org/10.1080/1606635021000021322.

Branwen, G. (2016). *Darknet market mortality risks.* https://www.gwern.net/DNM-survival.

Carnwath, T., & Smith, I. (2002). *Heroin century.* London: Routledge.

Coomber, R. (2003). There's no such thing as a free lunch: How 'freebies' and 'credit' operate as part of rational drug market activity. *Journal of Drug Issues, 33*(4), 939–962.

Cubrilovic, N. (2014). *Large number of tor hidden sites seized by the FBI in operation onymous were clone or scam sites.* Retrieved from https://www.nikcub.com/posts/onymous-part1/.

Davis, D. E. (2011). Irregular armed forces, shifting patterns of commitment, and fragmented sovereignty in the developing world. In M. Hanagan & C. Tilly (Eds.), *Contention and trust in cities and states* (pp. 249–265). https://doi.org/10.1007/978-94-007-0756-6_17.

Dupont, B., Côté, A.-M., Savine, C., & Décary-Hétu, D. (2016). The ecology of trust among hackers. *Global Crime, 17*(2), 129–151. https://doi.org/10.1080/17440572.2016.1157480.

Granovetter, M. S. (1973). The strength of weak ties. *American Journal of Sociology, 78*(6), 1360–1380.

Granovetter, M. (1983). The strength of weak ties: A network theory revisited. *Sociological Theory, 1*(1), 201–233.

Hall, S., Winlow, S., & Ancrum, C. (2013). *Criminal identities and consumer culture: Crime, exclusion and the new culture of narcissm.* London: Willan.

Hamilton, K. (2017, September 26). *Jamaican lottery scammers suspected in slaying of retired U.S. teacher.* Retrieved 26 May 2019, from Vice News website: https://news.vice.com/en_us/article/mb9588/jamaican-lottery-scammers-suspected-in-slaying-of-retired-u-s-teacher.

Hammersvik, E., Sandberg, S., & Pedersen, W. (2012). Why small-scale cannabis growers stay small: Five mechanisms that prevent small-scale growers from going large scale. *International Journal of Drug Policy, 23*(6), 458–464. https://doi.org/10.1016/j.drugpo.2012.08.001.

Iglesias, R. M., Szklo, A. S., de Souza, M. C., & de Almeida, L. M. (2017). Estimating the size of illicit tobacco consumption in Brazil: Findings from the global adult tobacco survey. *Tobacco Control, 26*(1), 53–59. https://doi.org/10.1136/tobaccocontrol-2015-052465.

Joossens, L., & Raw, M. (2012). From cigarette smuggling to illicit tobacco trade. *Tobacco Control, 21*(2), 230–234.

Kshetri, N. (2010). *The global cybercrime industry: Economic, institutional and strategic perspectives.* Berlin: Springer Science & Business Media.

Lum, C. (2008). The geography of drug activity and violence: Analyzing spatial relationships of non-homogenous crime event types. *Substance Use and Misuse, 43*(2), 179–201.

Mansfield, D. (2002). *The economic superiority of illicit drug production: Myth and reality—Opium poppy cultivation in Afghanistan.* In International conference on drug control and cooperation, Feldafing, January 7–12.

Martin, J. (2014). *Drugs on the dark net: How cryptomarkets are transforming the global trade in illicit drugs.* London: Palgrave Macmillan.

May, T., & Hough, M. (2004). Drug markets and distribution systems. *Addiction Research & Theory, 12*(6), 549–563. https://doi.org/10.1080/16066350412331323119.

Moeller, K. (2012). Costs and revenues in street-level cannabis dealing. *Trends in Organized Crime, 15*(1), 31–46. https://doi.org/10.1007/s12117-011-9146-9.

Moeller, K., & Sveinung, S. (2017). Debts and threats: Managing inability to repay credits in illicit drug distribution. *Justice Quarterly, 34*(2), 272–296.

Netherland, J., & Hansen, H. B. (2016). The war on drugs that wasn't: Wasted whiteness, "dirty doctors", and race in media coverage of prescription opioid misuse. *Culture, Medicine, and Psychiatry, 40*(4), 664–686.

Newmeyer, K. P. (2014). *Cybersecurity strategy in developing nations: A Jamaica case study* (PhD thesis). Walden University.

Passas, N. (2003). Cross-border crime and the interface between legal and illegal Actors. *Security Journal, 16*(1), 19–37.

Reuter, P., & Kleiman, M. A. (1986). Risks and prices: An economic analysis of drug enforcement. *Crime and Justice, 7*, 289–340.

Ruggiero, V., & South, N. (1997). The late-modern city as a bazaar: Drug markets, illegal enterprise and the 'barricades'. *The British Journal of Sociology, 48*(1), 54. https://doi.org/10.2307/591910.

5

The Cultural Drug-Crime Confection

Illicit Markets Involve New Approaches If Not More Stuff

The informal economy is the half-visible, semi-monetised, irregular but vital activity that surrounds and underpins the formal economy. Illicit markets are an outgrowth of informal economies, rather than the other way round. They are the bits of informal economies that have been criminalised. The move to digital economy has changed illegal and informal markets in new ways. Informal markets increasingly broker digital processes such as microwork and distribution of mobile airtime. Cryptomarkets mimic and embed some of the values of the formal economy and other systems such as crimeware leverage large-scale network effects. One of the ways cryptomarkets work is to test what goods are viable. For example, weapons are rarely sold on the cryptomarkets, but not for want of trying. To do this, a shared cultural understanding is needed for what is, and what is trying to be achieved.

© The Author(s) 2020
A. Bancroft, *The Darknet and Smarter Crime*, Palgrave Studies
in Cybercrime and Cybersecurity, https://doi.org/10.1007/978-3-030-26512-0_5

Illicit Intoxication and Normal Addiction in the 'Machine Zone'

Culture is created materially, through the devices we interact with, and embedded in our bodies (Dennis 2016). A part of algorithmic and material cultures is the zone aspect, a place which creates separation from everyday rhythms, networks and places. Markets are zones in this sense, with their own rules, cultures and systems. Schüll (2012) identifies 'the machine zone' in her study of gambling machines in Las Vegas. The zone is where the players enjoy total focus as they sit in front of the screen and interact with the machine. They play in front of gaming machines that by proxy deliver jolts of dopamine. The setting is designed to focus attention through a combination of tactile and sensory design which obliterates the periphery and speeds up play. The machines and the environment are carefully designed to maximise 'Time on Device', their metric of value. This is a devilish bargain the players willingly sign up for. It turns out that the players do not like winning, and are not in it to win it. Winning is troublesome for them as it breaks the machine zone. The player is atomised, focused on the interaction with the machine. Schüll saw that people kept playing when someone is having a cardiac arrest and being treated. The machine zone is designed to maintain a flow of attention and also a financial flow, using handy cash machines and electronic payment systems to keep the money going.

I was struck by the similarities between the machine zone and conversations I have had with student smart drug users, who report similar effects when taking modafinil. Modafinil was introduced as a treatment for the sleep disorder narcolepsy. It is one of a set of smart drugs or study drugs that are popular among university students in North America and Europe. The drugs are taken to improve memory, recall, and task salience (Jensen et al. 2016). Students taking modafinil report experience a simplifying, satisfying task salience in which they focus wholly on what is in front of them, whether exam cramming, reading or writing. There is a deep delight in separating oneself so wholly from other stimulation. As with most intoxications, the benefit is also a risk. Gamblers and study drug users forget to eat, drink, interact with friends or so much else and have to carefully plan to remind themselves to do these things. When you forget to eat, you realise how much memory and habit is embodied. Pharmaceutical companies produce a new drug indicated for a specific condition such as anxiety and immediately seek to expand the zone of its application to other conditions like dieting. Smart drug users are doing much the same and indeed a common illicit use of medical amphetamines is for weight reduction. We can see then the illicit as produced by the licit, for example, in demands to use smart drugs. Uber drivers, Amazon workers, cam girls, and all will face working requirements that are often fast paced and require them to be always 'on'. It is uncertain as to whether these drugs improve cognitive ability or just keep people on task or awake for longer. In this way the capitalist economy creates demand, or a need, for illicit drugs.

Likewise, the economy is intertwined with intoxcation. As the work of Dennis and Farrugia (2017) and others shows, intoxication is rooted in culture and nature, which gives it its partly involuntary feel. This involuntary element, the sense of being swept along, of having the body respond separately from the mind to triggers, is what makes it so potent. Each form of intoxication is a material culture. Intoxication experiences are systematised and designed into environments. The historically novel binge-drinking cultures of the 1990s and early 2000s in the UK were a product of the creation of new alcohol commodities and spaces (Measham and Brain 2005). Alcohol companies allied with local and national governments to drive changes in the law allied with product innovation to permit intense, focused consumption. That was the machine zone of alcoholic intoxication. Illicit intoxication has been both a rider on those processes and an escape from them.

The Work of Culture in the Context of the Illicit

A common perspective shared by many drug, alcohol and tobacco users is the presentation of the drug as an agent: it is doing something to them. The viewpoint is shared both by sympathisers and those with an interest in portraying illicit drugs as alien, disease-like entities. In fact drugs have to have cultural work done to them before they can be consumed. Work just means the activity that surrounds the drug and the user, which makes drug use palatable and desirable. From seeking out the substance, haggling, swapping or just posing at a bar to obtain it, practicing holding smoke in one's lungs and injecting, these activities are shared, practical and symbolic. All users do that, all of them work on themselves and the drug they consume. We often submerge this aspect of drug use because it raises difficult questions. It is not so easy for outsiders to be sympathetic, or to place blame at door of the usual culprits—alcohol and tobacco industries, government failures to regulate the market—when we understand the huge work users put into using drugs.

Culture might seem redundant in the machine zone or in a material context. However, I argue that it performs crucial functions and in a sense the material context of intoxication is congealed culture and politics. Intoxicants have a quality of in-betweenness. Culture does the work of legitimation and normalisation, and de-legitimation and stigmatisation. It can reconcile the desire for pleasure with the needs to display order and compliance (Pennay 2012). The illicit context makes some of these functions much more salient. Shared cultural understandings are needed to communicate tainted knowledge and to manage economies of scarcity (Bourgois 1998). Cultural competence and recognition is important in managing drug supply and consumption where those functions are not served by the formal governance system. One way we can think of this critically is the extent to which the concepts researchers use are coherent: are addiction, recovery intoxication, pleasure, and harm coherent concepts or are they quite contingent? What is their contingency built on? It is helpful to view them as concepts with historical and cultural stability, supported by socially validated systems such as the medical system, the legal system, institutions like psychiatry and addiction treatment, academic disciplines like sociology, pharmacology and so on. They act together to produce a stable ontology, reifying their logics and symbolic structures (Manderson 1995; Seddon 2016).

The stability and shared understanding is structured through ritual, a set of defined acts that are functional and meaningful (Collins 2004). Consumption rituals are powerful tie signs indicating in/out group membership and marking social time and space (Gusfield 1987). The array of practices and knowledge around an intoxicant produce it as an effective object with characteristics that vary by time and place and are not solely dependent on its physical nature (Gomart 2002). Almost all accounts of intoxication include a ritual aspect (Becker 1953) but this perhaps reflects a research bias. By its nature, ritual is observable, describable and account-able, and the ethnographic methods used with drug users will tend to pick up on ritual. Culture also manifests in cue reactivity, risk management, and dose titration. These activities which are vital to make intoxication effective are part of embedded algorithms shared by users. They can be seen on internet message boards, darknet discussion forums and in the unspoken learning that takes place when users gather.

These rituals transform. Lévi-Strauss (1969) defined civilisation as the distinction between the raw and the cooked. Drugs are likewise cooked, transformed. The argot of heroin users has 'cooking up' as the process of preparing heroin for consumption. Cooking techniques vary depending on form (Strang et al. 1997). Brown heroin requires heat and acid, white heroin less heat and no acid. Cooking is any transformation. Mixing a cocktail is cooking. What I mean by 'cooking' here is the combination of preparation, memory work and body work that goes into preparing intoxicants and making intoxication experiences. Both the drug and the user's body is 'cooked' in this process, turned into a system for drug con-sumption. It transforms the user between two states.

Transition is a common feature as transitions exist between multiple states. There are age transitions as part of the life course. One is the shamanic ritual inducting an adolescent into adulthood which pushes the body of the subject of the ritual using drugs. Yage, tobacco and ayahuasca may all be employed. The adolescent goes through death and rebirth, visits the spirit world and returns with their status changed permanently. The process of transforming the self necessitates looking inward. The value of intoxication is in making the user become more what they are, or should be; or getting away from themselves, or taking themselves out of the self. Transitional rituals are about inducting adolescents into culture, into society. The transformational drinking that goes on in Western adulthood is justified in terms of stripping away socialisation, getting one out of one's 'stuck in a rut' adult habits.

The process involves evoking multiple cues. Cue reactivity has been examined as an automatic response that is often activated by ritual cues or elements of ritualised practice. Cues are the tastes, sights, interactions and actions that have attached to conditioned associations with drug use in the mind of the user. In the case of the group of largely recreational users and examples of use in recreational contexts used here, the cues are built up as part of the process of drug associated learning. Cue reactivity studies foreground sensory inputs such as images, smells, tastes and textures. Cues can also involve familiar conversational terms, money, paraphernalia and other associations. Cue reactivity has been explored as promising an apparently objective measure of extent of substance dependence. However, self-reported addicts may show both aversive and appetitive responses to the introduction of familiar intoxicant-related cues (Rodríguez et al. 2005). Users become skilled in generating these effects along with making the substance itself a usable drug through ritualised practices such as preparation and sharing. Thus cue reactivity is a process that provides an element of somatic feedback in ritual practice. The somatic feedback element is a mediator of sensual practice, exploring the combination of preparation, sequence, setting, expectation and working on the body that produces a desired, or sometimes unwanted, outcome.

Ritual is also present at other aspects of the illicit intoxication. The legal process is highly ritualised, with expected denunciations, appeals to rehabilitation, and performances of suffering and penitence. Diagnosis also has its ritual element when it links generalised diagnostic categories of addiction, infection and overdose to the specific case (Rosenberg 2002). The disease entity of addiction is made culturally recognisable and inscribed in the body of the user in that moment of judgement.

Like 'substance' and 'set', the setting of intoxication is malleable and situated. This is most commonly approached in terms of spatial settings—coffeehouses, crack houses, clubs, parties, pubs and nightscapes. Criminalisation creates material realities of surveillance, opacity and punishment. Prison is a site of drug use and exchange (Fleetwood 2009), as are illicit consumption sites which involve a material culture of harm and harm reduction (Parkin 2013). There is an intoxication topography of these spaces and examines how they combine with ritual practice and social habit. It argues that a key element in setting is other people, specifically other users. In some settings, such as nightclubs, the presence of others is part of the setting to be consumed, intentionally developing a collective emotionality. In the new experience economy, these settings are closely managed in order to contribute to a commodified intoxication experience. Settings like hospitals, rehabs clinics function as re-inventive institutions (Scott 2010). Rather than having the self mortified, as in the total institutions, the client gives up their pre-institutional self voluntarily.

Symbolic Order and Power

One function of illicit intoxicants is their role in classification of objects and experiences into a symbolic order that divides the sacred from the profane. They are powerful mediators of social structure. Power and resources come to the fore in when managing a marginal existence. In situations of structural violence, adaption and survival are managed and negotiated. Female Thai heroin users find that socially prescribed role as woman conflicts with male heroin user role. They have to be public rather than domestic (Haritavorn 2014). Women users cannot live alone because of their role in a patriarchal society so are dependent on violent men. The male heroin user is more culturally recognised and acceptable than the female (Taylor 1993). Social sorting, structuring and marginalisation shaped the cultural valuation of drug users. Older drug users are typically marginalised (Anderson and Levy 2003) whereas older male drinkers in drinking cultures are valorised (Campbell 2000). Racial blackness and whiteness play a role too, particularly in the governmental response (Netherland and Hansen 2016).

There is a symbolic order to protect (Gusfield 1997). Ritual deferment is built into cultural practice, as in when women heroin users injected by partners. There is a gift economy here which is related to power. Giving a 'gift' without reciprocity asserts power (Mauss 1954). Colonial administrators and Muslim imams in South Africa proposed no-alcohol drinking for the Africans, but permitted it for whites. Continued drinking is a claim of personhood (Nugent 2014). Controlling accesses to alcohol was key to social hierarchies in imperial Ethiopia. Peasants were required to supply nobles with a form of alcohol. Later on, colonial mine owners tried to produce alcohol to keep miners in their compound, undermining the role of African women who produced alcohol. 1928 in Natal it was illegal to sell alcohol to black Africans. The shebeen was created, a liquor shack, illegal but important to black African life. White cultural discourse about alcohol undermined the sociality of black people. Black Africans were not considered to be 'full people', and it was thought that they could not drink alcohol responsibility. Later in the twentieth century, black South Africans were targeted as a growing consumer market by the alcohol industry, and drinking then became re-coded as a symbol of black modernity, subordinate but legitimated.

Related to that structuring aspect, culture makes behaviours and experiences legible, or impenetrably illegible. They may do this through mythic statements, origin stories, journey narratives that circulate and shared in user cultures. One narrative is that of recovery from addiction. Drug users perform legibility, for example, when users proclaim they are competent subjects because they bleach their injection works (Campbell and Shaw 2008). Users show to the researcher what they know to be a legible cultural performance directed at outside ethnographers, law enforcement, therapists or public health workers. In doing so, they make themselves partially legible. That action is also a strategic one and may hide other equally significant motives such as using drugs for pleasure which is hidden by the dominant cultural narrative of the desire-less addict (Dennis 2017). Treatment programmes have their own cultural norms and performances which make the user legible and 'worthy', as a drug user who uses without pleasure and wishes to reassert their agency over the drug. Initial studies treated drug users' gratification as unintegrated and anti-social (Robbins 1969), and there is quite a bit of that still. Does legalising cannabis in Uruguay change the culture? Should we ignore it? The way in which it is legalised or decriminalised is crucial. In Spain and Uruguay, there is a requirement to join a cannabis club in order to consume legally. This enforces specific locations for sharing knowledge and learning the ropes. The legal context then generates sites for cultural transmission, much like a British pub would have at one time been the main site of reproducing a male-dominated alcohol consumption culture.

The instrumental/recreational dichotomy may come into play there. The main feature distinguishing smart drug use from other kinds of illicit intoxication is that it is motivated by external demands: fitting in rather than standing out. This legitimates it in the eyes of many users, but not for some fellow students who consider it simply cheating. In my research, more experienced smart drug users were keen to differentiate themselves from novice users who they saw as not being fully in charge of their smart drug use and as purely responding to immediate demands such as having to take several work shifts in a row combined with essay submissions or study for exams. In some cases, their reason for smart drug use was to reject perceived conformity with alcohol intoxication culture and to allow them to take part in social events without drinking. The norms of leisure culture in developed societies drive smart drug use, as do the structural demands placed on students: to combine work and study, to graduate with qualifications enabling them to get good jobs to be pay off debt Instrumental drug use is more legitimated because it corresponds to the demands of an economy driven by monetisation of education, of leisure, of interaction. In the digital age this is the context, one of live tracking data which means those who participate in the economy are valued as algorithmic performers, showing structured, directed fun on Instagram or Facebook. Culture is then about value. It allows people to make value judgements, and the process of economic valuation is fundamentally a shared agreement about meaning.

A crucial part of sharing cultural understandings is the value and quality of the drug itself. The make-up of chemical potency is subjective. Higher pharmacological strength does not necessarily mean a 'better' or 'stronger' effect for the user. Street heroin is often cut with additives to enhance the pharmacokinetics and the psychoactive experience such as caffeine, theophylline and procaine. For that reason, a less chemically pure dose may be experienced as much more effectively 'potent' or desirable. Heroin is engineered for different regional markets and by new players in the market (Furst 2000). There are various other physical features and attributes of the substance (name, brand, colour, texture, taste, viscosity) that may or may not have an effect on the user's experience. Each of these supposedly objective, separable physical qualities blur into each other. They are created and modified by various factors. In some cases, in response to clinical need, in others marketing, taxation, regulation and surveillance. I observed this when analysing how cryptomarket drug vendors showed the ways in which their business model produced value. Some were keen to demonstrate it had instrumental rational value, in the form of economic profitability and sustainability. By contrast, others sought to show the cultural value to their work. A group of cannabis vendors were especially adamant on this point and sought to differentiate both their operations and their product from commercial operations. This quote captured how the value had to be demonstrated by educating others about what made for a good drug:

> There is a persistent myth about the trade which is that your top notch weed is dank, fat, thick smelling crystal covered nugs. It isn't a coincidence. Dealers, big commercial growers, seedbanks and breeders keep this myth alive. Commercial farmers who trade in large volumes. We are more like an artisan collective. Our aim is making the best product not the most money. There is vast and deep gulf between commercial indicas which grow rapidly and sativas. Commercial growers use indica because it will grow quickly and they push that as defining what is high quality. Vendor 'HomieGrown'

In this case, the seller cannot rely on the buyers' cultural knowledge about cannabis quality to signify what they mean by quality and wants to differentiate it from potency, seen as a cheap trick of commercial growers. In this example, we see a conflict about motivation and value and whether commercial growing of illicit cannabis is lower status than the more ideologically motivated kind of grower (Ancrum and Treadwell 2017).

Looking for Culture

The material culture of intoxication is created within global flows, technoscapes and the residue of past efforts. There is no natural, herbal high here, untroubled by cultural norms, political economies and human meddling. Opium, cannabis and coca are all cultivars, plants bred to enhance their intoxicant qualities. Objects have the power of embodying all kinds of relationships and dispositions, of pleasure, pathology and recovery. They can delimit, though not dictate, the terms of their use. Intoxicants mediate such issues as social class (wine), gender (sugar) and savoir-faire (absinthe). In the rhetoric of intoxication, each quality is constructed in relationship to others such that the sweetness of sugar only exists in relation to the bitterness, acidity, saltiness, sourness and umami of other substances. Material culture reproduces and affirms these social relationships. Social relationships become in part relationships between objects. The complex back-and-forth constantly regenerates the materiality of intoxication within an algorithmic culture.

The category of the illicit has also had an impact on scientific knowledge and in particular has tended to reduce knowledge about illicit intoxication to the behaviour selected samples of users in treatment or otherwise performing as chaotic, unstable and un-functional (Decorte 2011). Academic research has its cultures and priorities, and while research showing controlled illicit drug use is likely much more common than chaotic or addictive use, that does not endear academics to governments (Stevens 2007). A part of the culture of illicit intoxication is therefore the cultures of civil service departments, lecturers and researchers who act as gatekeepers to knowledge about the illicit and who give that knowledge force and structure. While users of different drugs share knowledge, academic tribes are quite culturally homogenous and tightly bounded (Becher and Trowler 2001). They maintain their shared ideology through rituals of reproduction at conferences, in meetings and in academic journals and through in-group terminology. Like drug users, academics share folk tales and war stories. Academics are also made up through algorithms. The power of the performance metric and citations core grows stronger each passing year.

The concept of culture has to be adapted. There has sometimes been a background assumption that much contemporary illicit drug use such as smart drug use and the use of recreational drugs bought over the internet lead to de-cultured drug use, without the rich folklore of the urban righteous dopefiend (Agar 1971). However, research had tended to focus on the public, the street junkie and the male. So we look for the cultural in flamboyant performance. The domestic, the private and the female drug user were rather missing or subordinate or thought of as without culture in this sense. Culture is just as much a part these places however, and of relatively atomised and instrumental uses of drugs. What there is less of is a sense of drug using culture as a separate set of spaces and values with its own demographic, performances and symbols. In that sense, my view is that the validation of illicit intoxication culture is going to be needed, an approach that traces it throughout different spaces, both digital and material.

Drug Markets in Institutions

The array of practices and knowledge around a psychoactive substance produce it as an effective object with characteristics that vary by time and place and are not solely dependent on its physical nature (Gomart 2002). Almost all accounts of intoxication include a ritual aspect (Becker 1953) but this perhaps reflects a research bias. By its nature, ritual is observable, describable and accountable, and the ethnographic methods used with drug users will tend to pick up on ritual. The way to move the discussion on is the role of cue reactivity in ritual, uses in risk management and titration.

In terms of risk management, it appeared that the more potent a substance was perceived to be, the more precise and measured the rituals surrounding it were (Carnwath and Smith 2002). Sensory dose titration was based on the experience and skill of users and the perceived potency of drug (for example, one that causes pain in consumption is potent). Smoking was a more practiced cue. Cannabis is taken to be a 'soft' drug, with a wide variation in effects, and generally of low risk. The ritual preparations described by participants were fairly lax about the amount used, and emphasised the performative nature of the ritual. Other users accepted whatever the roller decided to put in. They would then comment on the quality of the 'smoke'. A 'good smoke' had the right combination of smokeability and potency, but was not too strong or too mild. In the examples given of snorting substances, the group members took much more care over the titration of the dose, carefully ensuring lines are evenly distributed. There was greater concern here with managing the dose, as the drug and the method of consumption were seen as more risky. Perceived chemical potency equated risk. The ritual had the function of managing risk, ensuring an adequate level of intoxication while avoiding overdoses or other problem reactions. In other cases, such as ecstasy in pill form used in a clubbing setting, there was no opportunity to titrate the dose. Instead, sometimes a part of one pill would be consumed by one group member in order to test its quality and content.

Drug users perceived it being more possible for illicit drug use to be normatively integrated into an otherwise alcohol-focused party or other social gathering than cigarette smokers. This perception may be a bias reflecting the relatively drug and alcohol savvy make-up of the group. Nonetheless it does fit with more general sense in which smokers are seen as merely 'unhealthy' while illicit drug users are seen as risk-taking. Illicit drug users were not necessarily outside the ideology of healthfulness, provided they were seen to manage the risks of their drug use and confine it to social settings. Rituals were used to manage and mediate risk. From a public health perspective, it was notable that the most personal damage was associated with drinking in the night-time economy, in the form of sexual harassment, vomiting, being excluded from nightclubs and hospitalisation.

The ritual was part of the learning process for new users and the process of generating anticipation for experienced users. Rituals could be designed to combine the drug, set and setting (Zinberg 1986), for instance by preparing the 'set' ensuring the 'drug' is distributed and consumed and that the setting supported the desired form of intoxication. This aspect of the ritual further heightened anticipation, the 'buzz' and excitement of looking forward to intoxication. In the case of alcohol, skill was demonstrated through consumption, such as that of the drinker supremely able to handle large quantities of alcohol in the pre-drinking ritual. To contrast, in the case of illicit or unlicensed drugs such as cannabis, methoxi and medicinal drugs rituals focused much more on the preparation of the drug. Skill was demonstrated through confident, competent processing of the drug into a state fit to be consumed. Authenticity and expertise was demonstrated in this way (Haines et al. 2009). A rough equality of consumption was sought in snorting and smoking joints. Splitting lines into equal measure, those who hold onto a joint too long will be reprimanded as 'Bogarting' or smoking the joint far more or for far longer than considered fair (Sandberg 2013).

Sexual divisions and sexual scripts are part of nightlife (Ronen 2010). There is a distinction between the recreational drug economy and the commodified night-time economy. There was sense of illicit drug rituals themselves being gendered in these accounts. Men and women bought and sold drugs, cut lines and rolled joints. However, this probably reflects the kinds of drug rituals recorded. Skilled drug preparers are predominantly male in the research literature, though in the examples given here women were skilful drug procurers and producers. There was a clear gendering in dress and demeanour in preparation for going out to mainstream clubs. Female accounts in particular recognised the different pressures exerted on women in the heterosexual night-time economy, and this was also noted in the accounts of some male students. Disciplined embodied femininity was demonstrated though the considerable effort fake tanning required. In contrast, the atmosphere of the underground club could be experienced by both men and women as a valued time-out from some of the demands of the heterosexual economy of display.

One function rituals serve is to maintain social order and legitimate power (Hearn 2012). Some of the rituals described maintain a status hierarchy though performed egalitarianism. In this example, power relations are affirmed through invoking equality. These accounts emphasised senses in transition, for example from childhood to adulthood, through different taste cultures, from private to public femininity. Disgust and distaste were present in many accounts. Distaste could be a warning sign of a mismatch between intoxication and setting, or an undesired femininity, a gender order that reduces female subjectivity to writhing display. Taste and disgust was a way of judging sociality and evaluating the 'worth' of situations. Sensory responses, in particular embodied disgust and repulsion, can be explored as ways of enacting social scripts.

Conclusion

Drug users and dealers took to the digital rather faster than researchers did. That may have been because it short circuited both the econmic restrictions and the cultural stigmatisation of their activity. Markets have cultures, and criminal activity is culturally mediated and materially embedded. Economic exchanges may take a second to happen, but their consequences last a lifetime. They may be seen in the bodies of long term injecting drug users, or the culturally disconnected spaces of deprived and left behind areas. Cultural forgetting is a the way people at the core of the global economy have of dealing with people and places that are troublesome and peripheral. One of the cultural advantages of criminal markets is they link to and create economic life around some of these spaces. They can give cultural meaning and direction, or they can be ways of people achieving culturally normal goals, showing themselves to be entrepreneurs or high rolling consumers (Merton 1938).

References

Agar, M. H. (1971). Folklore of the heroin addict: Two examples. *The Journal of American Folklore, 84*(332), 175–185. https://doi.org/10.2307/538988.

Ancrum, C., & Treadwell, J. (2017). Beyond ghosts, gangs and good sorts: Commercial cannabis cultivation and illicit enterprise in England's disadvantaged inner cities. *Crime, Media, Culture, 13*(1), 69–84. https://doi.org/10.1177/1741659016646414.

Anderson, T. L., & Levy, J. A. (2003). Marginality among older injectors in today's illicit drug culture: Assessing the impact of ageing. *Addiction, 98*(6), 761–770. https://doi.org/10.1046/j.1360-0443.2003.00388.x.

Becker, H. S. (1953). Becoming a marihuana user. *American Journal of Sociology, 59*(3), 235–242.

Becher, T., & Trowler, P. R. (2001). *Academic tribes and territories.* New York: McGraw-Hill.

Bourgois, P. (1998). The moral economies of homeless heroin addicts: Confronting ethnography, HIV risk, and everyday violence in San Francisco shooting encampments. *Substance Use and Misuse, 33*(11), 2323–2351. https://doi.org/10.3109/10826089809056260.

Campbell, H. (2000). The glass phallus: Pub(lic) masculinity and drinking in rural New Zealand. *Rural Sociology, 65*(4), 562–581. https://doi.org/10.1111/j.1549-0831.2000.tb00044.x.

Campbell, N. D., & Shaw, S. J. (2008). Incitements to discourse: Illicit drugs, harm reduction, and the production of ethnographic subjects. *Cultural Anthropology, 23*(4), 688–717.

Carnwath, T., & Smith, I. (2002). *Heroin century.* London: Routledge.

Collins, R. (2004). *Interaction ritual chains/Randall Collins.* Princeton, NJ and Oxford: Princeton University Press, [2004], ©2004 (Main Library (STANDARD LOAN)—2nd floor HM1111 Col.).

Decorte, T. (2011). Blinding ourselves with science: The chronic infections of our thinking on psychoactive substances. In G. Hunt, M. Milhet, & Henri Bergeron (Eds.), *Drugs and culture: Knowledge, consumption and policy* (pp. 33–51). Farnham: *Ashgate.*

Dennis, F. (2016). Encountering "triggers". *Contemporary Drug Problems, 43*(2), 126–141.

Dennis, F. (2017). Conceiving of addicted pleasures: A 'modern' paradox. *International Journal of Drug Policy, 49*, 150–159. https://doi.org/10.1016/j.drugpo.2017.07.007.

Dennis, F., & Farrugia, A. (2017). Materialising drugged pleasures: Practice, politics, care. *International Journal of Drug Policy, 49*, 86–91. https://doi.org/10.1016/j.drugpo.2017.10.001.

Fleetwood, J. S. (2009). *Emotional work: Ethnographic fieldwork in prisons in Ecuador*. Glasgow: University of Glasgow.

Furst, R. T. (2000). The re-engineering of heroin: An emerging heroin "cutting" trend in New York City. *Addiction Research, 8*(4), 357–379.

Gomart, E. (2002). Methadone: Six effects in search of a substance. *Social Studies of Science, 32*(1), 93–135.

Gusfield, J. R. (1987). Passage to play: Rituals of drinking time in American society. In M. Douglas (Ed.), *Constructive drinking: Perspectives on drink from anthropology* (pp. 73–90). Cambridge: Cambridge University Press.

Gusfield, J. (1997). The culture of public problems: Drinking-driving and the symbolic order. In *Morality and health* (pp. 201–229). New York: Routledge.

Haines, R. J., Johnson, J. L., Carter, C. I., & Arora, K. (2009). "I couldn't say, I'm not a girl"—Adolescents talk about gender and marijuana use. *Social Science & Medicine, 68*(11), 2029–2036.

Haritavorn, N. (2014). Surviving in two worlds: Social and structural violence of Thai female injecting drug users. *International Journal of Drug Policy, 25*(1), 116–123. https://doi.org/10.1016/j.drugpo.2013.09.008.

Hearn, J. (2012). *Theorizing power*. Macmillan International Higher Education.

Jensen, C., Forlini, C., Partridge, B., & Hall, W. (2016). Australian university students' coping strategies and use of pharmaceutical stimulants as cognitive enhancers. *Frontiers in Psychology, 7*. https://doi.org/10.3389/fpsyg.2016.00277.

Lévi-Strauss, C. (1969). *The raw and the cooked: Introduction to a science of mythology* (Vol. 1). Harper & Row New York.

Manderson, D. (1995). Metamorphoses: Clashing symbols in the social construction of drugs. *Journal of Drug Issues, 25*(4), 799–816. https://doi.org/10.1177/002204269502500410.

Mauss, M. (1954). *The gift: The form and reason for exchange in archaic societies*. London: Routledge.

Measham, F., & Brain, K. (2005). 'Binge' drinking, British alcohol policy and the new culture of intoxication. *Crime, Media, Culture, 1*(3), 262–283. https://doi.org/10.1177/1741659005057641.

Merton, R. K. (1938). Social structure and anomie. *American Sociological Review, 3*(5), 672.

Netherland, J., & Hansen, H. B. (2016). The war on drugs that wasn't: Wasted whiteness, "dirty doctors", and race in media coverage of prescription opioid misuse. *Culture, Medicine, and Psychiatry, 40*(4), 664–686.

Nugent, P. (2014). Modernity, tradition, and intoxication: Comparative lessons from South Africa and West Africa. *Past & Present, 222*(Suppl. 9), 126–145.

Parkin, S. G. (2013). *Habitus and drug using environments: Health, place and lived-experience.* Retrieved from https://www.dawsonera.com/abstract/9781409464938.

Pennay, A. (2012). Carnal pleasures and grotesque bodies: Regulating the body during a 'big night out' of alcohol and party drug use. *Contemporary Drug Problems; London, 39*(3), 397–428, 346.

Robbins, T. (1969). Eastern mysticism and the resocialization of drug users: The Meher Baba cult. *Journal for the Scientific Study of Religion, 8*, 308–317.

Rodriguez, S., Fernandez, M., Cepedabenito, A., & Vila, J. (2005). Subjective and physiological reactivity to chocolate images in high and low chocolate cravers. *Biological Psychology, 70*(1), 9–18.

Ronen, S. (2010). Grinding on the dance floor. *Gender & Society, 24*(3), 355–377.

Rosenberg, C. E. (2002). The tyranny of diagnosis: Specific entities and individual experience. *The Milbank Quarterly, 80*(2), 237–260. https://doi.org/10.1111/1468-0009.t01-1-00003.

Sandberg, S. (2013). Cannabis culture: A stable subculture in a changing world. *Criminology and Criminal Justice, 13*(1), 63–79. https://doi.org/10.1177/1748895812445620.

Schüll, N. D. (2012). *Addiction by design: Machine gambling in Las Vegas.* Princeton: Princeton University Press.

Scott, S. (2010). Revisiting the total institution: Performative regulation in the reinventive institution. *Sociology, 44*(2), 213–231.

Seddon, T. (2016). Inventing drugs: A genealogy of a regulatory concept. *Journal of Law and Society, 43*(3), 393–415. https://doi.org/10.1111/j.1467-6478.2016.00760.x.

Stevens, A. (2007). Survival of the ideas that fit: An evolutionary analogy for the use of evidence in policy. *Social Policy and Society, 6*(1), 25–35. https://doi.org/10.1017/S1474746406003319.

Strang, J., Griffiths, P., & Gossop, M. (1997). Heroin in the United Kingdom: Different forms, different origins, and the relationship to different routes of administration. *Drug and Alcohol Review, 16* (4), 329–337.

Taylor, A. (1993). *Women drug users: An ethnography of a female injecting community.* Oxford: Clarendon Press.

Zinberg, N. (1986). *Drug, set, and setting: The basis for controlled intoxicant use.* New Haven, CT: Yale University Press.

6

Cybercrime Is Not Always Rational, but It Is Reasonable

Digital Crime Is Structured More Than Organised

A challenge for researchers and law enforcement has been understanding criminal activities that are adaptive, resilient and well motivated but not 'organised' in a routine sense (Raab and Milward 2003). A powerful explanation examines their economic logic as sophisticated, rationally governed operations with business-like structures and functions that leverage adaptive network qualities (Kraemer-Mbula et al. 2013; Kshetri 2010; Yip et al. 2012). However, there tends to be an elision between 'markets' and 'economic rationality' as if the two are co-produced. Markets in neoclassical theory are theorised as pure rational exchange when they are in fact institutionalised, culturally located, socially embedded structures (Beckert 2009; Fligstein 2002). In order to function markets do not need rationality, in the sense of calculable judgements that respond to price/cost signals, and do not necessarily breed it either (Beckert and Dewey 2017).

In terms of how we theorise illicit markets, criminology has increasingly recognised the many ways that dynamics of criminal economic entities are shaped by market relationships such as supply/demand relationships and economic opportunity structures (Becker 1968; Reuter 1983) and of

© The Author(s) 2020
A. Bancroft, *The Darknet and Smarter Crime*, Palgrave Studies
in Cybercrime and Cybersecurity, https://doi.org/10.1007/978-3-030-26512-0_6

criminals as rational actors (Winter 2008). The contention is that economic rationality in illicit markets should be seen as one possible situated, localised logic of action among others, and as the product of a range of practices, ideologies and technologies which are employed by users. These are: the development of a hybrid infrastructure of licit and illicit systems and technologies, sufficient weak network ties to ensure the diffusion of knowledge about trusted actors and of comprehensible business practices, formalised and informal regulatory processes, and shared cultural norms (Beckert 2009).

Cryptomarkets are suitable case studies as they are a place where the business structures involved are designed to be reproducible and are picked over by buyers, sellers and interested commentators in public discussion forums (Aldridge and Décary-Hétu 2014; Martin 2014a). Cryptomarket site administrators and vendors display various business-like attributes, such as entrepreneurship (Afilipoaie and Shortis 2015), business efficiency (Van Hout and Bingham 2014), reputation management (Décary-Hétu and Leppänen 2016) and risk assessment (Cunliffe et al. 2017; Décary-Hétu et al. 2016). Cryptomarket users themselves increasingly identify a move away from libertarian political motives to those of economic calculation (Munksgaard and Demant 2016). Administrators, vendors and drug buyers in the cryptomarkets often praise business-like and customer-focused attitudes and face challenges such as quality signalling (Wendel and Curtis 2000).

However, participants' self-representation may not capture the way in which markets are constructs with their own cultures and politics which shape the justificatory logics market participants apply (MacKenzie 2014). I define them as assemblages of software and hardware systems, networks which form around monetary and knowledge exchange and social support, and shared practices and norms, all of which embed social and economic relationships. Cryptomarkets are not just 'where things happen' but their structure and logics are part of what happens.

The cryptomarkets' appearance as open retail spaces belies complex underlying interrelations and structuring factors which may not be apparent from the 'front end'. For example, a large proportion of trades by value are wholesale dealer to dealer so for many drug users cryptomarkets mediate rather than substitute the offline market (Aldridge and Décary-Hétu 2014). This draws attention to the different factors shaping the actions of market actors and how they address various challenges such as coordination problems, maintenance of trust and interfaces with other systems. The Tor darknet is a relatively concentrated social and physical space, with 20–50 groups hosting most of the content (Lewis 2016). Within and across cryptomarkets, groupings of vendors cooperate and share trade. Just as legal, free markets are not feverish hives of individualised competition, and are in fact composed of cooperating stable entities far more than competitive and disrupting entities, so members of cryptomarkets spend a significant amount of time making them stable and predictable.

I examine that resilience in the context of the social and technical structuring of the cryptomarkets. I look critically at what the 'market narrative' might say and what it misses out. I argue that the impression of a frictionless, buyer responsive free market in illicit products is illuminating and attractive to but incomplete and in some ways incorrect (*The Economist* 2014, 2016). Bonds of trust, obligation and support still exist, need to be worked and govern users' actions and decisions (Tzanetakis et al. 2016). The cryptomarkets have a role in regulating and marshalling the behaviour and self-presentation of buyers and dealers and embedding these behaviours in the technical infrastructure of the market.

Organised Crime Is a Useful Performance for Cops and Criminals

Law enforcement tends to target high-value, low volume players, reflecting a 'strong tie' approach, rather than lower value, high volume activities (Hutchings and Holt 2016). Studies of the cryptomarkets show that there are few big players (Soska and Christin 2015) so most activity is of the small-value, high volume type. Organised crime is a convention, agreed by cops and criminals with relevant labels applied but which may not have much resemblance to reality (Lusthaus 2013). There are some common features. Organised crime groups are persistent and seek to generate profits from one set of activities that can be invested in others, so they are investment-oriented operations. There is some permanence or persistence in their activities. This requires some control, staking of claims, argument about organised crime staking claims over literal or business territory, organised as in social control rather than coordination. Organised crime limits some kinds of crime, that directed against protected members of the organisation. It provides an interface for corruption of law enforcement agents so it can employ them in the regulation of crime. It is about the distribution of power over the illegal and semi-legal spheres.

A common quip is 'organised crime is not very well organised' but it is patterned and sometimes coordinated. There is a meshing of cybercriminal infrastructure, globalised commerce and finance. This meshing emphasises complexity and standardisation, the monetisation of risk, and involves a great number of digitally skilled interested, underemployed or indebted individuals. Drug money provides a core resource for criminal groups to fund further criminal activity and support them moving into new areas such as human trafficking. The organisation of it is driven by economics, culture and association. Tightly associated groupings focus on volume production, whereas more value driven or opportunistic groups are loosely organised or act as associations rather than organisations.

Associations come together for specific opportunities that allow them to coordinate skills and resources (Fleetwood 2014). Cartel organisation in digital crime markets is not strong, partly because they lack the skills but also using cryptomarkets and cryptocurrencies represent a huge threat exposure for them. They are well served by existing shadow banking and money laundering services. Cartels are quite risk averse and the digital crime markets lack or are hostile to many of the established control agents they use.

That does not stop people making the claim of course that they are very well connected as in these quotes from two different markets:

> Connected to a mafia family? You? i'm over here crying laughing at your stupid ass. You ain't tied in bruh! I think we all know that. You know a guy who knows a guy. Complaint over a month ago was blue flakes in your dope. That ain't mob. sleeping pill tricks. You think by saying you use dope it helps you identify with us. your a certified clown. Enough of my hood rant, it's not adding any significance to this thread. I do one better. Done

posting all together. on the dope side realsupremesmoke got some fiya! right now! No i'm not him or any other vendor Dopechick i mean Dopeman can throw fud at. just my review.

The epitome of drug related feuds on the internet. Tersely worded posts. Beats shooting at each other. On a side note The PowerCartel made good of their promise and gave a 50% refund. Bastards. I only got 30%.

Digital society permits a move away from place-based crime control by organised crime groups but just because there is a route does not mean they want to take it (Choo 2008). Globalisation is one effect that pre-dates digitisation and which has extended the operational reach of organised crime groups. A work of caution on the data context is needed, policing and policy focuses a lot on asset forfeiture/recovery so there is a tendency to inflate the estimated value of organised crime proceeds (Levi and Osofsky 1995).

Trade Associations Exist Alongside Cartels

One of the problems cartels have with the darknet is it is hard to control your assets and how buyers and sellers deal with a market in 'lemons' where quality cannot be verified (Akerlof 1978). The illicit drug markets represent this problem given the difficulty of verifying drug quality and the impermanence of typical quality markers such as branding which do not allow people to confidently gauge reliability. There are not enough incentives to stop it becoming a predatory market. Profits on the retail side are low to non-existent (Reuter 1983; Reuter and Caulkins 2004).

Trade associations exist to manage their customer base and ensure supply chain security, sharing precursor chemicals, sharing seeds, and in some cases lab space. Here is a UK cannabis grower and dealer on a cryptomarket:

We are building a room inside a stone building. Plenty of insulation on top of our room to reduce any thermal tell tale signs. Then growing in soil under 600W lights.

if it's u and a mate I'd look into a bigger setup…maybe 2×600w in the flowering tent n have a 400w mh veg tent n maybe a few cfls in a clone station. I run a 600w for myself lol ok I've a few extra grams to sell but if u looking to make a nice tidy few pound I'd say perpetual is the way to go. I'd look into a few grow tent since its easier to work with (in my opinion) Setup wise n ur not gonna be making any holes in the wall. Clones are a good Routh especially if ur planning to be a cash cropper since you'll have consistent,strong hardy strains n guaranteed winners in any.

Anyway, I have lots of BC Big Bud (a UK favourite), lots of Critical Mass (usually it all goes to customers in the US fast, so jump on this stuff), Caramelicious, White Widow XTRM and AK47 XTRM. All seeds except Critical Mass come from Amsterdam Marijuana Seeds. The Critical Mass is from Mr. Nice seeds. All great genetics.

Criminal networks typically consist of individuals and small, loose groupings who come together around specific opportunities (Sparrow 1991). These opportunities are managed through the role of network brokers, individuals who connect denser criminal networks to each other (Coles 2001). Weak ties, acquaintanceships known to one but unknown to each other, are crucial in maintaining functioning networks and diffusing information. The low background noise of informational gossip is crucial for how criminals receive intelligence about market risks and law enforcement actions and adjust their behaviour (Dickinson and Wright 2015). My hypothesis is that this is true of cryptomarkets. The weak ties embedded in cryptomarkets reduce the cost of establishing trust which makes them highly attractive to criminal entrepreneurs. The success of cryptomarkets is in part because they marshal these weak ties in a very effective manner. Crucially these weak ties function both within specific markets and between markets. This explains some of the surprising resilience of the cryptomarket systems in the face of both law enforcement intervention and attacks from other cybercriminals.

Illegal Markets Come in Different Types

Beckert and Dewey (2017) set out a useful typology of illicit markets, along two axes. They compare the degree to which criminality is central to the market process, and the extent to which the trades are socially legitimated. Selling counterfeit clothing is generally legitimate, but illegal. Markers in human wombs are more stigmatised. Trafficking in child pornography is both heavily criminalised and taboo. Hunting rare animal trophies is legal in many places, but attracts widespread social condemnation. To this other dimensions could be added, such as coercion and collaboration.

Infrastructure and platforms matters more than technologies which can be swapped in and out. Specific escrow systems or vulnerability exploits are the vectors through which digital crime can happen. However, criminals have got much better at replacing technologies as needed, relying instead on crime platforms (Dittus et al. 2017).

There are different kinds of illegal market depending on the transaction, the people involved and the source of the illegality. A typology produced by Beckert and Wehinger (2012) break them into illegal products (such as illicit drugs), illegal commodification (selling human organs), illegal exchange (selling stolen goods), illegal production (slavery) and third-party corruption (selling access). Each has different value structures, ethics and interrelations with the legal and semi-legal and different ideas of value. Illegality can exist at one point in the supply chain, it does not have to be something all actors are complicit in.

Mostly illegal markets are treated as parasitical, circumventing regulations and leaching value from the formal economy. However, illegal markets have always contributed value. They might distribute labour and marginal employment opportunities. In the case of drugs they introduce new products and create use value. Law enforcement action can be perceived as an attack on a community as well as on a lucrative financial opportunity. Illegal markets can therefore provide security, meaning, purpose and commonality: ones that do are probably the stickiest and hardest to shift.

From Kingpinning to Routine Crime

In terms of the internal labour structure, inequality is typical. Tochka market admin pays staff under $1000 per week, a poor return for very high risk. Admin also uses external developers to maintain the site for even less (Caleb 2019). People involved put up with exploitation in the hope of future large gains. One of the temptations of cryptomarkets is to allow a dealer to monopolise their local market, called king pinning. Kingpinning is one way people try and use the darknet to mimic this lifestyle but largely is held in contempt by darknet users as ultimately futile and likely to lead to sudden arrest or deposition from one's pedestal by rivals.

I wonder how the windblown thieves who seek to hold consumer items and touch them cope with the world where much value is held digitally and there just isn't that much to steal? The group of largely successful crooks seen in various research studies have wealth pouring through and out of their hands in the form of expensive clothes, cars and tat. They don't put it aside because this is the aim, to be seen and envied by others. Their potlatch consumption is superficially successful but eats itself, and its community. Individualistic, hostile to local government, university, schools: what do these institutions have in common? A bit socialist, unnecessary from their point of view and probably also hindering their hoped for transformation from small time criminals to the big time. I wonder what has happened to them now there are some routes into the medium big time through the darknet and other rather easier ways of conducting one's business out of sight? Has the bling crime been replaced by the internet crime with a slightly different set of values? After all, being on the darknet means one cannot display one's wealth to others. Some have done this e.g. Alphabay's Casezes but online. Their glory days are generally brief—there's always someone younger, tougher, fitter to take over, relegating some in their early 20s to menial drug dealing after some hog days. Those who are 'oppositional' in these areas tend to hold down jobs and standard political views.

Crime is more typically embedded in routine. The focus of is often on the high disruption one off crimes that never happen in the same way twice.

Mostly however it is just low level heartache. Criminal markets have functional motives and psychological rewards. Criminal activity is routinised and scripted. As with other aspects of the illicit markets, reducing motives to economic gain is limiting. Economic gain can come in unexpected ways. For example, many drug dealers find returns from soaring bitcoin prices are greater than returns for drugs. Participating in markets then changes people's preferences and motives in a feedback loop. They learn to be 'players'. Some participate and become badder, some less bad. Everyone changes through interaction and learning, testing themselves against decisions that come up.

Normal Scammers and Legit Vendors

Scams were normal risks. They were expected and victims were expected to look out for themselves. There were two kinds of market scam. The 'normal scam' was an expected part of the crypto market experience. There were a range of normal scams. An otherwise reliable vendor selectively failing to deliver to a customer was thought of as irritating but a normal part of the business ethic for large vendors. A vendor with a poor or no reputation scamming a buyer was likewise expected and nothing the buyer could complain about. A market administrator conducting an exit scam, leaving with bitcoin in escrow, was disruptive but not overall cataclysmic. Scams in this sense are business models rather than market deviance. They were scams that the markets could recover from and that they were resilient towards.

Another class of scams began to emerge in 2018–2019 and were extra-normal scams where a scammer manipulated the data held by the market or its trust mechanism. For example, using market data to blackmail customers and vendors was seen as catastrophic. The scam would work by the attacker making the users' data public. Doing so would lead to the buyers or vendors not being able to operate in the cryptomarkets at all. These were attacks that the markers were not resilient to and which are hard to recover from.

Business Strategy and Trajectory

> One market vendor describes his or her situation: I require FE because I cant afford to lose money on BTC fluctuations. If I do, then I'm out of pocket and customers lose out on savings and such things. I need to meet profit targets and stick to a business plan or else there is no point in being here. Maybe I will have happy customers but I dont want to vend forever, I have a business plan and once I reach a certain amount in savings then I'm done. I'll stay around the forum cause I like it but I wont vend anymore. Not that its any of your business, it's my business and I will run it whatever way I want and I'm certainly not going to let someone with no life who thinks he is some kind of darknet robin hood but is only right 15% of the time by pure chance.

There are a range of business types present in the cryptomarkets which combine technical and organisational systems in different ways (Moeller 2012). They can be differentiated by size and also internal structure, their trajectory and how they link with other criminal operations and supporting services such as couriers and bagmen. Greater predictability in their operations means skills of capital management, stock control, customer responsiveness come to the fore. A vendor's market strategy is constrained or enabled by financial factors such as their access to startup capital, their ability to secure product through the drug distribution chain, and proximity to distribution systems. A simple way of categorising market relations is to look at the internal structure of vendor businesses. Common business types were single vendors with one person in charge of product sourcing or production and distribution, extended organisations with sourcing and distribution separate, and franchises or secondary distribution systems. Franchising allowed a vendor to maintain their market position while limiting the size of their operation and manage risk by minimising cross-border traffic.

Related to the business strategy is the vendor's concept of the life-cycle or trajectory of their own business. Some vendors have a growth trajectory and an end point in mind, and some plan an open-ended trajectory that responds to market demand. These are not fully separate as vendors change their approach depending on changes in the supply chain, perceived risk of law enforcement interception, and changes in the cryptomarket itself. I divided trajectories into the end point the vendor is aiming for: long-term stability, scam, pump and dump (trying for low-quality rapid sales followed by a swift market exit), and going private or off-market, meaning selling to a restricted, vetted client base. Vendors' network position helped maintain their trajectory. Lone vendors could be quite successful economically but did not exist in a network of supportive sellers while others have more complex business models with separate departments for production, distribution and shipping involving numerous ancillary staff (Reuter and Mark 1986). Separating out distribution can have benefits in allowing the vendor to concentrate on customer service and operational planning but it also creates human resources problems:

> CaptainBeard had someone doing his drops for him and that person was not a good choice for him and the first package never arrived. CaptainBeard had some problems with that guy and got rid of him. So now shipping has been rectified. CaptainBeard send out another package, this one FedEx next day and it arrive AOK for my drop situation. Buyer 'Alscarpets'

Some have clearly expressed longer-term visions for their business which balance the benefits of higher turnover versus the risks it represents such as lower profit margins, greater business complexity and attracting the attention of law enforcement and rivals. For those reasons they can seek to stay small and focused on retail level customer orders. Others have a plan to move from retail to bulk orders over time. These vendors that are trying to break into the bulk sales market seek to develop a close relationship with a selected client base.

A network strategy allowed vendors is to leverage network effects by identifying what I have termed 'super-reviewers', forum members who are particularly active and trusted by other users in the market who can be targeted with free samples and discounts. They are a kind of key reputation actor common in online criminal networks (Dupont et al. 2016). They are identified and acted on by the vendors in order to maximise reputation and sales for example by using free samples, a good way of building a reputation and are an effective entry strategy for new players (Coomber 2003). Reputation capital in the cryptomarkets is mediated through the reputation systems and forums. As many users noted, however, it is hard to differentiate between the many vendors who have almost the same highest possible score. They then turn to super-reviewers for judgement. Super-reviewers play a significant role in mediating a vendor's transition from small to bulk sales, and from being on the public market to taking their business private. Their role is akin to 'power reviewers' on licit platforms, a role that is deliberately created and rewarded by the platform designers. They have many weak ties to other market participants so act as diffusers of reliable knowledge.

Various factors affected whether they could follow their planned trajectory. A threat to vendors was becoming overextended and not having the staff to maintain throughput, and access to capital and the restrictions of the market feedback system which mean it was a risky investment.

> I'm waiting for more good reviews before I start selling in larger weights. If official tests are positive then I'll move into bulk. This takes time. The purest coke costs more and sells quickly compared to my standard product. The standard coke takes up most of my capital. The connoisseur market is tempting but I'm not ready for it yet. Vendor, Hazmates

So although the driving factor for some was making large profits as quickly as they could, many were self-limiting, seeing a distinct cut off point in their business trajectory, and for others there were inbuilt limitations of capital or ability to manage their customers and the feedback system (Hammersvik et al. 2012). They could limit their business size to avoid the risks of having other employees, or having to commercialise. A final point in some vendors' trajectories is closing or passing the business on. Some have a set aim in mind and leave the market having achieved a desired level of profit. A good business can be sold to another vendor which allows the vendor to depart with minimal disruption to their client base.

Underpinning their market strategies were business practices that manage customer demand (Martin 2014b). I have divided these into demand facing and market-oriented practices. Demand facing business practices sought to manage the business identity and the customer base, such as through branding, pricing strategies and product quality management. Market-oriented business practices involved managing challenges arising from the market infrastructure. They included practices of hedging against bitcoin fluctuation and extended to strategies to damage rivals' businesses through distributing negative reviews and all the way to cyber attacks on rival markets.

To some extent their practices were a function of market position in the sense of the relationship to the market overall rather than the size of the business. Positioning could be seen as a function of the business type but there were more complex factors at work in terms of the dynamics involving others in the market. Market position was therefore partly out of the control of vendors and was sometimes a function of business type and in other cases was due to the opportunities that came up and their ability to exploit them. Many vendors moved from retail to bulk operations as they were able to access larger quantities in the supply chain or as their customers changed their requirements. A different approach was the vendor developing their ability to control different steps in the supply chain. Some were able to take charge of most or all of the supply chain from production to retail distribution. This was the exception. Most vendors represented different steps in the chain, including the cryptomarket service industry. They provided precursor chemicals, or took other roles in the supply chain, or provided hosting or ancillary services such as bitcoin tumbling services which launder bitcoin.

Building a Hybrid Infrastructure to Cope with Uncertainty

A big part of user activity is threat identification and avoidance (Aldridge and Askew 2017; Holt et al. 2016). Ripoffs and predation are present and have to be protected against (Moeller et al. 2017). Scams are the deliberate manipulation of trust or market systems to create a profit without delivering product. It could be a business model in itself or an end point of the trajectory of otherwise reliable vendors or markets. Administrators shuttered several markets in this way. Although not common, there are vendors for whom the exit scam is a goal. In this model, they build up their client base with free samples or inducements before leaving with multiple large orders unfilled. Lucrative exit scams also work at market level. Selective scamming also exists, which allows the vendor to increase profit margins while maintaining a reasonable reputation. A smart scammer can manipulate the feedback system, for example by changing the delivery date until it is too late for the customer to give feedback. In those situations, the only redress was to appeal to the market administrator. In terms of business, scamming is not just an ethical issue. It is sometimes forced by the closure of a market, or is a final goodbye from a vendor leaving the market. Market participants recognised a distinction between businesses set up to milk market users and those where the vendor quits their obligations due to external factors. The latter were thought of as normal scammers driven by changes in the cryptomarket and its infrastructure rather than a commitment to scamming as a business strategy as such.

The market infrastructure is composed of a number of different technical and social network interfaces that mediate the drug market as a whole. This is more than just increased transactional efficiency compared to offline markets but also involves a set of practical stances which play out and are reproduced within the cryptomarkets and their associated discussion forums. One way this shaped the judgements vendors make is when a sufficiently trustworthy relationship is established they can go private have an invited only clientele within the cryptomarkets or move their client base entirely off the market. Doing so allows them to manage their turnover and operate without relying on one single cryptomarket. This reduces risk for vendors from market-based scams and from closure due to law enforcement activity or cyber attacks. In contrast to that densely structured approach, other vendors reduce risk by reproducing their business across multiple cryptomarkets (Broséus et al. 2016). They rely on resilience through replication and hedge against market failure. Super-reviewers also operate across different markets and track and share information about vendors on the forum.

A major problem for vendors is the risk to profits from Bitcoin fluctuations. Bitcoin is a volatile currency. A deal might be finalised at one value and shipped at a lower one, sufficient to wipe out the vendor's profit margin before they can convert the bitcoin into another currency. The risk can be mitigated by offering buyers incentives to Finalise Early (FE). FE shortcuts the market's escrow system. Typically a buyer's payment is held until they confirm receipt of the product or a certain amount of time has passed. FE means payment is immediate. It puts a risk on the buyer who then only has the goodwill of the vendor to rely on should the shipment not arrive. Some buyers do not have the choice of avoiding it. Buyers who are rated low and are assumed to be less reliable may have to pay a premium or take on risk by being required to FE. Those who decide not to take on the risk of FE have a smaller and also less reliable selection of vendors from which to choose.

Other vendors create strategic relationships to limit risk. Some become suppliers for smaller scale vendors. This can be used as a way of mitigating the risk of shipping across international borders (Décary-Hétu et al. 2016). Pairing up with a domestic distributor allows fewer, larger shipments to be made with the aim of reducing the risk of interception. The logic is that a greater number of shipments increases the chances of a random intercept by customs inspectors which will then draw attention to the whole operation. Bulk volume sales also allow for great liquidity in the business

> Until we do reach these volume customers, our business model is capital locked, unable to source additional volume product (the only reliable way to import) and facing delays when it comes time to re-inventory. Vendor 'Babezinclubland'

Larger vendors may use couriered drop shipments that allow them to operate outwith the postal system so avoiding possible law enforcement surveillance and ensuring correct delivery.

Coordination and Cooperation

Vendors make strategic use of their relationships with others. Small-scale sellers rely on shared knowledge and resources with others on a similar level. Smaller scale, more artisan cannabis producers would share recipes and material using specialised, closed discussion forums on the darknet or on social media. They would club together to buy growing material, giving themselves more buying power. In this they acted like trade associations which leveraged buying power and shared knowledge about the market and products. Groupings of larger and more 'professional' operations exist which see their position as constantly under threat from hostile vendors attempting to undermine their reputation.

Trade was sustained by vendors being willing to share knowledge and customers, creating resilience without organisation. Here is a vendor stepping into fill the gap when another vendor is unexpectedly offline:

> As I said I will keep two brands of #4 [heroin] available to fill [vendor] Afghantracy's gap. I will list it today, get your orders in by 10 pm GMT if you want me to ship it by Tuesday. Good going Tracy, I'm happy she is okay and all is well. The market is a big banquet and there is enough custom for all. The two of us are steady and robust. Vendor, Mixican

Individual cooperation was supplemented by a more generalised commitment to cryptomarkets as a system which needed to be maintained and protected. There are frequent statements in favour of the working of the free market that highlight the benefits of competition as 'being good for everyone':

> Cyber attacks on Merkat damage market diversity. Reduced range of cryptomarkets is AWFUL for the darknet. Perfect markets do not exist. Nobody who cared about the darknet would attack a market. Having just one cryptomarket is very very risky. Buyer '3MT'

Many users had a sense of obligation to other users and the community as a whole. One interviewee was a trained chemist and tested the drugs he bought using various reagents. He then posted the findings online with more information about the drug's characteristics.

These was some ideological disagreement about the value of competition. Users discussed risk and economic theory, hypothesising what lies behind fluctuations in drug prices and quality. Among forum lectures about the value of the market in supporting free choice, there were also users who valued cooperation and support among market participants. There is an awareness that market behaviour is rooted in the deep structure of the darknet, and a sense of the market as not inherently rational:

Customers are in the main not very rational in what they do. They do not act on information but their sense of the vendor and the appearance of the product. Vendor 'GlobalMegaCorp'

The different approaches vendors had can be seen as straightforward economic strategies and on one level they are. They are also strategies promoted by the structure of the markets with feedback mechanisms and mimicry of clearnet markets. There are different ideological stances were at work, in the sense of coherent value-oriented positions. Many are pragmatic and looked to the market as a source of income. A second group seek to demonstrate that the markets were a viable libertarian space for contract-driven relations (Munksgaard and Demant 2016). A third adhere to a resistant ideology which was a counter to the capitalist imperative of the market. They are critical of commercialisation and see the cryptomarkets as a place to conduct business without capitalist ideology being ever-present. Many respondents and those buyers and sellers commenting on forums consciously chose to resist what 'crime as business' might imply. Although they welcomed many aspects of the market relationship, they also valued the better social relationships and positive community activities that would go on around the market exchanges themselves. These included harm reduction initiatives, supporting people in decisions about drug use and desistance, and supporting less profit-driven and more artisan or responsive producers (Barratt et al. 2016).

Structuring Opportunity

Key to understanding how criminal opportunities are structured in cryptomarkets is contextualising economic motives and understanding how they are self-limited and restricted by the overall market infrastructure. Cryptomarkets are deviant social enterprises in that they are a context of exchange that is in part but not wholly structured by economic opportunity. Cryptomarkets are a location, rather than an organisation, in that there is little control over members (Lusthaus 2013). While the technical organisation can be highly structured, the social organisation of the cryptomarkets combine formal 'jurisdictions' of administrators (Valverde

2014) with less defined but still significant social 'beats' within the cryptomarkets and lateral regulation and social sanctioning by users. There is no natural logic of ever expanding supply. Some vendors choose trust and predictability over obtaining the biggest orders possible. Many market-related actions are not financial, calculated or exchanges at all. They involve reciprocity, sharing knowledge about risks and opportunities, sharing startup resources, and maintenance of the hybrid social and technical infrastructure. Conversely there are many monetary exchanges that are not exchange related such as scams, extortion, or more benignly, gifting and reciprocal exchanges of goods that do not even involve the distant prospect of financial settling up. One tempting conclusion is that the cryptomarkets solved some problems that drug users and dealers used to have. For example, social supply is the non-exchange distribution of drugs in friendship or reciprocity networks (Coomber et al. 2015). It might be assumed that the retail aspects of the cryptomarkets replaced social supply since this kind of distribution is not market friendly. However, it is very much in evidence both within the markets and mediated by them (Barratt et al. 2016).

Cryptomarkets enable and disable different types of crime and different orientations towards the illicit market. In this they function as formal and informal regulators. Conflict management strategies are highlighted by Morselli et al. (2017) as informal social regulation, consisting of 'tolerance, avoidance, ostracism, third-party intervention, negotiation, threats.' The act of excluding competitors or types of criminal activity that are perceived as low-value or carrying a high risk of law enforcement attention acts to constrain some types of criminal activity such as banning the sale of weapons. This might be motivated by moral revulsion about particular crimes but also by knowledge of the fact that these crimes bring with them unreliable and unprofessional users who are likely to attract the attention of multiple law enforcement agencies. A combination of moral pressure from users and self-interest encourages market administrators to regulate the items and services being sold. Critical to the development of business models in the cryptomarkets is the diffusion of knowledge about anonymity and security practice. There is a collective effort made up of many individuals and organisations that are not directly connected

(Granovetter 1973). That provides these markets with notable resilience in the face of technical and law enforcement disruption.

Key to self-regulation is small-scale performances of market norms. Cryptomarkets marshal the entrepreneurial dealer in the direction of performing as a customer service operative, emphasising secure packing, timely dispatch of product and accuracy of claims made about the product. They do this partly through the structure of the market itself and also through the community of practice that encourages this kind of representation and action on the part of sellers and buyers. They share much with clearnet marketplaces in that the apparently neutral, automatic referencing and rating system requires quite a lot of management by vendors. A critical point for the study of drug market is whether it is still useful in the light of this to divide the crime market into big men, middlemen and small fry, when we know the relationships are dynamic. Hence, we might move from studying market position to market action such as the role of mediation, franchising, supply chain control strategy and leveraging/arbitrage action such as exploiting differences in control regimes.

'Following the money' does not then necessarily lead to the biggest fish as cryptomarkets are a structure of mediation and embedding rather than a structure of business. Mediation works through network roles, weak ties therefore going beyond the traditional 'brokerage' function identified by Pearson and Hobbs (2003). Brokers ensure flexibility, avoid networks becoming brittle; they also act as innovators and introduce or validate innovations in the market (Morselli and Roy 2008). The networks have high functional differentiation between for example purchasing, processing and export. Market intelligence is necessarily limited. It cannot be assumed that online markets are inherently more transparent to market actors than street-level markets, but it is the case that they are mediated in different ways and the knowledge used can come in different forms. Mediation involves coordination and here it is interesting that vendors are often guided by indicators from other actors and not market signals. The embedding of cryptomarkets in other systems shapes the dynamics of vendor businesses and market activity. Cryptomarkets are a flexible and resilient crime architecture (Kenney 2007). A development within cryptomarkets is how they are changing the role of trust (Décary-Hétu and Dupont 2013). Maintaining trust is a perennial challenge in criminal networks. Lack of trust creates high transaction costs (Yip et al. 2013). This should point towards criminal networks being very dense and tightly bounded, with minimal links to other networks which could compromise criminal operations. However, this is not the case. While criminal networks, including transnational networks, are often highly embedded (Kleemans 2012), they are rarely hierarchal or controlled by a 'big boss' and they have porous, fluid boundaries. Indeed a smart vendor would try and maximise weak ties and minimise strong ones. Super-reviewers had a key role and it was notable that unlike licit web services which replicate the same role there was nothing in the technical infrastructure to recognise them. Instead, buyers and vendors sought their opinions out and looked to reward them.

Economic rationality, like other logics of a criminal marketplace, is performed when suited. Like violence it is a signal deployed where appropriate to generate desired effects among one's peers, victims, police and rivals. There are many logics overlapping in cryptomarkets. There are market-focused logics of customer service, professionalism, market forces as independent forces in the marketplace. There are non-market logics of cooperation and community that emphasise cryptomarkets as illicit social enterprises. Maintaining and acting out these logics is central to the work of vendors and buyers and supports the market as a functioning social space. The form these logics take vary between cryptomarkets depending on their configuration. Some promote greater experience sharing and non-exchange-based cooperation, particularly those focused on psychedelics and cannabis. Others emphasise instrumental logics and tangible economic benefits. Economic rationality is an outcome of particular configurations, rather than a driving force in the motives of criminal market actors. Those involved deploy and arrange the market architecture to fine tune the interface between the technical and social network aspects of the online criminal infrastructure.

Conclusion

If cryptomarkets are deviant social enterprises then, as Haller (1990) asks, other than the subject matter, exactly what difference does it make that the enterprise is illegal? Research has examined business practices among criminal networks such as malvertising (Zabyelina 2016), techniques which have much in common or sometimes are exactly the same as the same techniques in licit business activity. The illicit is not an external force shaping these enterprises, but is one feature of the background that vendors try to design out using encryption, stealth and security practices. Hence we cannot fully understand the decisions made by cryptomarket vendors if we rely on the licit/illicit distinction as the main driving force shaping criminal markets. Many of the processes I explored show cryptomarket enterprises adopting processes common to the licit business world. In answer to Haller's question, many of the differentiating factors he identified are not present. Both vendors and buyers showed role specialisation. Indeed the enterprises may be more stable and internally organised than was characteristic of 'organised' crime.

References

Afilipoaie, A., & Shortis, P. (2015). *The growing industry of darknet marketing.* Swansea: Global Drug Policy Observatory.

Akerlof, G. A. (1978). The market for "lemons": Quality uncertainty and the market mechanism. In *Uncertainty in economics* (pp. 235–251). New York: Elsevier.

Aldridge, J., & Askew, R. (2017). Delivery dilemmas: How drug cryptomarket users identify and seek to reduce their risk of detection by law enforcement. *International Journal of Drug Policy, 41*(Suppl. C), 101–109. https://doi.org/10.1016/j.drugpo.2016.10.010.

Aldridge, J., & Décary-Hétu, D. (2014). *Not an 'e-Bay for drugs': The cryptomarket 'Silk Road' as a paradigm shifting criminal innovation.* Rochester, NY: Social Science Research Network.

Barratt, M. J., Ferris, J. A., & Winstock, A. R. (2016). Safer scoring? Cryptomarkets, social supply and drug market violence. *International Journal of Drug Policy, 35*, 24–31. https://doi.org/10.1016/j.drugpo.2016.04.019.

Becker, G. S. (1968). Crime and punishment: An economic approach. In *The economic dimensions of crime* (pp. 13–68). https://doi.org/10.1007/978-1-349-62853-7_2.

Beckert, J. (2009). The social order of markets. *Theory and Society, 38*(3), 245–269. https://doi.org/10.1007/s11186-008-9082-0.

Beckert, J., & Dewey, M. (2017). Introduction: The social organization of illegal markets. In J. Beckert & M. Dewey (Eds.), *The architecture of illegal markets: Towards an economic sociology of illegality in the economy* (pp. 1–34). Retrieved from http://www.oxfordscholarship.com.ezproxy.is.ed.ac.uk/view/10.1093/oso/9780198794974.001.0001/oso-9780198794974.

Beckert, J., & Wehinger, F. (2012). In the shadow: Illegal markets and economic sociology. *Socio-Economic Review, 11*(1), 5–30.

Broséus, J., Rhumorbarbe, D., Mireault, C., Ouellette, V., Crispino, F., & Décary-Hétu, D. (2016). Studying illicit drug trafficking on darknet markets: Structure and organisation from a Canadian perspective. *Forensic Science International, 264*, 7–14. https://doi.org/10.1016/j.forsciint.2016.02.045.

Caleb. (2019, May 7). *What do we know about the DeepDotWeb seizure?* Retrieved May 8, 2019, from Caleb website https://medium.com/@c5/what-do-we-know-about-the-deepdotweb-seizure-98ca45de9987.

Choo, K.-K. R. (2008). Organised crime groups in cyberspace: A typology. *Trends in Organized Crime, 11*(3), 270–295. https://doi.org/10.1007/s12117-008-9038-9.

Coles, N. (2001). It's not what you know—It's who you know that counts: Analysing serious crime groups as social networks. *British Journal of Criminology, 41*(4), 580–594. https://doi.org/10.1093/bjc/41.4.580.

Coomber, R. (2003). There's no such thing as a free lunch: How 'freebies' and 'credit' operate as part of rational drug market activity. *Journal of Drug Issues, 33*(4), 939–962.

Coomber, R., Moyle, L., & South, N. (2015). The normalisation of drug supply: The social supply of drugs as the "other side" of the history of normalisation. *Drugs: Education, Prevention and Policy, 23*(3), 255–263. https://doi.org/10.3109/09687637.2015.1110565.

Cunliffe, J., Martin, J., Décary-Hétu, D., & Aldridge, J. (2017). An island apart? Risks and prices in the Australian cryptomarket drug trade. *International Journal of Drug Policy, 50*(Suppl. C), 64–73. https://doi.org/10.1016/j.drugpo.2017.09.005.

Décary-Hétu, D., & Dupont, B. (2013). Reputation in a dark network of online criminals. *Global Crime, 14*, 175–196. https://doi.org/10.1080/17440572.2013.801015.

Décary-Hétu, D., & Leppänen, A. (2016). Criminals and signals: An assessment of criminal performance in the carding underworld. *Security Journal, 29*(3), 442–460. https://doi.org/10.1057/sj.2013.39.

Décary-Hétu, D., Paquet-Clouston, M., & Aldridge, J. (2016). Going international? Risk taking by cryptomarket drug vendors. *International Journal of Drug Policy, 35,* 69–76. https://doi.org/10.1016/j.drugpo.2016.06.003.

Dickinson, T., & Wright, R. (2015). Gossip, decision-making and deterrence in drug markets. *British Journal of Criminology, 55*(6), 1263–1281. https://doi.org/10.1093/bjc/azv010.

Dittus, M., Wright, J., & Graham, M. (2017). *Platform criminalism: The 'last-mile' geography of the darknet market supply chain.* ArXiv:1712.10068 [Cs]. Retrieved from http://arxiv.org/abs/1712.10068.

Dupont, B., Côté, A.-M., Savine, C., & Décary-Hétu, D. (2016). The ecology of trust among hackers. *Global Crime, 17*(2), 129–151. https://doi.org/10.1080/17440572.2016.1157480.

Fleetwood, J. (2014). *Drug mules: Women in the international cocaine trade.* New York: Springer.

Fligstein, N. (2002). *The architecture of markets: An economic sociology of twenty-first-century capitalist societies.* Princeton: Princeton University Press.

Granovetter, M. (1973). The strength of weak ties. *American Journal of Sociology, 78*(6), 1360–1380.

Haller, M. H. (1990). Illegal enterprise: A theoretical and historical interpretation. *Criminology, 28*(2), 207–236.

Hammersvik, E., Sandberg, S., & Pedersen, W. (2012). Why small-scale cannabis growers stay small: Five mechanisms that prevent small-scale growers from going large scale. *International Journal of Drug Policy, 23*(6), 458–464. https://doi.org/10.1016/j.drugpo.2012.08.001.

Holt, T. J., Smirnova, O., & Hutchings, A. (2016). Examining signals of trust in criminal markets online. *Journal of Cybersecurity, 2*(2), 137–145. https://doi.org/10.1093/cybsec/tyw007.

Hutchings, A., & Holt, T. J. (2016). The online stolen data market: Disruption and intervention approaches. *Global Crime,* 1–20. https://doi.org/10.1080/17440572.2016.1197123.

Kenney, M. (2007). The architecture of drug trafficking: Network forms of organisation in the Colombian cocaine trade. *Global Crime, 8*(3), 233–259. https://doi.org/10.1080/17440570701507794.

Kleemans, E. R. (2012). Organized crime and the visible hand: A theoretical critique on the economic analysis of organized crime. *Criminology & Criminal Justice, 13*(5), 615–629. https://doi.org/10.1177/1748895812465296.

Kraemer-Mbula, E., Tang, P., & Rush, H. (2013). The cybercrime ecosystem: Online innovation in the shadows? *Technological Forecasting and Social Change, 80*(3), 541–555. https://doi.org/10.1016/j.techfore.2012.07.002.

Kshetri, N. (2010). *The global cybercrime industry: Economic, institutional and strategic perspectives*. London: Springer Science & Business Media.

Levi, M., & Osofsky, L. (1995). *Investigating, seizing and confiscating the proceeds of crime*. London: Home Office Police Research Group.

Lewis, S. J. (2016). *Untangling the dark web: Unmasking onion services*. Presented at the HackFest 2016, Quebec City.

Lusthaus, J. (2013). How organised is organised cybercrime? *Global Crime, 14*(1), 52–60. https://doi.org/10.1080/17440572.2012.759508.

Mackenzie, S. (2014). Conditions for guilt-free consumption in a transnational criminal market. *European Journal on Criminal Policy and Research, 20*(4), 503–515. https://doi.org/10.1007/s10610-013-9229-z.

Martin, J. (2014a). *Drugs on the dark net: How cryptomarkets are transforming the global trade in illicit drugs*. London: Palgrave Macmillan.

Martin, J. (2014b). Lost on the Silk Road: Online drug distribution and the 'cryptomarket'. *Criminology and Criminal Justice, 14*(3), 351–367.

Moeller, K. (2012). Costs and revenues in street-level cannabis dealing. *Trends in Organized Crime, 15*(1), 31–46. https://doi.org/10.1007/s12117-011-9146-9.

Moeller, K., Munksgaard, R., & Demant, J. (2017). Flow my FE the vendor said: Exploring violent and fraudulent resource exchanges on cryptomarkets for illicit drugs. *American Behavioral Scientist* (early online version). https://doi.org/10.1177/0002764217734269.

Morselli, C., Décary-Hétu, D., Paquet-Clouston, M., & Aldridge, J. (2017). Conflict management in illicit drug cryptomarkets. *International Criminal Justice Review*. https://doi.org/10.1177/1057567717709498.

Morselli, C., & Roy, J. (2008). Brokerage qualifications in ringing operations. *Criminology, 46*(1), 71–98. https://doi.org/10.1111/j.1745-9125.2008.00103.x.

Munksgaard, R., & Demant, J. (2016). Mixing politics and crime—The prevalence and decline of political discourse on the cryptomarket. *International Journal of Drug Policy, 35*, 77–83. https://doi.org/10.1016/j.drugpo.2016.04.021.

Pearson, G., & Hobbs, D. (2003). King pin? A case study of a middle market drug broker. *The Howard Journal of Criminal Justice, 42*(4), 335–347.

Raab, J., & Milward, H. B. (2003). Dark networks as problems. *Journal of Public Administration Research and Theory, 13*(4), 413–439.

Reuter, P. (1983). *Disorganized crime: The economics of the visible hand*. Cambridge and London: MIT Press.

Reuter, P., & Kleiman, M. A. (1986). Risks and prices: An economic analysis of drug enforcement. *Crime and Justice, 7*, 289–340.

Reuter, P., & Caulkins, J. P. (2004). Illegal 'lemons': Price dispersion in cocaine and heroin markets. *Bulletin on Narcotics, 56*(1–2), 141–165.

Soska, K., & Christin, N. (2015). Measuring the longitudinal evolution of the online anonymous marketplace ecosystem. In *Proceedings of the 22nd USENIX Security Symposium.* Presented at the USENIX Security 2015, Washington, DC.

Sparrow, M. K. (1991). The application of network analysis to criminal intelligence: An assessment of the prospects. *Social Networks, 13*(3), 251–274.

The Economist. (2014, November 1). The Amazons of the dark net: Business is thriving on the anonymous internet, despite the efforts of law enforcers. *The Economist.*

The Economist. (2016, June 16). Shedding light on the dark web: The drug trade is moving from the street to online cryptomarkets—Forced to compete on price and quality, sellers are upping their game. *The Economist.*

Tzanetakis, M., Kamphausen, G., Werse, B., & von Laufenberg, R. (2016). The transparency paradox: Building trust, resolving disputes and optimising logistics on conventional and online drugs markets. *International Journal of Drug Policy, 35,* 58–68. https://doi.org/10.1016/j.drugpo.2015.12.010.

Valverde, M. (2014). Studying the governance of crime and security: Space, time and jurisdiction. *Criminology & Criminal Justice, 14*(4), 379–391. https://doi.org/10.1177/1748895814541899.

Van Hout, M. C., & Bingham, T. (2014). Responsible vendors, intelligent consumers: Silk Road, the online revolution in drug trading. *International Journal of Drug Policy, 25*(2), 183–189. https://doi.org/10.1016/j.drugpo.2013.10.009.

Wendel, T., & Curtis, R. (2000). The heraldry of heroin: "Dope stamps" and the dynamics of drug markets in New York City. *Journal of Drug Issues, 30*(2), 225–259. https://doi.org/10.1177/002204260003000201.

Winter, H. (2008). *The economics of crime: An introduction to rational crime analysis.* London: Routledge.

Yip, M., Shadbolt, N., & Webber, C. (2012). Structural analysis of online criminal social networks. In *ISI 2012: IEEE International Conference on Intelligence and Security Informatics* (pp. 60–65). IEEE.

Yip, M., Webber, C., & Shadbolt, N. (2013). Trust among cybercriminals? Carding forums, uncertainty and implications for policing. *Policing and Society, 23,* 516–539. https://doi.org/10.1080/10439463.2013.780227.

Zabyelina, Y. G. (2016). Can criminals create opportunities for crime? Malvertising and illegal online medicine trade. *Global Crime,* 1–18. https://doi.org/10.1080/17440572.2016.1197124.

7

Managing Trust Relationships in Digital Crime

The dominant story of technology goes: new technology creates new configurations of work and society, and new threats. These configurations cannot rely on interactional trust. Instead, new technologies must be developed to manage human relations, technologies such as double entry bookkeeping, life metrics, and now the blockchain. These technologies promise 'trustless' interactions. They do no such thing. I show the work that needs to go into maintaining so-called trustless technologies. I draw on my research on organised crime and criminal markets to show how trust is generated in a cybercriminal market that explicitly rejects several technological 'tricks' commonly used by online illicit markets.

A key problem with the management of trust in the digital, algorithmic age is that the algorithm is designed to reveal information about ourselves that we have not explicitly agreed to disclose (are you pregnant?! Here's a product…). So showing trust in the sense of revealing information about oneself is not so effective, instead we reveal data about ourselves to others. There is a lot that can be inferred without our consent or knowledge that it is happening at all.

© The Author(s) 2020   **129**
A. Bancroft, *The Darknet and Smarter Crime*, Palgrave Studies
in Cybercrime and Cybersecurity, https://doi.org/10.1007/978-3-030-26512-0_7

Seeing like a Blockchain: The Problem of Trust

How do you send money abroad? Or receive it? Western Union? WeChat pay? IBAN? In a hurry? What if you have no address? Somalia remittances are the largest capital in-flow to the country, a place that lacks payment systems, financial institutions, fixed telephony, very low bandwidth even where government institutions exist like Somaliland and Puntland. Xawiladda money transfer companies are able to deliver to no fixed address using a network of agents (Hammond 2016). It sits on hawala, an honour system for transferring money, which uses no instruments and relies solely on ostracism as a sanction. Money remittances bind families together over global distances. Remittances redraft family and social relationships. Money flows are not just one way traffic, they change power at source, destination and in-between. These systems have been attacked by money laundering and anti-terrorism regulations, so security can undermine lateral trust and development.

In situations like that, networks limit growth to avoid detection—though there is a logic of growth that's hard to avoid. Detection means detection by tax and excise authorities, but also detection by bigger networks keen to protect their turf or tax big operations. Outlines the role of specialist brokers who can link specialised parts of the networks e.g. manufacturers, wholesalers, distributors. They are highly knowledgeable and make use of contacts and perceived reliability, so this is a high trust-high function part of the network. In agile networks the emphasis is on the quality of the relationship involved—purely temporary, pragmatic and mechanical, but also brittle.

Smart Contracts, and Machine Laws

Trust is future oriented. It means an agreement has been reached that something will reliable happend. Markets only work by suggesting a better future. That might be one second away, or next year. Financial crimes involve systemic misuse of trust. In recent times Banks and financial institutions systematically manipulated trusted indicators to their own advantage. Trust signals work when they are simple to produce but expensive to fake (Gambetta 2011). The big problem in any market is how easy or difficult it is for bad actors to produce these signals themselves and to 'earn' trust either interpersonally or through the inbuilt reputation system. The higher the cost, the less incentive to scam. At one time, it was thought the problem of digital trust was solved by crowd reviews, big data. Crowd-sourcing reviews is unworkable and easily hacked, as we are seeing. Hence the opportunity for trustless tech and smart contracts which should cut through all that and mean trust signalling is cheap.

We are used to digital objects being infinitely abundant, copyable. Instead the blockchain created scarcity, traceability and uniqueness (Maxwell et al. 2017). We actually work with trustless technology a lot without knowing it, such as certificates, used to install 'trusted' software. These can be modified and allow malicious installs.

The hope of trustless technology is that code will replace decision making. The term is used for a specific subset of tech. A section of code loaded into the blockchain to be executed by every node on it. However, it is impossible to encode laws, transactions, contracts because you can't enumerate possible outcomes in ways that are recognisable. Examples of smart contracts: a vending machine (which then fails to vend), software that locks access to the premium layer, self-driving cars with the trolley problem incorporated into them. Everyone says they want the car to save the greatest number of people, unless it is the car they happen to be in (utilitarianism vs objectivism). Smart contracts are trustless, self executing contacts that follow a basic if > then structure (Szabo 1997). For example, you rent my car, if it is not released then your money is not released to me, if the sensor detects you have run my car into a wall, penalties are triggered. Smart contacts offer that they should be incorruptible and have a permanent or defined end-state, so if you use a blockchain for your smart speaker it won't just pack up without wanting when the company does.

They have some fairly obvious problems. They still rely on trustworthy inputs. One could fool an input to trigger contract execution. How do you settle disputes? Agree penalties? What if the sensor picked up something incorrectly? How do you compensate for security holes, as happened in a 2016 hack of the Distributed Autonomous Organisation and a 2018 freeze of the Parity wallet service. What does blockchain do to social relations? It pushes us to use code rather than agreement to reach an agreed definition of the situation. It also may change how we frame laws and regulations so we start writing them in the expectation that they will be encoded (De Filippi and Hassan 2016). Laws and regulations might be written in a 'code like' way, with the blockchain acting something like a compiler to talk to the machine. Machine law. In that sense the blockchain becomes an operative paradigm. What we are doing is thinking about our digital lives in a more code-like way. It has also some unintended effects. In the current climate it functions as austerity tech. Much of the developments in e.g. administering justice digitally are austerity driven. We have a whole area of tech that is largely motivated by the desire to do things cheaper with less human labour. It is assumed that doing so will not reduce the quality of decision making, a highly tendentious claim. AI is also spoken about in this way in higher education—it will get rid of those pesky professors.

Trust in Cryptomarkets

Successful transactions and mutual reliance are often more a result of functional coherence than trust, in that people need others to work the network associations. There are some preexisting associations that help, such as involvement in legal business arrangements, or just being in the same place. Clan or family associations are part of that. One focus has been on ethnicity but this is misleading: white British is the major ethnic group involved, others are able to corner particular bits of the market because of their coherence rather than special qualities that might be cultivated in their ethnic group (such as Sicilian 'honour'). Lusthaus (2015) notes in relation to Eastern Europe and Russia how ethnicity may be a problem: national political conflicts harmed trust relations within networks that contained Russian, Ukrainian and other post-Soviet nationalities.

Trust can be based on: time predictability—a person has proved their reliability in the past and will be assumed to do so in future; shared/perceived interest—it is calculated to be in the interests of all parties to act together, either because of a shared culpability or because of other consequences such as punishment by another actor. Trust does not therefore require repeated interactions. It does depend on a sense of the routine. Reputation is a kind of criminal capital that can be transferred from one setting to another (Johansen and Lampe 2002). Certain features can enhance trust such as shared subcultural language and state priorities, though some of these signals are more about showing competence than demonstrating trustworthiness.

Part of the pleasure of using cryptomarkets is the enjoyment of transgression and performing oneself as a responsible person with agency, in charge of their drug use purchasing and use. Most important, lots of labour goes into making these things work—cultural performance, policing boundaries, etc. which are the subject of our article. As in the formal economy, violations of trust do not lead to individuals withdrawing from the market. They often factor it in as a cost of doing business.

Differential power and resources are also of overarching importance. Those interpersonal trust signals don't help a jot when one is robbed or cheated. So it is assumed that they are reliable when they may not be. They do not stop someone using their physical or organisational power. They may have an effect on future transactions but that only occurs if the injured party has access to another vendor or buyer. The initial characterisations of Silk Road as an e-Bay for drugs in the sense of retail market, then as not being that, as dealer to dealer, but later on understood as a market that transforms the exchanges and communities that go in within it. Thus the 'device' (Law 1990) of the cryptomarkets reshapes. Illegal markets matter because they are ways of increasing the reach, effect and coordination of crime. The concept can be misleading if not used carefully as it can imply that we do not have to think further about the organisational and cultural structures involved.

Conclusion

Criminals operating in the cryptomarkets and elsewhere know about vulnerabilities and how relying on technology to do the job is the fastest way to create them. Markets depend on centralised social and technical systems are tempting targets and relatively straightforward to compromise. There are lessons here for the vision of a trustless technology future. Code is unlikely to replace bureaucracy any time soon.

References

De Filippi, P., & Hassan, S. (2016). Blockchain technology as a regulatory technology: From code is law to law is code. *First Monday, 21*(12). https://doi.org/10.5210/fm.v21i12.7113.

Gambetta, D. (2011). *Codes of the underworld: How criminals communicate.* Princeton University Press.

Hammond, L. (2016). *Obliged to Give: Remittances and the Maintenance of Transnational Networks Between Somalis at Home and Abroad. 10, 27.*

Johansen, P., & von Lampe, K. (2002). *Is there honor among crooks? On the importance of trust in criminal relations.* Chicago: American Society of Criminology.

Law, J. (1990). Introduction: Monsters, machines and sociotechnical relations. *Sociological Review, 38,* 1–23. https://doi.org/10.1111/j.1467-954X.1990.tb03346.x.

Lusthaus, J. (2015, August 5). All's Fair in Love and War? Retrieved 11 July 2018, from Industry of Anonymity website: https://industryofanonymity.com/2015/08/05/alls-fair-in-love-and-war/.

Maxwell, D., Speed, C., & Pschetz, L. (2017). Story blocks: Reimagining narrative through the blockchain. *Convergence: The International Journal of Research into New Media Technologies, 23*(1), 79–97. https://doi.org/10.1177/1354856516675263.

Szabo, N. (1997). Formalizing and Securing Relationships on Public Networks. *First Monday, 2*(9). https://doi.org/10.5210/fm.v2i9.548.

8

How Knowledge About Drugs Is Produced in Cryptomarkets

Drugs are a great internet commodity as, much like Jeff Bezos' decision to start Amazon by selling books, they are relatively straightforward to warehouse and distribute, if not to produce. The challenges come in consistently communicating with consumers and ensuring information is reliably passed along the supply chain. Information feedback is limited due to being clandestine. Online and offline information sharing functions best where markets are relatively heterogenous and involve multiple unconnected players, allowing consumers to compare with each other and assess the validity of different quality claims.

Drug users are knowledgeable consumers. They have to be, due to the limits of the market. Therefore, the internet provides an effective knowledge overlay for users own experiences and a check on their expectations. Drug use is mostly still a mutually learnt activity, like most other kinds of intoxication. The internet allows users to extend their knowledge into different fields and adopt new kinds of substance use with greater ease. It does have an effect on how fungible drug use is, and the extent to which users are willing to move from one drug to another.

Knowledge is a contested by everyone involved in the market. There is a continuous discussion about other players' motives, whether they are

© The Author(s) 2020
A. Bancroft, *The Darknet and Smarter Crime*, Palgrave Studies
in Cybercrime and Cybersecurity, https://doi.org/10.1007/978-3-030-26512-0_8

honest actors or malicious, and what the effects of particular drugs signify about its qualities.

Cryptomarkets host a knowledge-focused culture. The markets for a range of products. They give users the ability to select specific products that are not available on the street market. This is where one of the positive effects for users is to be found. Users take personal enjoyment in making use of the cryptomarkets. The process of expanding and refining their technical know-how and their knowledge about the different varieties of drug for sale was rewarding for them.

Saying cryptomarkets are knowledge-focused means more than like any market they need information to work. Some key knowledge actors do not have anything to do with drug use but see a role and obligation for themselves to make things work. There is an informational community composed of users, sellers, and also those with a more technical interest or who see their role as part of a public obligation to make things work in the best way possible. These key knowledge actors provide vital information to market users. They post test results and also provide vital context as discussed in this cryptomarket:

> As always I will concede that these tests are not definitive, but they are better than nothing (as was evidenced by yesterday's fiasco with Suited Vendor) and for those misinformed people who believe that other caine's will react to this test and appear to be cocaine – giving a false positive, the website addresses this directly:

> The EZ Test Cocaine Purity test is very insensitive to the usual cuts such as mannitol and such, but will as a bonus, not react to any other substance from the family of cocaine (lidocaine, procaine,etc.), which are frequently used to fool the poor soul who wants to taste it. These other -caines will only produce a numbing effect (at best) and contribute to really bad hangovers!!

As Energy Control, a harm reduction organising operating on the cryptomarkets point out to users, it is easy for vendors to make supportable but misleading claims. Vendors sometimes send samples to Energy Control for testing and use the label of 'EC Tested' when they post the test results. Vendors might do this to test for toxicity of a batch, to ensure they themselves are not being scammed by someone higher of the food chain, or to illustrate the quality of their product to customers. There are plenty of ways in which they may select and post test results showing just the best results for them, or they may flat out inflate the results: 'By some strange, unknown cause, data in vendors pages are often around 10% higher than test results provided' (DoctorX 2019). Drug checking services are one useful instrument which helps users and vendors and is a piece of the information puzzle, but only one. Like any other data point, its relevance can degrade quickly, or it just be wrong. Drug user communities spent a lot of time on comparative epistemology as a result.

Quality Is an Unstable Quality

As the testing debate shows there is no one tell-all indicator that will resolve debates about quality. Nobody really agrees what drug quality means. That does not stop people trying. One of the claims made about cryptomarket supplied drug is that they are of a higher quality than street drugs. However, what that means is not in itself consistent. Quality can stand for consistency, qualities of chemical purity, strength of effect, predictability of effect, dependability of supply and value for money. Users know drugs through the body and the body becomes the store of experience. Buying drugs on the cryptomarkets involves creating a stable, interpretable quality from these many possible qualities. Committed cryptomarket users often say that quality is higher when purchased on the darknet. 'Street quality' is used to refer to poor quality, fizzy, adulterated products of little worth. However, many drug users have tried and found little difference between the two sources and decided to stick with their local dealer. The two markets share much of the same supply chain. The benefits of operating on the cryptomarkets are partly dependent on how well one can realise the advantages it offers.

This also means understanding that quality is never going to be wholly predictable. Supply chains adopt new suppliers, producers innovate refining techniques, and users bodies and expectations change as well:

> Here is the thing tho, by bestman's own admission on his vendor page, and backed up by reviews on forums and his feedback, the quality of bestman's

gear is not consistent, it goes up and down. Due to his glowing feedback, I wouldn't say it is ever BAD, but sometimes it is not as strong as others. Right now, I believe, he is selling g's for $125. Now would be the time to go try him out people, but read his profile, based on what he is saying, I think he knows this gear is not his best batch. I am sure it is just fine tho, especially for the price of $125 for a full g. That is less than what some people on the streets near me are charging for a bundle, and there is usually less than .5 of a g in those bundles, so I don't think you can go wrong, really. Just know for anyone who is interested in trying bestman that his quality changes, but his prices are nice and low, where I like them. His gear is legit and it will give you a good rush, I get a good nod myself, and the legs are long long long. Almost too long, I got to wait so long to take another hit to get another nice rush again because of how long the gear lasts. And I don't know about you guys, but for a guy like me who likes to get the most out of his gear, cheap heroin with a good rush and long legs is all I need. I am with kitty, I def recommend giving bestman a shot.

Novice users sometimes start from an understanding that any change in the drug effect must be the result of a malicious dealer adulterating the drug with another substance to pad it out. More experienced users come to the understanding that quality is always going to be malleable and in part it is up to the user to ensure their experience is the one desired by them.

Understanding the drug being taken is necessary for there to be a consistent effect so in that sense knowledge is recursive. We know drug X has Y effect as long as we are sure that drug X continues to be drug X. When users of drug X now use drug Z and want Y effect, then does that mean both drugs in the same class, or are effectively the same drug? Drugs cannot be reduced to one element.

Drug markets share and shape knowledge. This is true of offline markets and cryptomarkets. Cryptomarkets have the advantage of doing so much more readily and publicly. Drug categories change what drugs are. The make-up of drugs is a politically contested issue. This is relevant when attributing actions to drugs such as 'drug related crime'.

Paraphernalia and Preparation

There are three elements of preparation described in users accounts, preparation of the substance, of the setting, and of the user. Preparation rituals invoked somatic cue responses. Many accounts note the stimulation of immediately anticipated drug and alcohol consumption. Others emphasise the 'buzz' that comes from contemplating the night ahead. Accounts of illicit drug use described the importance of employing skill and judgement to create a 'good drug' out of the raw materials (Grund 1993). In this case, a medicine is transformed into to a recreational drug in the process of cutting and snorting:

Product-- I went to cut open the MBB and spilled some of the cola. Luckily it was over my mirror plate so no loss but y'all be careful if you do order. The smell wasn't as strong as other colas I've had but remember that you shouldn't judge cola based on smell. It definitely had that cola taste to it and the numb was just right IMO; not too strong, not weak, and doesn't set in immediately. It was powder but it stuck very well together. No burn on the inhale which was amazing for me as I've had a destroyed nose now for over 2 weeks after having some bad cola. The euphoria was mellow at first, not leaving me strung out. It wasn't as mellow as others I've had but surely didn't have me bouncing off the walls. No jitteriness and no fiend. Definitely a quality cola. 40 minutes in, I wanted a little more zest so I had some of the shatter that he threw in (I know my concentrates and the shatter was FIRE, better than the cola) for free and this was the exact cocktail I needed. I feel the cannabis accentuated the cola experience and I was just so happy and energetic. (maybe it was doing more cola :--D)

I had this daunting task of dishes to clean and there was no shortage of motivation when the cola got me just right. Dogs could even sense the state of mind and almost seemed happier too! Definitely gave me that feeling we look for in cola. And as with any quality cola, it just faded off and left me back to normal. I do recommend this stuff, friends, if you're tired of the pickings here on S.

In this account, there is a range of expertise involved. The vendor provides the substance and the user the skill and knowledge required to make it into a drug. Users demonstrate responsibility for the their ability to use it in an effective way. The figure of the expert is a common one in accounts of illicit drug use rituals. Obtaining an illicit drug requires the expert to be in the know, to know who to talk to and how, and to be skilled in judging the quality of a potential purchase. In cases of shared ritualised consumption, other members of the group show how they value these skills by deferring to the expert's judgement.

Asha illustrates the common pecking order of consumption. One goes first as she provides and prepares the drug. In some accounts, the provider of the drug is different from the person who prepares, which was more frequently the case with cannabis. In those accounts the preparer usually went first, followed by the provider. Less experienced users are often left, or leave themselves, until the end, having had a chance to observe the consumption process in action. In several accounts, snorting has the element of sequence common to many drug use rituals. In this case, it continues until the table is clean, ensuring there is no incriminating evidence and also that the ritual is completed with the drug being entirely consumed. The consumption must be complete for the ritual to be satisfactory, something of a general feature in the accounts and also noted in the wider literature (Du Toit 1977).

For contrast here is another account collected from a drug user's diary, collected by me:

> Before leaving [for the remainder of the evening], my friend Dahlia reaches into her purse and pulls out a small, clear pill bottle of Adderall, her physician prescribed bottle of ADHD (attention deficit hyperactivity disorder) medicine. Carefully, she lays out five little blue pills, and, using a ring taken from her finger, she crushes the pills with precision and skill. I pull out a credit card and dollar bill from my wallet and lay them on the table for Dahlia to use. She picks up the card and cuts the crushed pills into four straight lines. She stands back and we all gather round, admiring her work. I grab the dollar bill from the table, roll it tightly, and hand it to Dahlia, who initiates the process as she bends down, puts the bill to her nose and snorts, then, using the credit card again to arrange the bits she missed into a smaller line, she repeats. One by one, we follow suit, until the table, once covered with the fine grain blue powder, is inconspicuously clean. (Asha)

The substance in use in Asha's account is Adderall, a prescription medication available in the USA for narcolepsy and Attention Deficit Hyperactivity Disorder (ADHD). It is a psychostimulant made up of various amphetamine salts. It is available in quick-release tablet or slow-release capsule form. The preparation described by her involves crushing the tablets and cutting the resulting powder into a form small enough for absorption by the mucal membrane. The process effectively changes the medicine into a recreational drug with properties similar to 'speed' (street amphetamine) by altering its pharmacokinetics so that the drug is rapidly absorbed into the bloodstream without metabolisation.

Asha gives a typical account of the precise, careful and measured ritual preparation involved in consuming a drug by snorting. Diarists gave other accounts of snorting drugs, such as cocaine, MDMA/ecstasy and unclassified legal highs. Each account had similar features of expertise with the expert as the person who measures and cuts up the drug having some responsibility for ensuring the ritual is completed. The same person has responsibility for caring for others' drug use and the care of naïve users. The user who possesses the drug-making paraphernalia—in the case of drugs prepared for snorting, commonly a mirror, a razor blade and sometimes a currency note or straw—is validated and governs the group dynamic. The paraphernalia provides a group focus. All participants get a line from the same mirror and of (as far as possible) the same size. The person doing the cutting demonstrates their skill and equanimity by dividing the lines equally. Paraphernalia is a technology which is part of the drug use technoculture. Paraphernalia used in these rituals were often described as 'storied', memorialised with past intoxication scenes, shared memories and relationships. The act of bringing out a storied bong or a waterpipe may spark conversation and recollection about friends present and absent. Storying can attach to form or brand rather than a continuous object, such as a brand of cigarette paper.

Drug quality is interpersonal and locally situated. These elements of the ritual prepare the drug and the group to engage in consumption. They also prepare the individuals for intoxication by heightening anticipation. In Lara's account, we see how the preparation process generates a sense of stimulation, described in terms of somatic cue reactivity:

My skin tingles a little at the crisp sound of the two cigarette papers I lick and stick together, this is followed by a third paper delicately placed in the middle overlapping the other two. I open the cigarette in my hand with one smooth sweeping lick and empty a good part of its contents into the cradled papers. I unwrap the cellophane from the hard brown block resting next to my papers. The smell of earth and wood is singed with my lighter, crumbled between my fingers spread evenly into the joint. I roll the package between my thumb and forefinger. I start from the middle and gradually work my way to the end applying the suited amount of pressure, satisfied I lick the papers together and place a custom made piece of cardboard 'roach' into one end and twist the other. ('Lara')

The satisfaction described by Lara comes from the delicate and precise preparation. Part of the anticipation, represented by her skin tingling, is heightened in the sensory experiences she describes: the sound of cigarette papers rustling, the texture of hash burnt and crumbled between her fingers, and the wholesome smell given off by singeing it. Hash, short for hashish, is a solid preparation of cannabis. Burning the hash generates a distinctive smell that indicates its quality and makes it easier to crumble into a joint. The smell is taken as evidence of hash being a natural preparation, in contrast to artificial 'chemical' drugs like mephedrone and Ecstasy, with their associations of potency and risk.

Lara is describing the common British method of preparing a joint mixed with tobacco that necessitates the hash being finely crumbled so it can combust evenly. These actions contribute to it being a 'good smoke', a joint that burns evenly, produces a good high and does not burn up too quickly.

I 'spark up' the joint. My first inhalation is short and light. I inhale again except this time tightly holding it deep in my lungs and finally exasperating the smoke from my mouth with a pleasurable and sensual delight. I continue to smoke, my head feels light and my eyes heavier, the sounds in the room open up, I become aware of the hard floor beneath my feet and of my body as part of the room. The feel and texture of everyday material objects become more intense and interesting. I pass the joint to my partner… I feel part of my true essence, free to express myself and be who I am. My thoughts and ideas come to my mind and evolve quicker than I can excitedly express them. An idea leads to another idea, until I have so many ideas! I'm eager to share new found truths about the things that have always been there however insignificant or monumental they might be. ('Lara')

Lara experiences a profound sensation of transcendental immanence, more than can be expressed by words. The sense of experience intoxication as 'beyond words' is something also common in accounts psychedelic drug use. It may reflect a genuine aspect of the experience of being ineffable, or the lack of a cultural language with which to name these experiences. This is in contrast to the extensive and rich language in use in Scotland to describe the many variants of drunken intoxication and its consequences.

With cannabis there is an extensive, evocative sensory terminology. Drugs snorted in powdered form were accounted for in less explicitly sensory terms than in accounts of cannabis use. However, there are sensory elements such as colour and texture viewed as indicators of quality, and the sensations involved when snorting:

A crystallised residue is laced into the mirror top. With it lays a curled up twenty pound note. I reach into my purse and pull out a credit card and small packet of MDMA. I tap some crystals out onto my cherished mirror and crush them flat, transforming it into white powder. I cut and spread it into equal lines; two for each person sitting in the circle. I lick my finger and run it down the side of the card, gumming the residue I lift off. I take the note between my fingers, lean over the mirror, and quickly inhale the two lines. I sniff. I feel a sharp pain shoot through my nostril followed by a cooling liquid oozing down my throat. I blink. I pass the loaded mirror to my left. All I care about now is the sense of euphoria flooding through my body and soon it will encompass the entire room. ('Nina')

In Nina's account, the act of snorting the drug is somewhat unpleasant. There is a physical challenge to her, as the drug is difficult to consume. It induces brief pain, followed by a cold, oozing sensation. The distaste response is an expected part. However, the physical sensations are quickly overshadowed by the sense of euphoria she experiences. She describes the euphoria as occurring throughout her body, one that extends to encompass the whole scene, a totalising sensation that submerges the self. This drug ritual reduces the salience of self in the interaction between self and object.

These accounts describe a dual preparation of drug and user. There was direct use of and commentary on cue reactivity in the preparation process. This commentary could be a way of overcoming ambivalence, dealing with negative cue reactivity by invoking it.

In the drug field, the question of 'there is a thing there, but what is it' seems to be far more complex, recursive and sticky. For example, the phenomenon of needle fixation among heroin users is hard to reduce to simple observation and response. Injecting drug use is a multiple activity consisting of rituals, habits, fixations, demonstrations of skill, dependence, and cultural myths.

Repair work was a central part of the intoxication experience for men and women. In the hours following their drug taking, the following morning and throughout the days that followed, groups of friends would review and 'repair', re-tell stories in ways that minimised harm to bodies and reputations, and emphasised fun and excess. Social media were used in what is called 'playbour' (Kücklich 2005). Photographs and videos shared via Facebook or other social networking sites such as Instagram and Twitter would mediate the retelling of the night out. Social media provided references for others to 'work towards' what ended up being deemed a 'good night' or a 'good drunk'. This shared learning provided a model for working towards, a display of a good night which those involved would strive to recreate, reliving the best nights through specific drinks, music, locations, conversations, jokes and anecdotes.

The memory work done by individuals in groups is fundamentally different from the data collection carried out by administrators, which produce a thoroughly different impersonal record with no scope for recoding. Instead it is additive. Institutional administrative memories do not change in the way that individual recall does. For health administrators, the problems of binge drinking are problems at the time, and for ever more. Calculating risk for health researchers, medics and other responsible adults involve a very different kind of memorialisation.

How Users Share Knowledge and Assess Quality

Why do 95% of vendors claim their coke is pure or uncut then you get it and there is no shine or "flakey" appearance? i havent personally bought any on agora yet so no disrespect to the vendors on here selling it as i cant judge but on the road that was the case and that was on [Silk Road] SR1 and 2. I've been asking myself the same question. JustSmuggledN's coke met those standards but he received a thorough bashing and 73% purity report on SR2. Not sure where the hell the guy is now with SR2 being down but his blow was very very clean, shiney, and flakey.

What users call purity is in fact many different kinds of potency. Pharmaceuticals tended to attract quantifiable claims, cannabis much less so:

This is the big one, the one we are all here for, bestman365's product. I am going to judge the product somewhat critically, and I feel I was being a bit generous with the score of 8, but when it comes down to it this is some quality dope for a very reasonable price, and we need more domestic USA #4 vendors like that in the markets. Overall, this dope is a great score, and you will be satisfied with your order. The vendor advertised the gear I ordered as "Raw", "Pure", and "Uncut". I would say "Uncut" is the most accurate of those adjectives, because I believe what bestman means is that he himself has not stepped on this heroin, it is pure in the sense that it is purely the dope the vendor picked up from his supplier, and he has not added any cuts himself. The dope is a beige color and when you add water it becomes a dark brown. When drawn up, the spoon is left pretty much clean, but there is a very dark brown residue that will collect on the cotton. The only thing bestman has written on the product's page for its description is, "((((Warning Very Strong)))))" and for the most part that is accurate. It is not the strongest dope I have ever got my hands on, but it is not to be trifled with. I have only needed a very small amount, and it has had me nodding for extended periods of time. I believe the legs, or duration of the high is pretty long, but it is hard for me to say because I have lost all self control since I got the dope on monday afternoon and have booted up nearly every 2--4 hours since. This is not because it is weak dope, but because I am going thru a hard time and don't give a fuck. Let's put it like this, this dope has had me fucked up 24/7 since monday, and I still have more than a quarter of my gram left. I am not sure of the exact weight of my "gram", but I can tell you it is a very fat gram and I am surprised I have done as much dope as I have, with how much I have left. The first hit I took after getting the letter in the mail was my biggest hit, and when I weighed the dope, bag and all, after I took that hit, the scale read 1.25g. Not sure of the weight of the small baggie the gear came in, but it is safe t say my gram was over 1.0. The rush is decent, and very welcome after the trash I had been getting locally on the street, which has done.

Heroin vendors would grade their products, presenting them as different strengths and forms for different markets. Some would sell 'potency' and 'extreme' versions or types for smoking and injecting.

Typical drug listings would make claims about the drug's purity. In the quote above, it is presented as meaning the drug is in its raw form, unadulterated by the vendor. There are many problems with making that claim, especially as a drug like heroin does not come out of the laboratory in a pure state. Its raw form includes many other substances. Users commonly shared that understanding along with two others: that the drug is high potency, and also that it is in a state which will allow them to achieve the desired effect with minimal side effects. Unwanted effects were often interpreted as evidence of impurities, rather than the effect of the drug itself:

Alison, I ordered from beige last Thursday, so mine was shipped out on Monday, presumably with yours. So I would definitely expect it to arrive tomorrow. It's definitely really nice, amazingly clean. I'll have to do a proper review later, but for now I'll just say it's really nice. Not sure if its really worth the price, except as a novelty, because it's not really twice as pure as his Colombian stuff. However, being able to have something this pure is a real rarity with heroin, so its just nice to have.

Different drug cultures adopted different language regarding purity. Those selling cocaine, mephedrone, ecstasy and other drugs produced and refined as part of a laboratory process tended to make stronger claims about percentage 'purity' (90%+ pure and so on). Users drew on sensory imagery of white, clear purity:

Seriously, it is difficult to find heroin of this quality outside of a hospital. It may not be quite pharmaceutical grade, but its definitely some of the purest available. It is almost pure white, dissolves pretty much entirely in water, and draws up almost clear. I don't have a very high tolerance at all, and only the tiniest bit of this powder makes me feel nice and warm and totally pinned. My nose is all fucked up right now, so I've only been shooting it, but the legs are still decent. I haven't had enough to nod on it yet; instead I've been feeling energetic and euphoric all day. This China White fits all the symptoms of pure diamorphine; it's definitely over 90% pure. The price sucks, but you aren't going to get anything better outside of a clinic somewhere like Switzerland.

Cannabis vendors made claims about the overall qualities of the plant and its place of origin, rather than specific claims about THC and CBD. There is a claim to naturalness being made by those vendors.

It might seem logical that chemical potency is the main measure of drug purity. However, users when discussing the effects of different vendors' products noted that there was not a linear relationship between chemical purity and effect. Less chemically raw drugs could be more effective. That could be achieved by the user themselves combining different opiates. Less pure could produce a better rush:

As evening comes around, I decide to do maybe a third of the bag. I prep my shot, wipe my left elbow, insert needle and dig down until I get that lovely plume of blood. I push down the plunger, remove needle, and apply tissue waiting for that golden RUSH. Sure enough, 30 or 45 seconds later, waves of warmth course through my body while I smile at the world in pure joy. For the next few minutes I feel just like Jesus' son; not a thing in the world could bother me. For some reason, I find that less pure dope gives a better rush than the purer stuff. This shot, IMO, gave an absolutely amazing rush. Another few hours pass by, and I'm able to get another proper rush.

Purity could signify a practical quality, that of chemical strength or lack of contamination. It could also signify an ideal quality, the capacity of the substance to help the user locate their ideal desired high, rush or other effect.

Adulteration and Contamination

There was the sense from more experienced users that the drug in its state as bought from the vendor could never on its own produce that ideal, that the user had to work on it and cope with the inevitable impurities and adulterants introduced into the drug.

> Most vendors selling "fishscale" would result in such a test. Most cartels don't wash all the alkoloids out so you never get 89% coke to begin with. Then they usually add 10–15% of levamisole. This is so the typical fishscale sold on the darkents. Tier 2/3. Then you get the vendors that do acetone washes and they usually get a 10% leva with about 70% (sometimes higher with additional acetone washes), about tier 2. Then comes everything that is uncut and may just have some unflushed alkaloids that cause it to not test at 89% but is usually >80%; Tier 1 cola, the top of the market (rare but available)'.

There needs to be knowledge about what a 'pure' drug is and for users it depends on what it is being used for. The quality of the drug also indicated something of the motives of the vendors. Drug dealers have long been suspected of maliciously messing with their products to pimp their profits. Users of cocaine and heroin in particular were alert to the different motives of the vendors. Practically, cutting the drug could mean the vendor simply bulking it with less potent or inert agents to add weight, or it could mean adulterating it to change the high in response to customer demand (Coomber 1997a, b). They perceived an ethical distinction between different motives for adulteration. Adulteration could be seen as useful or as deceptive. When perceived as deceptive, users interpret adulteration as being used to mask the vendor's action bulking out the drug to increase profit and an attempt to give the false impression of potency. When seen as useful it could be interpreted as the vendor enhancing the drug's effects in some way. That might be increasing the length of the high, or changing the shape of the high, for example, creating a longer and more enjoyable 'tail' to the experience as described in this heroin thread:

> The other vendors that I've used who are still vending are bestman365, FattusCatteratus, Manuel Noriega, and subsrgood. beige is very similar to

subs in terms of quality and price, and are the 2 top shelf vendors. Pricey, but worth the price, with beige having better stealth and slightly cheaper prices. bestman and FatCat also have similar quality, which is still very good. Their dope gives a better rush, but doesn't last as long, and you definitely need more of it. FatCat is more expensive, and since they raised prices again, maybe not worth the price, although they also have pretty good stealth, while bestman's stealth can't even be called such, as Batin pointed out earlier. I got Manuel Noriega's stuff back when he was still sending out 'good' quality, but I still rank him at the bottom. It seemed potent, but I'm pretty sure that it seemed so potent because it was cut with some antihistamine or other sedative. Didn't really make me itchy or nauseous, which good dope always does. Had pretty amazing stealth, but not worth it. Definitely not up to the quality of the others.

Adulteration could also involve changing how the drug looked or felt: making lower quality powder methamphetamine look like crystal, for example; These characteristics were taken to demonstrate the authenticity of the drug and the production process, as a heroin buyer demonstrates:

> wrote this earlier but I purchased his 3.5g listing of MMF batch a little over a month ago and was shocked when I opened my pack and was staring at what seemed to be gunpowder. It had big black chunks of tar, that I actually smoked one of the large chunks and it ran just like BTH, it also had some brown powder that looked like and had the consistency of sand and then there were also clear granules that looked like table salt. They would not crush. I was expecting to get a bag of white powder that I had heard so much good about and was bummed to say the least when I saw this bullshit bag of gunpowder. I gave them a 5/5 but said that I was very dissapointed in quality and wrote them a pm saying I think they accidentally sent me the discount batch.

Crystal meth and cocaine were closely examined for these physical qualities, their colour, consistency and crystalline or powdered quality being tells for the production method. As this forum quote illustrates, a range of experience and knowledge is used to assess purity. However, potency was not completely analogous to the drug's chemical purity. Potency might indicate the drug had been adulterated, as did absence of negative effects:

It seemed potent, but I'm pretty sure that it seemed so potent because it was cut with some antihistamine or other sedative. Didn't really make me itchy or nauseous, which good dope always does.' Forum user 'Benzobeatz'

In this and similar accounts there is a direct link drawn between genuine, rather than apparent, potency and negative effects. In other cases, risk is a measure of potency: the stronger the drug, the greater the danger. The positive association between risk and effectiveness has been noted in relation to pharmaceuticals as well as recreational drugs (Martin 2006). Likewise, a heroin high that felt too 'clean' could be taken as evidence that it is adulterated and ultimately less effective. On the other hand many more sought the smooth, untroubled high as a sign of purity. Decorte (2001) suggests many users mistake side effects as signs of adulteration and so a high that feels pure is likely to be from a drug that is much less than pure. Different dynamics and expectations existed for different drugs. Heroin is expected to be higher purity than street heroin, but also to cost more. Cheap heroin is suspect as like to be cut. Cannabis is expected to be significantly cheaper for the quality. Many heroin users were willing to pay more for reliable quality. Heroin users adhered more to the idea that the drug has a set of consistent qualities that are hidden by adulteration, whereas cannabis users had a greater sense of the drug as multiple, and could perceive high chemical purity as working against effectiveness.

There are, then, a number of ways in which cryptomarkets affected the process of signalling and assessing quality. Drug vendors can 'grade' products, offering different quality products. Users employ different kinds of knowledge—craft, chemical and experiential. It is very different when assessing Xanax than meth, for example. In the case of meth, cocaine, cannabis, heroin and so on users are drawing on a rich body of shared experience to lock down the nature of the specific product they have in front of them. In the case of pharmaceuticals, the knowledge and the ability to act on it are more limited.

Conclusion

Drug markets focus on purity, predictability and potency, without necessarily having easy agreement about what those terms mean. There are lots of people who contribute knowledge in various ways, not always through knowledge work. Users crafted solutions for others, would recommend which drugs worked with which daily and weekly work cycle, or counselled others in dosing and other ways of managing the drug effects. None of these functions are unique to cryptomarkets or online spaces generally. Users gather and share knowledge and techniques where they can (Parkin 2013). The cryptomarkets scale up that process and also link it directly to specific vendors and products in ways that the local market has difficulty doing. While digital communities are effective sites of knowledge sharing and communication, they develop their own blindspots and myths as well.

References

Coomber, R. (1997a). Dangerous drug adulteration—An international survey of drug dealers using the internet and the World Wide Web (WWW). *International Journal on Drug Policy, 8*, 71–81.

Coomber, R. (1997b). The adulteration of drugs: What dealers do to illicit drugs, and what they think is done to them. *Addiction Research and Theory, 5*(4), 297–306.

Decorte, T. (2001). Quality control by cocaine users: Underdeveloped harm reduction strategies. *European Addiction Research, 7*(4), 161–175.

DoctorX. (2019). *Use and abuse of drug checking by cryptomarkets vendors.* International Energy Control. Retrieved 17 April 2019, from https://energycontrol-international.org/use-and-abuse-of-drug-checking-by-cryptomarkets-vendors/.

Du Toit, B. (1977). *Drugs, rituals and altered states of consciousness.* Rotterdam: AA Balkema.

Grund, J. P. C. (1993). *Drug use as a social ritual.* Rotterdam: Instituut voor Verslavingsonderzoek, Erasmus University Rotterdam.

Kücklich, J. (2005). Precarious playbour: Modders and the digital games industry. *Fibreculture, 5*(1).

Martin, E. (2006). The pharmaceutical person. *BioSocieties, 1*(3), 273–287.

Parkin, S. G. (2013). *Habitus and drug using environments: Health, place and lived-experience.* Farnham, Surrey, England: Ashgate. https://www.dawsonera.com/abstract/9781409464938.

9

Creating, Managing and Responding to Risk in Cryptomarkets

Cryptomarkets Are One Place Where Drug Risk Is Dissected and Reworked

Forums extensively examined both the risks of the drugs that they were consuming and the risk journeys that users went on.

> I should also mention that once the local tar I was getting no longer available to me I resorted to the shitty stuff at a new location and thats when I first tried mainlining it. Agora

> I snorted oxys for a few yrs until the oxy formula was changed in 2010, then switched to H for over a year. The bulk of my opiate use was approx $80/day habit. Trying to get clean, I took subs for a few mos but was unable to get off. To get clean, I took Iboga / Ibogaine and that immediately repaired my opiate receptors and got me off a 4 year opiate habit overnight without any WD. I have been clean ever since - - 3.5 yrs!! (feel free to ask questions about Iboga. it is an incredible plant and cures opioid addiction overnight... youtube it!).

© The Author(s) 2020
A. Bancroft, *The Darknet and Smarter Crime*, Palgrave Studies
in Cybercrime and Cybersecurity, https://doi.org/10.1007/978-3-030-26512-0_9

Risk is meaningful, symbolic behaviour. Risk is part of human interaction and the risk behaviour online should be understood as meaningful, communicative and identity forming just as much as any other aspect of life (Rhodes 1997). People are exposed to risks that are inherently unmanageable and unknowable. There is a contradiction here. All kinds of behaviour become quantified, informationalised, mined, performed and commodified through the digital infrastructure (Lupton 2016). However this does not reduce uncertainty. It creates new measures of social and political worth towards which people are enjoined and impelled to act (Lupton 2015) which create new uncertainties.

Drug users face various problems, stigma, multiple risk vectors such as to their health, legal and citizenship status and reputation. Rhodes outlines the risk matrix which is contextual. Heroin-related risks might be overdose, vein damage, which might be exacerbated by the context in which the drug is taken. Then there are the risks needed to obtain the drug and use it—the tradeoffs with others, the need to manage relationships with partners, children, social services, avoid police etc. Situated rationality should not be seen in individual terms then but rather as these elements being aspects of the context of risk—a social unit of analysis. Cryptomarket users think systematically about these risks and make use of the cryptomarket/darknet infrastructure and associated systems in order to mange them. The concept of responsible harm is introduced. I explore how the cryptomarkets intervene and create their own context.

The behaviour of drug users is regulated in pubs, homes, nightclubs, clinics injection rooms, schools and courts. Informal regulation happens through the risk infrastructure and the valuations of other users. Despite the role of cryptomarkets in de-stigmatising drug use there was still plenty of rage at the presence of people who others use the darknet to avoid, at those who are dependent uncontrolled users, junkies taking the rest for a ride. You might think that what other people do should not matter since it does not materially affect anyone else. However, it does. Any community has obligations and those who appear to break these obligations attract especial rage, as do those who sympathise with them. Those who break the obligations by acting in ways that are associated with junkies and who exhibit undesirable traits such as complaining or being unable to handle their drugs are reviled by others. They are reviled because they symbolically harm the community.

Limitations of this kind of approach being able to address the larger inequities that affected people such as access to services (refs) or to be recognised as a basis for doing that.

The vendors also include harm reduction information

1. I'm a beginner so what steroids should I use for building mass and gaining strength?

We advise all beginners to start with oral steroids first. In our opinion the best oral steroid for beginners is Anavar, followed by Turanabol and Winstrol. Danabol/Anadrol are a step above as they have the potential for fast results but with more side effects.

2. I want to lose weight. What do you recommend?

There are several products that can help you with losing weight. Clenbuterol, Ephedryne, Cytomel (T3) and T4. We suggest you use Cytomel (T3) in combination with Anavar, Turanabol or Winstrol. Aditionally, if you can tolerate it, then Clenbuterol is also really efficient.

3. Is it possible to help me create a steroid cycle?

Yes but only if you are serious about buying products. We've had a lot of back and forth conversations with potential customers that went on for days/weeks and no purchases were made. If you are serious get in contact with us and don't forget to mention your goals and previous experience with using steroids.

4. I'm looking for product 'X'. Will you guys have it in stock in the future?

We're always looking to expand our product variety so if you're looking for something that doesn't appear in the listings (the complete and updated list is available at Dream Market) send us a message and we'll see what we can do about it.

We have to be circumspect about this though as vendors are not consistent about the products they sell and the qualities they have. Some demonstrate a general interested in harm reduction while others are of the buyer beware view.

Structuring of Risk

There are four structuring axes which involve culture, chemistry, legal/policy context and market structure. The Merkat forum gave people a way of articulating and addressing risks on each axis. I framed culture as involving at one end normalisation and the other pathologisation of certain drug types and forms of use (Barratt et al. 2014). I defined chemistry as those effects attributed to the pharmacological characteristics of the drug and its interaction with the user, which can range from potentially dangerous but possibly rewarding potency to drugs that are attributed with manageable and predictable qualities. Users paid attention to the legal and policy context and its implications for risks from law enforcement activity (Aldridge and Askew 2017). The market infrastructure was also carefully analysed by them, comparing with other markets to asses its reliability and trustworthiness of market actors and technical architecture and its relationship to the rest of the illicit drug market (Beckert and Dewey 2017). Each axis is embedded in different ways in the cryptomarkets, the wider digital infrastructures and associated systems, and national and international policy structures and cultures.

Cultural normalisation of use and supply has been identified as part of recreational drug cultures in the UK and more widely (Coomber et al. 2015; Measham and Shiner 2009). It is the case on the cryptomarkets that many users operate in normalised drug cultures and see drug use as functional fun (Askew 2016). In these cases, risk is identified with uncontrolled use. However, many users who contribute to the forums are more isolated, and their drug use does not correspond to the picture of drug use legitimated by a time and space bounded, recreational purpose. Many heroin users on the forums describe isolated circumstances and daily use which is not part of a shared recreational culture that can provide a normalising narrative for their drug use. In those cases, the forums were the main focus of shared reflection and discussion of drug use for them. They discussed pathologisation risks such as stigma and the requirement for secrecy and the need to combine drug use with work and family life with non-drug users. As this user described, peer harm reduction was an aim but was hampered by the isolation and stigma many users experience:

And to [user] hanoi: I feel you man. It sucks having to keep quiet about it, makes it really hard for the average person to get quality harm-reduction information. But when you don't keep quiet about it you get estranged from so many people you knew and loved and the binge continues. We are not terrible junkies huddled between trash bins shaking and looking dirty and pathetic without a thought in our head besides who we need to rob to get our next fix. No, I want that perception to change, and the best way to try to get that to happen is to advocate for more responsible drug use from my fellow drug lovers. Opiates/heroin is, in my opinion, one of the greatest drugs in the world, a true gift from 'god'. It should be respected and used responsibly, not abused and taken for granted, or it will fuck up your world. Forum user 'Allysbaba'

This image of the user with responsibilities to others turned up frequently in users' conversations. Users are implored by each other to act smartly and treat the drug with respect in relation to chemistry-related risks. These are identified as stemming from the drug's potency, addictive qualities, pharmacokinetic action and interactions with other drugs and medications. Users can involve themselves in extreme drug use binges as long as they are temporary, and they are aware of what to expect and how to manage it without having to resort to a visit to hospital or involve other kinds of personal or legal trouble. Legal risks arose from law enforcement action. This was factored into the risk infrastructure as a risk that could be manageable with the right intelligence about the actions of law enforcement agencies. For example, that they prioritised particular drugs or user types as in the following posting:

You must have a super supply of will power if you've been an O [opium] chipper [user] for 7 years! O is extremely addictive just like the other opiates. I'm not trying to talk you into continuing your journey, but I feel you because from the sound of your post, I'm on the same journey. Making your own O is so much better and safer than having to risk coins every time you make a darknet purchase, not to mention you're putting your life in the hands of the vendor in a way. Look what happened to Phillip Seymour Hoffman. Plus less risk with LE [law enforcement]. And I would think O would be less taxing on your liver, kidneys and the rest of your body, since it's all plant based and no added chemical fillers… at least that's my experience with O. Forum user 'spangledust'

Spangledust writes about making your own opioids as a way of reducing risk of law enforcement attention.

Users identified market risks from the use of Bitcoin and the market escrow process used to guarantee sales. Bitcoin is a highly volatile currency. One of the ways of ensuring trusted transactions in the market was for the administrator to keep Bitcoin in escrow until the drugs were delivered, only releasing them when the buyer confirmed, or after a set period of time which vendors did not like. There was in the posts talk about the good etiquette involved in releasing payment when goods arrived and not delaying payment until the last possible moment. Currency volatility meant that the Bitcoin could have a very different value by this point. Some vendors had a 'finalise early' option to reduce the risk of losses due to currency fluctuations or to the market closing as the result of an 'exit scam'; the market administrator leaving with the vendors' and users' bitcoin (Moeller et al. 2017). The 'finalise early' option involved the release of the customer's Bitcoin as soon as the deal is agreed. This minimised the risks of the cryptomarket failing or going offline before the transaction was complete. However, this option transfers market risk from the vendor to the customer whose only recourse if the drugs fail to arrive is to leave a bad review or criticise the vendor on the forum. A high level of trust is required for finalise early to work. Market risks is also recognised by other users as stemming from phishing (falsely obtaining private information) or other predatory criminal activity that targeted cryptomarket users.

Users dissect and discuss risks in terms of each of these four dimensions. Users updated each other continually on what risks applied where and how to manage or mitigate them. The different risks were produced in different structural contexts. Normalisation developed through local drug use cultures and the varied acceptance of different drug types and use contexts and involved both drug users and non-users. Chemical risks emerged in the process of drug production and the user's personal drug history, so these risks were recognised as being embedded in biography as well as pharmacology. Legal and policy risks were shaped by the structure of drug prohibition, surveillance systems the user was exposed to and the priorities of law enforcement agencies. Market risks worked through the process of drug buying as an exchange and as an economic system which was located in the structure of the cryptomarket payment, escrow and review systems.

Each dimension worked at a different interface. Users talked about these harms as arising at these different interfaces and discussed harm reduction practice as taking responsibility for risks and harms at each interface.

Peer Support

An example of peer support was the way site users shared detailed experiences about heroin injecting techniques, how to avoid infection and accesses, and how to diagnose and cope with some of the immediate physical effects of injecting such as bruising. There were many sources of peer support, from those of experienced users to vendors. Some vendors provided harm reduction information with the drugs they sold but this was relatively basic content. The main sources of information for users were in the market forums and from other users. Cryptomarket forums use structural peer rating features that allowed users to be promoted because of their positive interactions with others and provision of harm reduction support. Silk Road had its 'Karma' rating, and Merkat similarly has user ratings for dependability, mimicking feudal chivalry (Chevalier, Scutifer and so on). Being active in the forums and posting harm reduction advice is one of the criteria for being nominated for these recognised roles.

> I'm as transparent as possible about the tests and always disclose if the sample has been bought anonymously or given by the vendor. Theoretically double blind tests would be best but that isn't feasible at this point. Please decide for yourself if you want to use the information or not. I refrain from publicly giving comments on cocaine vendors, their shipping methods and their products. I will only post the lab test results. There is no lab documentation available for the cocaine that has been tested, the lab results are only provided verbally. The only way to be sure what your powder consists of is to get it tested yourself. Forum user 'Bugout'

As this user and other users acknowledged, some of the tests were based on free samples provided by vendors in the hope of garnering positive feedback. Vendor testing is open to manipulation as they may provide samples they know are 'good' and there is no guarantee that batches are being retested regularly. Many of those users who posted tests stated explicitly that it as part of their commitment to making the cryptomarkets work as a community that was capable of identifying and managing drug-related risks. As one said 'we all have an interest in drugs, whether selling, buying, researching chemically' (tester HiKite).

Much of the discussion of drug safety in the Merkat forum was not explicitly badged as such. Users tended not to head for discussion threads on harm reduction or drug safety to discuss problems. They raised them in other threads on the forum, for example as part of discussions about drug quality, about how to use a particular product effectively, and the reliability of particular vendors.

Peer support discussions covered various practical problems. Complaints extended to the general postal and service infrastructure that affected the speed of deliveries, scamming by vendors and having shipments intercepted by customs. Scamming by vendors was not a typical interaction but it was an anticipated risk. Problems were attributed on a combination of naïve 'n00b' (new and inexperienced) users and weak or duplicitous management of the site. Other cryptomarket administrators could and did steal from customers and vendors (Duxbury and Haynie 2018; Soska and Christin 2015). During the study, several similar sites fell prey to theft by administrators, or were suspected as having been set up for that purpose in the first place. There are claims that one site had many staff involved in filleting Bitcoin from buyers and sellers who they could then plausibly claim were scammers themselves.

The effect of the various postings was to create counter-narratives in opposition to prevailing characterisations of drug users (Maddox et al. 2016). Forum users challenged the distinction between good and bad drugs. One heroin user shared his experience of his girlfriend who was a regular cannabis user looking down on him for his intravenous drug use. Users recognised the structural context of stigma that made it difficult to obtain harm reduction information and challenge the stigma that applied to injecting drug users.

> Hello all my underground friends and law enforcement agents who got nothing better to do than watch us citizens safely navigate the e-blackmarket and exchange information and anecdotes about which vendors are legit, our experiences with a variety of chemicals, and safety/harm reduction. Forum user 'ProfWhite'

Users also discussed the ways in which the design and working of the darknet itself mitigated risk and stigma. Many users discussed how they felt much safer and less stigmatised purchasing and interacting with vendors through the market. They reported much more respectful and business-like interactions with vendors than that which was felt to characterise offline markets. They felt most positively towards forum threads when they operated as a community.

> It's so nice that everyone here can talk openly, not be judged, help each other, provide tips and harm reduction tricks – even provide each other with some Bitcoin when they're short – it really is a beautiful thing:) I trust the people in this thread and they know they can trust me, so it's just a great feeling to be able to rely on others here. Forum user 'TrumPet'

For this group of users, harm reduction was a community-focused activity that involved a range of risks from the potential dangers associated with using the drug itself to the legal and social threats of personal exposure, shaming and stigma.

Risk Signalling and Responsible Harm

A drug's potential for harm can be taken as a sign of potency and effective-ness. Users incorporate the ability to manage what were perceived as more potent drugs into their drug use as a badge of experience. They empha-sise 'educated choices' in their normalised, risk-savvy approach to drug use. Such choices involve acting independently of both government sanc-tioned claims about blanket drug risk, and also of vendors' claims about their product. The 'educated user' has the ability to consume responsibly, with self-reflection and awareness which would manage the risk as in the following post:

> Buy some (House Lannister and Platinum Standard for me). Test it. Take it only if you are educated enough, conscious enough, and self aware enough to take it responsibly. Make sure you know how the meds that you take on the regular will be effected. Forum user 'ToddUnctous'

In users' posts, there is a move away from the idea of risk as an assessment of potential harm to risk as a manageable, normal challenge that comes about in the course of obtaining and using drugs. The educated user has the 'right stuff', the right personal characteristics to manage risk before, during and after taking the drug and to incorporate expected harms into their drug use biography. In these postings, the locus of risk is shifted from the drug and drug consumption process to the market structures and the operation of the market as a social process. Users who make points similar to those made by ToddUnctous are showing how aware they are of the market as a social infrastructure and risk as produced through this infrastructure. They acknowledge a range of potential harms related to the drug trade and drug consumption. For them, responsible harm means an approach that recognised that harm could only be minimised so far and that allowed for harm to exist as a likelihood in every user's drug use biography.

Users draw on a variety of sources for harm reduction advice beyond the Merkat forum. These include open-internet sites such as Reddit and Erowid, harm reduction services and directly from the scientific literature. Many users showed that they are familiar with current academic research. Users posts draw on expert knowledge but they did not cite the authority of experts in their assessment of the trustworthiness of advice given or received. This may reflect the success of public health harm reduction initiatives as a lot of good practice was taken for granted such as using clean needles and properly preparing injecting works accepted as normal.

Users' claims to responsible harm involve putting the harms of illicit drugs in the context of other harms they are exposed to and taking responsibility for harms caused by their drug use. One way of doing this is to draw comparisons between harms from illicit drugs with those of prescribed or over the counter medicines. Another is to emphasise that the harm caused was limited to the drug user and did not affect others, as one user indicted in a post:

This is probably the 3rd or 4th time I've done cocaine. I think nitrous oxide and ibuprofen have probably done more damage to my brain and body than any cocaine/cut I've snorted in the past year. Forum user 'flame&citron'

Users recognise the association between chemical strength, risk and desire, for example a more unpredictable drug could also be more effective and desirable. Such association is also recognised and evident in the advertising of pharmaceutical and alcohol companies. Users talk about potency as a sign of both risk and of quality. Their counter-public health discourse involved a narrative that was somewhat different from the public health harm reduction narrative. For the educated and informed user, harm reduction practice extends beyond avoiding harm to more effective and safe use of multiple drugs. An advantage of the darknet is that users can obtain a great variety of drugs, in varying strengths and forms. Some presented this as a form of harm reduction. For example, using smokeable heroin to preserve a low tolerance, or using kratom to mitigate the effects of opiate withdrawal.

Users posts often link personal good health and work success with being a responsible user as in the following post by hot4teacher:

So I got all the equipment (bulk syringes, needles, micron filters, alcohol swabs, tourniquet, sterile storage vials, sterile water for injection, BA, hand sanitizer for disinfection), put a using schedule into effect (no more then 3 days in a row and never during a workweek) and then got some nice #4 [heroin]. That was about 2 months ago and since then I have used pretty much every weekend. So far I have not had even the slightest inkling of physical w/d [withdrawal] symptoms. ... My job hasn't suffered the slightest (due to get a permanent contract along with a raise), I exercise regularly, eat healthy and continue to lose weight. And I actually learned a few things about medicine and pharmacology in order to be able to enjoy myself as much as I do using heroin while exercising a very high degree of harm reduction. But thats of course just the story of one person. Forum user 'hot4teacher'

There was in user posts a difference between the techniques of harm reduction and the narrative of better, safer use. For example, users referred to the complexities of interactions between drugs and the body and how these could be used to maintain heroin use and manage it using a range of supplementary drugs. For many users, the cryptomarkets are one source of such drugs. The could also obtain such drugs through the street market or acquaintances willing to sell, swap or give their prescriptions as loosenutz wrote:

> Methadone. Used to help wean addicts off heroin, but a very powerful opiate itself, some refer to it as pure evil, because of the terrible, painful, months long withdrawal symptoms you can experience if you abuse and become addicted to it. 'dones [methadones] are much better for recreational use than other opiates that are used to wean addicts off heroin in my opinion, such as suboxone. I would take about 10-15mg and I would get a mild euphoric buzz and I always noticed it seemed to come in waves. It can knock your ass out tho if you take too much, I remember being scared I was dying one time when I used it, hah. Forum user 'loosenutz'

Users discuss how drugs that were prescribed to control addiction and prevent pleasure such as methadone and suboxone could be re-used to attain pleasure and manage harm, for example by combining them with heroin and other opiates as part of a drug use repertoire. Suboxone is prescribed as an addiction treatment. Users not how useful the drug is for work. It operated in a slow way, tended to stay in the body, but did not have the debilitating qualities sometimes ascribed to methadone. GrimeReaper's post showed an understanding of what drug effects were and how to successfully combine them for example that suboxone is a partial antagonist as it contains naloxone

> I use very small amounts of sub in my hits. I am a little ashamed to admit, because it is sooo bad for you, and the mark of a worthless junkie, but I crush up the pill and IV it. But this is how little I use, I can make 1 of those 8mg pills last a week if I keep myself relatively under control. Forum user 'GrimeReaper'

Users of opium-derived drugs discuss how these drugs can substitute for each other in some ways and not in others, and how this is tied to the relative risks they presented. For example, heroin was fast acting and powerful but also presented a risk of addiction. That could be mitigated by using other drugs that worked more slowly, or which combined opioid agonists and antagonists. This attribute can be a positive. Users indicate that they can manage drug dependence by moving from injecting to smoking, or from heroin to opium, substituting other drugs as needed. Their posts indicate a complex understanding of the ways in which drug use history, personal biography, the user's body and the drug molecule and delivery system interact to produce particular effects, some of which they felt are desirable, others which have to be mitigated.

Dosing and the User's Body

The users' embodiment—their awareness of the body as an instrument and mediator of experience—is the focus for several different kinds of knowledge which are used and shared. In relation to heroin, it is recognised in how the drug responded differently depending on the user's tolerance:

> If your H is rubbish and you've not been doing opioids like oxy or subs you will have low tolerance. Take the right dope and a small dose, fifty to seventy five milligrams, and you'll have a mid-range high. Stick to less than a hundred mgs until you're sure of how the H you have works on you. Take care if your tolerance depends on rubbish dope. It's about how your body handles it and you're the only one who knows that. Forum user 'Snarkfish'

Tolerance was represented as an attribute of the user's body that they had to be aware of and both use to assess drug quality and properly titrate their use. It also is acknowledged in advice about dosing. The view that 'everyone is different' prevailed, and general rules of thumb are given out by users to advise on what might be expected at different doses. Users share advice on titration, discussing how to produce different kinds of effect with heroin using varying dosage and different injection and smoking techniques.

Users advised others to test small amounts of heroin to gauge quality in relation to tolerance:

> I expect you'd be okay taking one third of the bag, but it might make you sick if you have a low tolerance. In that case, best to snort a few bumps to test the strength. With a new batch I take small test shots or bumps. You won't waste much that way. Forum user 'Minajatrois'

In this quote and many others there is an understanding of tolerance as embodied, and that the user's own self-understanding is crucial to a successful and safe drug use experience. Pleasure was embodied and could be experienced at different stages of drug consumption. It could come in preparation and/or anticipation, such as watching the flow of blood into the syringe when a vein is reached. A clean high is sought, corresponding to the drug's appearance of physical purity. A combination of colour, smell, texture and form signalled quality. In the case of heroin, users looked for various attributes: whether it 'crunched' when cut, how it flaked, its colour, and when cooked whether it turned into a clear golden liquid.

> Is it lab grade? Maybe not quite there but certainly among the top gear and purest you can get. It's a beautiful white, when you put it in water it dissolves away completely, and it draws into the syringe nice and clear. Gives me that warm, pinned feels. Forum user 'Fakepants'

Impurities were 'dirt', in the sense of matter out of place (Douglas 1992). Dirt could include a physical residue left after dissolving heroin to inject it, or bodily reactions such as coughing and hacking. In our study, side effects could be dirt or could be taken as a sign of chemical purity. In this case, there is a difference between more casual users—who saw side effects and comedowns as unwanted dirt contaminating the desired experience—and more regular and experienced users of cocaine and heroin, who saw side effects as a signal of potency and effectiveness.

There is recognition of technique of injecting or smoking as part of the user's embodied disposition. Users share these techniques and judgements to evaluate the desired qualities of different vendors' products. Vendors make a greater contribution to these discussions, often defending the process by which they make claims about drug purity. This kind of knowledge is open to challenge. For example, vendors may suggest that critical users do not have the street experience to judge. Vendors and some more experienced forum users saw their role as policing some of the knowledge claims made about product quality and acted in the forum to shut down opposing claims.

Community Safety Net

Communities can provide moral support and sometimes they provide material support also. On the Reddit community r/opiaterollcall (now banned) there to arrange face-to-face opiate trades for users who are dealing with withdrawl. In several darknet forums it was the practice for some users to altruistically provide drugs for others. This quote captures the anxiety of a long term dependent user when their offline social connections begin to fall away:

> Being frustrated, having money to cop but having no connects & no where else to look is the fucking worst!! 2 months ago I had all the connects in the world. I couldve stocked up for a rainy day, but back then I also didn't have enough money to do so (plus I would've just done them all anyway). Now I have NOOO connects. Well, 1 connect. He was the back-up to my back-up guy. Now, he's the ONLY guy I have. It's damn near pointless buying 6,000,000 grams of Tylenol with 5mg of some damn Oxy.
>
> Second: He has that sweet sweet sweeeeeet brown powder. The problem is my long-time other doesn't do it and "will not stand for it if I were to do it (again)". I never IV'd it, only snorted. I know I know, thats a waste. But when you cant get your hands on anything else then why the fuck not?! My connect of 30 & 15mg oxy is lost. PLUS I can't find all the cool ass pills you guys have (which I am honestly jealous about), and the other connect who had random things whenever I called just fell off the map.
>
> Now I'm waiting on a call for the guy to get off work so he can "hook me up" with some shitty pills. I swear, I've been holding off not IV'ing brown, but I'm damn near close to it. I can't deal with this shit any more. It is worth users investing in community ties to form a safety net for hard times.

Cryptomarkets Are Meeting Points

Cryptomarkets have become meeting points where different kinds of knowledge can be combined and validated (Van Hout and Hearne 2017). They develop a risk infrastructure that provides technical tools, shared knowledge and shareable judgements to manage risk. Cryptomarkets when they work as advertised are protective against law enforcement surveillance, predatory dealers and third-party theft and enabling of drug use that is purposeful and pleasurable, or self-medicating, or for coping with life stresses. There were multiple framings of harm reduction, as avoiding punitive measures and moralising discourse (Keane 2003), and incorporating and promoting the voice of users (Friedman et al. 2007; Pauly 2008). As Munksgaard et al. (2017) state, cryptomarket forums are a place where users can define the 'normative context' for drug exchange and use.

In their posts, users focus more on harm management in this context, advocating complex drug use repertoires grounded in different sources of knowledge about drug effects. Some users rely on 'expert' knowledge derived from the scientific literature whereas others use personal experience or the reported experience of others. They discuss the ways that drugs typically prescribed for medical management purposes such as naloxone or methadone could be re-tasked for more involved harm management processes and for pleasure. This is typical of the way drug users routinely incorporate harm reduction into their drug using practice (Friedman et al. 2007). Users are a source of lay expertise for others (Jauffret-Roustide 2009), they develop and share protective strategies (Harris and Rhodes 2013), and provide care and support (Drumm et al. 2005). Users are producers of knowledge about harm reduction that can augment, run ahead of, and challenge that of experts.

Many of the findings mirror others about harm management serving broader purposes of community building (Gowan et al. 2012). User priorities are not necessarily those of mainstream public health which was sometimes seen as prioritising more abstract risks over immediate threats to the user (Harris and Rhodes 2012). Their discussion moves the focus of harm reduction from responsibilisation and discipline (Moore 2008) to building on community and self-care. Users are able to adapt medications used for harm reduction to their own needs. Faulkner-Gurstein (2017) outlines how naloxone was initially seen by its manufacturers and public health experts as a technical quick fix to be administered by medical personnel. Users in this way it induced rapid withdrawal in users which was perceived by them as a form of punishment. When they were able to access and administer it themselves users had adapted it and used it as a self-help tool. Such user-driven changes in the cultural context are typical of how it and other medications such as naloxone and subutex are discussed on the cryptomarkets.

In online discussions, some risk factors change or are missing. Risks from purchasing the drug are shifted. There is still the risk that having paid for the drug it is not delivered. However, there is some comeback. The buyer can dispute the order with the market administrator. That may or may not lead to satisfaction. It does change the emotional texture of the experience. The buyer is not at risk of a humiliating like it or leave it situation, so the power differential has altered somewhat.

This forum creates a set of shared systems, tools and knowledge practices that give meaning to and are used to manage risk behaviour: a risk infrastructure. In it users challenge prevailing 'expert' risk narratives thus produce a counter-public health. Counter-public health has a long history, under various labels, of examining the formation of health and risk management strategies and of political activism by counter-publics, meaning those marginalised communities exposed to risk (Epstein 1996; Robins 2004). It describes the logic of collective action around risk behaviours that emerges from peer-to-peer communication. It focuses attention on the formation of risk priorities and practices that address health risks but have priorities that differ from and sometimes challenge those of formal public health. For example, there are individuals who prioritise pleasure over stopping risky activities (Hunt et al. 2011), that challenge predominant individualising narratives of the meaning of risky behaviour (Bourgois and Schonberg 2009). This challenging can produce new knowledge that may add to or overturn existing scientific risk paradigms and develop alternative peer-to-peer harm minimisation techniques (Decorte 2001; Van Hout and Bingham 2014). These communities form and are formed from political engagement to varying degrees. The original Silk Road was a site of political and philosophical discussion which is less evident in the markers that have replaced it as the users of the new cryptomarkets become more driven by concerns about security and usability (Munksgaard and Demant 2016).

Seen in this way, cryptomarkets become the location for shared knowledge production formed around potential drug risks. They link to the wider 'demimonde' of alternative communities (Maddox et al. 2016) whereby participants enact alternative value structures and create protocols and knowledge sets in relation to drug exchange and use (Munksgaard and Demant 2016). Cryptomarkets are particularly interesting as they are both a mode of obtaining drugs and are at least in principle designed to promote professional and accountable transactions and interactions between buyers and users (Barratt et al. 2016). The design and use of cryptomarkets can be seen as a response to the generation and distribution of risks through drug prohibition and the discursive stigmatisation of them. They allow drug users to take risks and introduce deliberation and comparison into the drug buying process. There is co-production of harm reduction information and practice in the cryptomarkets between vendors, users and harm reduction experts who contribute to some forums. Some cryptomarkets also allow for some co-production of harm reduction products. For example, the now closed Alphabay market encouraged vendors to provide the opioid agonist naloxone by waiving the vendor bond for those who did (Gilbert and Dasgupta 2017).

Users of cryptomarkets can be seen as setting up an alternative, counter power structure to frame and manage risk which gives weight to the structural, political and legal factors which create risks for them (Munksgaard and Demant 2016). This draws on and integrates some important insights from public health and harm reduction but also challenges some of the values implicit in them, especially the idea of harm reduction and risk minimisation. Responsible harm is a useful way of thinking about these processes by providing an avenue for the articulation and analysis of user evaluation, minimisation and accounting for harm. The cryptomarket enables some users to make informed choices about the risks they want to take. Responsible harm meant constructing a risk agenda that incorporates some controlled risk but allows for a degree of unpredictability in drug taking. While users are motivated by harm reduction, they also question some of its implications. In their view, constructive risk taking can create a context which is supportive and controlled.

Conclusion

Competing ideas of harm exist under the same term. Harm reduction necessarily has to accommodate with competing political agendas. It emerged from and is sustained by activists, users and communities and explicitly concerns values as part of health (Boucher et al. 2017). Cryptomarkets do not remove risk but do they do reconfigure harm. Structural risks still exist, for example users may still have to engage in sex work to obtain money and expose themselves to attendant vulnerabilities. A user who earns cash through sex work and exchanges it for heroin is not in a position to leave that complex set of negotiations and obligations and simply 'buy it on the darknet'. So there are strict limits to the cryptomarkets' harm reduction potential to transform the power relationships that exist in the offline drug market. Indeed the offline market may serve existing users adequately in many situations. We should also move beyond background assumptions that the offline 'street' is automatically more risky and has no inherent advantages (Abel and Fitzgerald 2012).

The potential of the cryptomarkets is less their ability to systematically alter the harm-utility relationship and more their ability to de-link some of these overlapping structural elements. A key change is the separation of drug distribution from other environments, for example, from sexual exchange, nightclubs, and shooting galleries. New inequalities emerge. Users need resources to access cryptomarkets such as stable address for drug delivery, internet access and use skills or access to people who have them. One of the changes the cryptomarkets wrought is in relative power between different groups of users and vendors. Power has not flattened. Administrators have a great deal and there is suspicion by users of extensive collusion between them and vendors. Having said that, the relative dis-embedding from existing contexts that cryptomarkets have engineered does allow for users to combine a greater range of knowledge sources when they examine risk and harm in relation to specific products on offer. They are also able to articulate narratives of drug use that resist stigmatisation, pathologisation, and criminalisation. The benefits of the cryptomarkets therefore extend from being a novel form of illicit drug distribution and into their ability reconfigure the cultural meaning and recognition of drug use.

References

Abel, G. M., & Fitzgerald, L. J. (2012). 'The street's got its advantages': Movement between sectors of the sex industry in a decriminalised environment. *Health, Risk & Society, 14*(1), 7–23. https://doi.org/10.1080/13698575.2011.640664.

Aldridge, J., & Askew, R. (2017). Delivery dilemmas: How drug cryptomarket users identify and seek to reduce their risk of detection by law enforcement. *International Journal of Drug Policy, 41*(Suppl. C), 101–109. https://doi.org/10.1016/j.drugpo.2016.10.010.

Askew, R. (2016). Functional fun: Legitimising adult recreational drug use. *International Journal of Drug Policy, 36,* 112–119. https://doi.org/10.1016/j.drugpo.2016.04.018.

Barratt, M. J., Allen, M., & Lenton, S. (2014). "PMA sounds fun": Negotiating drug discourses online. *Substance Use and Misuse, 49*(8), 987–998. https://doi.org/10.3109/10826084.2013.852584.

Barratt, M. J., Ferris, J. A., & Winstock, A. R. (2016). Safer scoring? Cryptomarkets, social supply and drug market violence. *International Journal of Drug Policy, 35,* 24–31. https://doi.org/10.1016/j.drugpo.2016.04.019.

Beckert, J., & Dewey, M. (2017). Introduction: The social organization of illegal markets. In J. Beckert & M. Dewey (Eds.), *The architecture of illegal markets: Towards an economic sociology of illegality in the economy* (pp. 1–34). Oxford: Oxford University Press. Retrieved from http://www.oxfordscholarship.com.ezproxy.is.ed.ac.uk/view/10.1093/oso/9780198794974.001.0001/oso-9780198794974.

Bourgois, P., & Schonberg, J. (2009). *Righteous dopefiend.* University of California Press.

Boucher, L. M., Marshall, Z., Martin, A., Larose-Hébert, K., Flynn, J. V., Lalonde, C., et al. (2017). Expanding conceptualizations of harm reduction: Results from a qualitative community-based participatory research study with people who inject drugs. *Harm Reduction Journal, 14,* 18. https://doi.org/10.1186/s12954-017-0145-2.

Coomber, R., Moyle, L., & South, N. (2015). The normalisation of drug supply: The social supply of drugs as the "other side" of the history of normalisation. *Drugs: Education, Prevention and Policy, 23*(3), 255–263. https://doi.org/10.3109/09687637.2015.1110565.

Decorte, T. (2001). Quality control by cocaine users: Underdeveloped harm reduction strategies. *European Addiction Research, 7*(4), 161–175.

Douglas, M. (1992). *Risk and blame.* Routledge.

Drumm, R. D., McBride, D., Metsch, L., Neufield, M., & Sawatsky, A. (2005). "I'm a health nut!" street drug users' accounts of self-care strategies. *Journal of Drug Issues, 35*(3), 607–629.

Duxbury, S. W., & Haynie, D. L. (2018). The network structure of opioid distribution on a darknet cryptomarket. *Journal of Quantitative Criminology, 34*(4), 921–941.

Epstein, S. (1996). *Impure science: AIDS, activism, and the politics of knowledge.* Berkeley: University of California Press.

Faulkner-Gurstein, R. (2017). The social logic of naloxone: Peer administration, harm reduction, and the transformation of social policy. *Social Science & Medicine, 180,* 20–27. https://doi.org/10.1016/j.socscimed.2017.03.013.

Friedman, S. R., de Jong, W., Rossi, D., Touzé, G., Rockwell, R., Des Jarlais, D. C., et al. (2007). Harm reduction theory: Users' culture, micro-social indigenous harm reduction, and the self-organization and outside-organizing of users' groups. *International Journal of Drug Policy, 18*(2), 107–117. https://doi.org/10.1016/j.drugpo.2006.11.006.

Gilbert, M., & Dasgupta, N. (2017). Silicon to syringe: Cryptomarkets and disruptive innovation in opioid supply chains. *International Journal of Drug Policy, 46,* 160–167. https://doi.org/10.1016/j.drugpo.2017.05.052.

Harris, M., & Rhodes, T. (2012). Venous access and care: Harnessing pragmatics in harm reduction for people who inject drugs. *Addiction, 107*(6), 1090–1096.

Gowan, T., Whetstone, S., & Andic, T. (2012). Addiction, agency, and the politics of self-control: Doing harm reduction in a heroin users' group. *Social Science & Medicine, 74*(8), 1251–1260. https://doi.org/10.1016/j.socscimed.2011.11.045.

Harris, M., & Rhodes, T. (2013). Methadone diversion as a protective strategy: The harm reduction potential of 'generous constraints'. *International Journal of Drug Policy, 24*(6), e43–e50. https://doi.org/10.1016/j.drugpo.2012.10.003.

Hunt, G., Milhet, M., & Bergeron, H. (Eds.). (2011). *Drugs and culture: Knowledge, consumption, and policy.* Avebury: Ashgate.

Jauffret-Roustide, M. (2009). Self-support for drug users in the context of harm reduction policy: A lay expertise defined by drug users' life skills and citizenship. *Health Sociology Review, 18*(2), 159–172. https://doi.org/10.5172/hesr.18.2.159.

Keane, H. (2003). Critiques of harm reduction, morality and the promise of human rights. *International Journal of Drug Policy, 14*(3), 227–232.

Lupton, D. (2015). *Lively data, social fitness and biovalue: The intersections of health self-tracking and social media.* New York: Social Science Research Network.

Lupton, D. (2016). *The quantified self: A sociology of self-tracking cultures.* Cambridge: Polity.

Maddox, A., Barratt, M. J., Allen, M., & Lenton, S. (2016). Constructive activism in the dark web: Cryptomarkets and illicit drugs in the digital 'demimonde'. *Information, Communication & Society, 19*(1), 111–126. https://doi.org/10.1080/1369118X.2015.1093531.

Measham, F., & Shiner, M. (2009). The legacy of 'normalisation': The role of classical and contemporary criminological theory in understanding young people's drug use. *International Journal of Drug Policy, 20*(6), 502–508. https://doi.org/10.1016/j.drugpo.2009.02.001.

Moeller, K., Munksgaard, R., & Demant, J. (2017). Flow my FE the vendor said: Exploring violent and fraudulent resource exchanges on cryptomarkets for illicit drugs. *American Behavioral Scientist* (early online version). https://doi.org/10.1177/0002764217734269.

Moore, D. (2008). Erasing pleasure from public discourse on illicit drugs: On the creation and reproduction of an absence. *International Journal of Drug Policy, 19*(5), 353–358.

Munksgaard, R., & Demant, J. (2016). Mixing politics and crime—The prevalence and decline of political discourse on the cryptomarket. *International Journal of Drug Policy, 35*, 77–83. https://doi.org/10.1016/j.drugpo.2016.04.021.

Munksgaard, R., Bakken, S., & Demant, J. (2017). Risk perception in emerging markets for illicit substances in Scandinavia-The effect of available information through online communities. *The Scandinavian Research Council for Criminology.*

Pauly, B. (2008). Harm reduction through a social justice lens. *International Journal of Drug Policy, 19*(1), 4–10. https://doi.org/10.1016/j.drugpo.2007.11.005.

Rhodes, T. (1997). Risk theory in epidemic times: Sex, drugs and the social organisation of 'risk behaviour'. *Sociology of Health and Illness, 19*(2), 208–227.

Robins, S. (2004). 'Long live Zackie, long live': AIDS activism, science and citizenship after apartheid. *Journal of Southern African Studies, 30,* 651–672. https://doi.org/10.1080/0305707042000254146.

Soska, K., & Christin, N. (2015). Measuring the longitudinal evolution of the online anonymous marketplace ecosystem. In *Proceedings of the 22nd USENIX Security Symposium.* Presented at the USENIX Security 2015, Washington, DC.

Van Hout, M. C., & Bingham, T. (2014). Responsible vendors, intelligent consumers: Silk Road, the online revolution in drug trading. *International Journal of Drug Policy, 25*(2), 183–189. https://doi.org/10.1016/j.drugpo.2013.10.009.

Van Hout, M. C., & Hearne, E. (2017). New psychoactive substances (NPS) on cryptomarket fora: An exploratory study of characteristics of forum activity between NPS buyers and vendors. *International Journal of Drug Policy, 40,* 102–110.

10

Secrecy and Anonymity Online

Anonymity Is Desired but Not Achieved in the Cryptomarkets

What do you look like, from Google's point of view? Whatever your imagined self might be—an eclectic mix of unpredictable tastes—it is probably a set of rather predictable patterns and habits. Surveillance works through data so it is the qualities of data that matter. Data reconfigures power. It is better in a data driven society to be known. The data poor are not known, without access to credit. So privacy serves those who can afford to have their data double untroubled. Big Nudge is already here, in the many ways supermarkets arrange their shelves, design products and serve up solutions.

Women face a threat surface through digital media and devices. Our obsession with personal security means we forget that for some people it is never personal. A woman's partner could coerce them into giving up passwords and access to personal accounts or force a fingerprint-protected device. Abusers learn to use this as part of their strategy of coercive control. Using geoblocking and all the rest doesn't help when your partner will simply harm you if you don't have location data on at all times.

© The Author(s) 2020
A. Bancroft, *The Darknet and Smarter Crime*, Palgrave Studies
in Cybercrime and Cybersecurity, https://doi.org/10.1007/978-3-030-26512-0_10

In 2013 it was revealed that police in Skåne in Sweden built a family tree database of Roma, their connections and various details about them. What if a private company was building that using publicly available data? Or producing a public database of people's criminal records? The latter has been done. Guilt by association becomes very easy. Dark network characteristics raise interesting problems. Are we assuming that all criminal actors are effectively linked together in the network The darknet offers another model of security that is shared and relies on it as a mutual quality. That means it gives some superficial advantages to criminals but not a huge amount. Pedophiles can use it to share photos and information but find difficulty setting up hosting or bitcoin tumbling because nobody will serve them.

We are in digital societies that create an architecture of suspicion and deanonymisation. Anonymity has political and personal uses. People who have good reasons to be hidden can share a lot with criminals, spies and cops. The darknet exists in a longer history of the development of anonymity in modern societies, in relation to the formation of the modern state and economy. Anonymity has been an incendiary means for social protest.

Anonymity is wrongly seen as fearful. It can be framed in various ways: as a threat to predictable and coherent social order (Abbink and Sadrieh 2009), an unavoidable and normal feature of daily life (Natanson 1990), an intrinsic feature of private liberal citizenship (Froomkin 1999), and a necessary condition of protest (Thompson 1975). Historically, it has been assumed that anonymity is a fundamental part of the fabric of modernity with profound implications for social life. Sociology identified the emergence of anonymity as a feature of urban life (Simmel 1906) and of a complex division of labour that necessarily involves working relationships between unknown others (Durkheim 2013). As well as generating new forms of solidarity and self, it has also been presented as threatening social control, creating fleeting and passing interactions (Wirth 1938) and indifference (Milgram 1963), and leading to the creation of new forms of governance to defeat it such as surveillance assemblages (Haggerty and Ericson 2000). Some of the assumptions behind these claims have been challenged, such as that anonymity is a general quality of urban life (Gans 1962), or that it is an inherent quality arising out of certain settings and with definite potential in promoting certain kinds of behaviour. It is certainly not a characteristic of life online. We join this tradition, which challenges both anonymity's supposedly a-social character and its naturalising as a technical-structural trait (Karp 1973). There are plenty of ways anonymity can give a cloak to malicious mobs, as shown in Gamergate, various other troll attacks and sad communities who like to dox people they think are weaker than them. It has become something of a habit on the incel alt-right. The prevailing narrative is an individualising one which suggests that people given the chance will revert to a savage state of nature. This is not how trolling works however. These are conformist mobs who are outriders for the social order.

Some features of the early debate were reproduced in relation to historical development of the internet and social media. Early libertarian and feminist conceptions saw the severing of offline and online identities as freeing humans from the weight of real-world restraints and oppressions (Barlow 1996). The cypherpunk movement sought during the 1980s and 1990s to embed a libertarian concept of cyberspace, developing cryptography and trust mechanisms that were intended to replace or resist central control and management and to substitute it with network-based systems (Branwen 2015). The development of public encryption using Pretty Good Privacy (PGP) by Phil Zimmerman was a key moment in this. Zimmerman was subject to a criminal investigation under the US Arms Control Export Act, high strength encryption being considered a military technology. Ensuring public encryption is available and usable is part of a political movement that has related tendrils such as the campaign to retain net neutrality. There is a 'politics of code' where struggles over concepts like privacy are embedded in software. Government agencies seeking to build 'backdoor' flaws into encryption technology are engaging in a political move that embeds power (Hales 2014). However focusing on the machinations of state agencies downplays the anonymity defeating technology built into many privately owned systems.

Coinciding with the rise of social media, there has been a greater focus on online anonymity as personally malign (U. N. Broadband Commission for Digital Development 2015), supposedly promoting a range of damaging behaviours and stances from uncivil discourse to abuse (Reader 2012). Political discourse in the UK, USA, China, Russia and India, among other countries, focuses on anonymity as a problem. It is framed as a shield and encouragement for terrorists, hackers, traffickers and trolls: people who post harassing material online in a deliberate attempt to damage individuals and online communities (Department of Electronics and Information Technology 2015). Encryption has become the focus of some of these discussions as a problem technology. The Russian government has systematically tried to disrupt some anonymising systems whereas US government agencies been more circumspect and are constrained by unresolved legal questions (Çalışkan et al. 2015). These differences and disputes highlight the dual nature of the internet, both allowing counter-publics to emerge and also opportunities for state and private domination through control of the data infrastructure (Garrett 2006; Maddox et al. 2016). Researchers have identified new orientations and identities coming into being on the internet such as crypto-freedom (Beer and Burrows 2010; Coleman and Golub 2008). Many users respond with resignation to the brute fact of surveillance that is embedded in the infrastructure of the internet (Lee and Cook 2015). It is technical and personally difficult for an individual to separate their real-world identity and their online personae, even when it is experienced as a pressing use for them.

Secrecy Is Needed

Secrecy matters in ways we do not recognise. It may be more useful than privacy, which is inherently fragile. The darknet provides one way of doing this in ways that can be both harmful and beneficial. In some perspectives secrecy is productive or necessary. In Freudian psychology, repression is necessary for adult development. Secret societes can involve ethical lying. African-American street hustlers valorise deception of the Man, and toasts celebrate the ability to mislead and deceive. Classical poetry and history preserved ethical truth while happily lying about the facts (Pratt 1988).

Secrecy is a social strategy, which works by pooling hidden knowledge. In order to interact secretly you need a literal or figurative mask. The mask allows the wearer to decide what is concealed and revealed. Birchall's (2016) argument that a shift from privacy to secrecy as the focus of tech activism and practical action online has been going on which in some ways circumvents the discussion of privacy as a goal. It might seem a matter of course that darknet markets are 'secret' however many clearnet communities also have an expectation of anonymity in them. What was distinct about cryptomarkets was the continuous focus on the infrastructure and practice of secrecy, on stealth, anonymisation and untraceability.

Anonymity's Techno-Politics

Secrecy combines technical and social aspects. Secrecy practices involve blending, spoofing and scrubbing. The cryptomarket infrastructure is designed to strip out identifying data from photos. Cryptomarkets place a premium on the ability to act anonymously, without being unknown. The capacity to do this has raised concerns about the way in which consistent deanonymisation in digital spaces limits privacy and autonomy. From the another angle, anonymity is viewed as a factor that disinhibits abusers and allows terrorists and pedophiles to operate with ease. However the ability to operate anonymously is relatively rare and becoming more so. Private companies assemble de-anonymisng techniques or simply employ their user data to block and limit users who may be embarrassing for them (Froomkin 2015). So there is a shift in power away from individuals and states into corporate entities operating with and enforcing norms of good behaviour that they develop on the fly. Recent changes in the policy of Twitter, Facebook and other companies has been towards banning users who violate norms of civility; civility as determined by those companies. There is a tendency then to reduce this to a question of platform technology and moderators equipped to make the right call. This reduces political questions to technical ones, and obscures how technical and social infrastructures are created in ways that de-anonymise.

A crucial distinction is that users can value anonymity without wishing to be secret. The difference between anonymity and secrecy is one with consequences in the area of the blockchain. Anonymity should allow for multiple identities. The blockchain allows for multiple but not infinite pseudonymous identities. The more one has, the more they can be tied together. So the blockchain and the pressures of the drug market online limit people's ability to exploit anonymity. The search for verifiability is starting to eat at the anonymity of the darknet. Can verifiability be preserved along with anonymity?

Cryptomarket users develop anonymity and use it as a resource that enables market interactions and allows for useful exchange of knowledge about drug consumption techniques, quality and safety. Anonymity is one part of their community of practice, which assembles technologies that allow them to operate freely.

Anonymity can be broken down into different qualities that can be more suited to some activities and orientations than others (Pfitzmann and Hansen 2010). Often in discussions of online anonymity it is used to mean pseudonymity, when individuals have a consistent, but disguised, persona. Multiple pseudonymous identities can be adopted to further obfuscate identity, to create desired effects through for example sock puppetry, creating multiple personae to give the impression of multiple support for one's viewpoint, or to emphasise different roles and personas. De-linking separates different interactions by the same user and prevents them being connected by an outside agent. Undetectabilty disguises the content of hidden activity and unobservability the participants, such as the origin and recipient point of hidden communications. Ruppert et al. (2013) usefully class digital social activity into actions and their traceability. Anonymity within the darknet preserves actions while it is intended to disrupt traceability. When we use the term anonymity here we use it to refer to the recognised state of being hidden, which includes these different aspects of anonymity: we use these more precise terms when picking out relevant aspects of it. These different elements, though relevant, each describe a technical quality of anonymity. Previous research, not related to the darknet, into the nuances of anonymity on the internet has found a singular term to be left wanting because of the difference between a user being anonymous and them feeling anonymous (Kennedy 2006). Barratt's (2011) distinction between 'technical anonymity' and 'social anonymity' allows for a better understanding of the different effects of anonymity. Technical anonymity exists when individuals are untraceable: there is no link between their actions and a singular identifiable and accountable persona. Social anonymity is the shared sense of operating anonymously.

Technical and social anonymity are pervasive features of the darknet (Barratt). Users aim to be anonymous from each other and from the prying eyes of internet service providers, government agencies and other surveillance bodies. Cryptomarkets are often framed as the product of a few geeks and some devilish entrepreneurs. However, that focus on their technical and entrepreneurial achievements misses out how these markets came into being as a result of a combination of the technologies with structural conditions. These were the changes in illicit market structures and the meshing of illicit and licit economies called deviant globalisation (Gilman et al. 2011).

The Pleasures of the Hidden

Cryptomarket users build a secure space in which they can experience a more pleasurable means of interacting in the drug market. There are benefits of use in terms of security, quality and the reduction in need for violence (Van Hout and Bingham 2013a, 2014). A consistent admonishment on the forum was not to mistake social anonymity for technical anonymity. The latter needed continual curation. The technology is used as a means to avoid violence and personal risk but it is also used to engage with others in a more palatable way. Cryptomarket market sales and interactions do not have face-to-face contact but may, because of technical and social anonymity, allow for types of exchanges users are not able to have in other markets. This different social space allows for an atypical set of relationship constructions; the social context of market performance and subcultural capital required to buy drugs on cryptomarkets is different from offline modes of purchasing or acquiring drugs.

Many forum discussions concerned security and its potential breaches. Users and vendors compared notes and discussed stealth. Vendors were rated on their stealthiness and this was the basis for many discussions. We asked interviewees to describe the whole process from initial exploration through purchasing and delivery. Interviewees gave detailed accounts of how they went about using the darknet and their motivations for using it. Forum discussions were only one place where information about anonymity was exchanged. Related clearnet sites such as reddit hosted extensive discussions of security and users frequently posted warnings and advice there. As well as these practical orientations, users gain personal satisfaction from successfully using the darknet while maintaining anonymity and vendors show their customer service quality by engaging in security signalling.

The role of forum administrators in managing relationships between participants was key: blocking and banning deviant individuals from engaging in forum communications and regulating the marketplaces (Holt et al. 2015). Forums facilitated 'nested support systems' that provide a place for information exchange, connections with other users and mutual support from those that have or have experienced similar difficulties (Van Hout and Bingham 2013b). Less experienced users are able to benefit from forum sections that have 'how to' instructions, and it is possible to find out which vendors have better products or more secure packaging (Martin 2014).

Interviewees recalled discovering and becoming involved with the darknet as a moment when their technical skills could be used. The recognition of the darknet as a potentially shadowy place prone to scams was acknowledged but as a challenge that could be overcome by using the right combination of trust practices and checks. Scamming was expected, but buyers were in practice rarely the victim of scams by vendors. It was more common for consignments to go astray or be intercepted by law enforcement, than for users to fall victim to scam vendors or sites as one buyer explained when interviewed.

> Well I was always interested in things like bitcoin and then I found out about Tor and things like that expanded like the knowledge base of it and then I found out just how open it was. I went onto the hidden wiki which is a site which used to document loads of Onion [Tor] sites. That's dead now, that's been hacked, so it's just loads of scam sites now which I found out to my cost. They had this huge list of things like, you could get people assassinated on the internet … I mean it's not something I'm interested in but wow [laugh], it's the knowledge that you can. So yeah, I gravitated towards like, hey I could get my weed really cheap delivered to me from the Europe. And yeah ended up getting into it from there. Interviewee 'Al'

Interviewees and users described the personal satisfaction that came from avoiding surveillance and showing one's digital nous. Interacting with others online can allow for membership of a subculture without the risk of stigma or exposure that might be associated with the related activity in a more visible setting (Adler and Adler 2008). Users who were sufficiently savvy and confident could take on a technology management role where their skills were acknowledged by others. They mediate and broker the street-darknet market relationship. One interviewee did this by selling his digital skills to local dealers, another by using them for social supply.

The type of activity possible with darknet activity is best conceived of as not being limited to specific instances of law breaking or interactions with others online. Rather, darknet markets and forums provide technically proficient users with another space in which to exist socially, a different outlet for interactions that are made difficult or impossible by their circumstances when not online. This outlet is not the detached cyberspace conceived of in the 1990s, where it was believed that the physical body could be released from the corporeal concerns and constrains imposed by everyday life. However, it does provide space for a community of technically skilled individuals to thrive.

Technical anonymity hinges on an empirical question: is it possible for someone to connect a darknet user's activity to their legal identity? If the answer is no then they have technical anonymity, if they can be then they do not have technical anonymity, a binary outcome. With social anonymity, the user's own perception of being anonymous is determined by a combination of factors. The extent of the user's technical knowledge and skill will determine how well they understand the encryption methods or software they are using as a means to avoid detection. One interviewee had used cryptomarkets with someone else guiding the main technical elements, and reflected on how it would feel to be completely alone:

The fact that you're giving people your address over the internet to buy class A drugs is also something I wouldn't want to do without fully understanding how it works. And then also hiding your IP [internet protocol] address, because you know that government, governments and stuff like that are monitoring these sites like you know that they are monitoring the traffic, lets not lie about that. And so you want to be able to hide your IP and stuff like that effectively and know you've hidden it well and I would just be relying on what I'd read on the internet basically to understand that I'd hidden myself well enough and I don't feel that's good enough. Interviewee 'Sel'

More experienced users are more likely to feel secure in their methods to ensure security and to enjoy the benefits of being able to engage with likeminded people. When users experience social anonymity, they are able to engage in the forums without the inhibitions experienced when fearing the exposure of information that will lead to social stigma.

Attesting Persona

Users have personas without being identifiable. Vendors benefit from establishing consistent but disguised personae. The expectation that users who wish to buy and sell on the darknet maintain a consistency of behaviour and etiquette towards other users shows the difference from what might be expected from a large face-to-face criminal marketplace. Geser's (2007) outlining of the tendency in successful online interactive circles for avatars to have continuity links to the type of anonymity employed by darknet users. Though a vendor will strive to completely separate their profile from their legal identity and 'public' life, the markets are structured so that trust is built up through user reviews and so buyers expect sellers to live up to the records of their previous transactions recorded prominently on each vendor's profile and in the associated discussion forums.

Darknet market users try and ascertain the consistency of the vendor's identity. In this instance, the continuity of a persona and its 'attestability' by others is key to acceptability and trustworthiness. Well-known vendors would establish themselves across different markets and market administrators would allow for this by reserving the usernames of well-known vendors when a new site was created. Good vendors would have an entourage of users on the site attesting to their reliability. Buyers use sites like reddit and Grams that work across different markets.

Multiple Identities Are a Challenge for Users and Vendors

Lol, it must be a mess having to keep up these shills, you chubby little loser. Perhaps I could call you out with your Christian name? Or get the cops? Have you worked out how I am yet, wanker? No chance – you don't recognize your own mug in the mirror. Forum user 'vphelps'

Holding multiple personas across different markets could be interpreted benignly. Having several in the same market was thought to be suspicious and the act of scammers, fake vendors and hostile vendors producing smack talk about rival vendors. So although anonymity was prized, singularity was as well, in the sense that vendors having a single, pseudonymous identity with which they could be held account. Users valued having one voice and one chain of responsibility.

The salience of anonymity varied among users. Some users had an active, 'total' approach to anonymity and would for example use anonymising methods when viewing clearnet sites that hosted information about the darknet. Others took a more relaxed approach and assumed that much of the work was done for them by the market itself and the software they used to access it. Doxxing is when a person's anonymous online persona is linked with their real-world identity and address. Some vendors make threats of doxxing but this is mostly seen as beyond the moral norms of the community and akin to snitching. Partial doxxing could be a threat:

I know that was an over-reaction but I had run out of options. This user has been trying to wreck my reputation. Merkat forum mods wouldn't do anything. So I let the person know that I had his full address and he should drop it. I never gave out their complete doxx despite what the Merkat mods say. I just gave out part of their phone number – nothing that would doxx them. Vendor 'Pigtime'

On the one hand doxxing is forbidden. On the other, forum users will claim a knowledge of a vendor's real-world identity to call out scammers.

One approach was to identify the vendor consistently through these different personae without doxxing them. Doxxing was technically possible for vendors and market administrators, however it was a rare occurrence. The threat of doxxing to social anonymity was greater than any passing benefit from doxxing an individual.

Maintaining Opsec Through Defeat and Deniability

The total process for securing transactions on the darknet was 'opsec' (operational security). As forum users often reminded each other, opsec was active, not passive. Using the right software on its own would not guarantee functioning opsec. Users had to apply opsec principles to the whole of the supply chain. It could easily be compromised. Sloppy practices included using the same username in darknet and clearnet sites, and using clearnet email addresses for darknet transactions.

Two techniques are salient: technical defeat and socio-legal deniability. Defeat techniques are the kind of encryption, stealthing and evasion that shields them from the gaze of law enforcement. 'Tumbling' bitcoin to ensure it was not traceable is a technique of defeat. Without tumbling, users can be traced through the blockchain if another part of the transaction is compromised. It is a form of money laundering, and could be done through a service like Bitcoin Fog that effectively creates a break in the chain through which users can transfer funds to different wallets to pay vendors, or payment can be transferred directly to the vendor's wallet. Some users saw it as overkill for the casual buyer.

There was a sense among more involved users that defeat on its own was inadequate. As Al pointed out, there were too many potential security holes:

> Everyone would view reddit through Tor or something so unless they are an idiot of course. But it's generally, you get the same level of security viewing the clearnet site through Tor. There are other mechanisms for them to track you, using cookies or javascript that could be used to track you. But if you're on something like Tails, that's automatically blocked anyway. So if

someone was to view it on it, even through Tor, they would still be trackable, even if you maximise the screen then the website can tell the resolution of your monitor. So that can be used to track you. So you can't have anything maximised, ever. So they would know exactly the size of the screen, right someone viewed this with a resolution of this, you had a resolution of X, so we have reason to believe that was you. And obviously that's not going to work on its own, you need other evidence but that is circumstantial. There's actually a specific warning when you go to maximize a window on Tails, it says hey maybe not. Interviewee 'Al'

Ideally PGP encryption is used to send buyers' addresses to vendors so it should not be linked to the purchase directly through the market. When vendors are arrested, suspicion is expressed on reddit that they may have kept buyers' details. In contrast, some users were very relaxed about opsec, using their own computers with a mainstream operating system, Tor, and having drugs delivered to their home address.

Deniability is a way of engineering interactions that involves severing personal legal responsibility for drug shipments and introducing plausible deniability. For example, using a false name for deliveries and scrubbing stored addresses is a technique of deniability, as is wording messages in a deliberately vague way.

[Discussion of secure email systems] I've been told that particular server has been infiltrated by the NSA as well. To be safe always avoid the kind of words that might trigger a search. I make sure I'm VERY vague in emails. Forum user 'Hilarysgusset'

Much of the discussion around security on the darknet focuses on techniques of defeat. However, arrests are more likely to happen because of failures of deniability: being caught with large quantities of drugs clearly destined for consignment, making large cash purchases, having others give evidence leading to a warrant and so on.

Defeat on the vendor's side involves stealth. Good stealth is an important measure of vendor quality. Shipping in good 'cover', such as a DVD case or another innocuous item, is praised, as is having a legitimate-looking return address. The more it appears to be a plausible shipment from an online retailer the better. Various techniques are used to avoid detection of shipments: vacuum sealing, use of moisture barrier bag, and good practice such as cleaning vacuum seals, are commented on. Good stealth is held to go right through the supply chain and involves the vendor using untraceable systems when paying for postage. Buying postage through an online retailer is seen as sloppy. If the vendor uses their real details to purchase postage and is compromised then the addresses of customers can be exposed to law enforcement. The technique of defeat is also key here, ensuring no link in the chain of identification will lead back to the vendor. There is a sales and trust aspect to what is done. Many of the techniques used are part of what we have termed 'security signalling'. There is heavy signalling done by security measures. Security measures by vendors are a signal of the vendor's reliability and professionalism. Those who did not work opsec throughout the supply chain were seen as amateurish.

The Inadequate Shield of Technology

Two technology 'backbones' underpin the cryptomarkets. The internet backbone—the system of routers and cabling connecting the different hosts around the world—and the global postal system. Each could link the users to their real-world identities in various ways and vendor and user opsec was crucial in stopping this from happening. Successful use of the technology was a combination of the right hardware, software and good practice. There were a set of technologies and infrastructures involved, from specialised software, burner phones and the postal service. Encryption which scrambles the data packets being sent via the internet backbone is the magic invisibility cloak that 'noobs' (new, inexperienced users) are constantly being reminded about on the forum.

> The first time as a vendor was on Evolution. I set up a simple vendor page, not much on there because I didn't think much needed to be said. After the first few orders were sent in unencypted I told the buyers never to do that. I put a post in all my listings – use PGP or don't order. It was amazing how many people don't bother with the simplest encryption. Vendor 'diamondsogs'

However anonymity is not synonymous with encryption. Embedded metadata in a document can reveal much about its author. It is simple to geolocate using camera data embedded in photos which records the camera type, date, time and often the location unless this metadata is stripped out or not recorded in the first place (Julian 2015). Frequently using the right technology could lead to lax real-world security practice. Real-world security holes were neglected as long as the person thought they had got the digital security set up correctly. For example, one vendor might store the names and addresses of clients in unencrypted paper form with product.

Bitcoin is often represented as a technology of anonymity. Unlike Tor it is not designed for anonymity, but it does permit it (Reid and Harrigan 2013). Various techniques and practices have to be applied to make bitcoin anonymous. The first possible identity leak is at the point of converting government backed fiat currency such as British sterling or the US dollar into cryptocurrency. Cryptocurrencies use a publically available blockchain to record transactions. Law enforcement can follow the blockchain and monitor large transactions that can then be matched up with darknet users using brute force data matching.

One method of de-linking the connection between blockchain transactions and one's real-world identity is to use local bitcoin:

[Bitcoin vendor] picked me up, drove to another cafe, bought a pot of tea while we had a little chat about Bitcoin and the general crypto-economy and all that jazz because the transfer was taking a while to come through. The transfer came through, and there was a verification code that I knew but he wouldn't get until he had sent the coins and the transaction had been confirmed. So he then showed me the code and they matched up with one that I already had, so I knew the Bitcoins had been transferred successfully. And I was able to go home. Interview 'Al'

There is a theatre of security aspect to some of the precautions taken by interviewees, vendors and forum users, where anonymising activities become ritualised (Amoore and Hall 2010). Some aspects of encryption and stealthing are undertaken because they give the impression or feeling of protection, and 'that's just what you do' when you are using the market.

Security practices are part of the expected comportment when interacting with the market. There is similarity with the legal security market. Security signalling is part of the theatre of security that has become a common part of social life in many societies. Public and private security services engage in a variety of techniques that signal that they are taking security seriously. As security has become privatised and spread throughout society, these theatres of security are becoming more common (Schreier and Caparini 2005). Darknet vendors adopted security signalling as mark of vendor and product quality. In addition to signalling, we also identified the satisfaction and pleasure some users gain from applying a comprehensive anonymisation strategy to their operations on the darknet. Personal pride and social status can come from successfully handling the layered systems of encryption and anonymisation. Darknet users' rituals of anonymising could also be seen as disrupting the normalised, ritualised surveillance which has been embedded in the fabric of social life (Bajc 2007). In these ways, anonymity becomes a resource for both sellers and buyers, who use it to signal quality, trustworthiness and competence.

Various implementations of encryption are presented as troublesome technologies that encourage a dangerous anonymity that is corrosive of the social order. As we have shown, this misrepresents both the history of those technologies and how they are used today. It is also a political claim. Treating anonymity as inherently suspicious brushes aside critical perspectives that point to government mandated publicity of individual identities and behaviours as a tool of social control (Cobb 2007), which are features of new forms of governance that target conduct (Flint and Nixon 2006), and the ethics of cryptography (Rogaway 2015). There is also a long history of anonymising practices and technologies themselves as tools with a political purpose (O'Brien 2001). We started with the argument that anonymity, often presented as a kind of withdrawal from social life is through and through a form of social engagement (Marx 1999). What it does is sever the relationship between one persona and others. It 'functions as a variable means for negotiating identities and interests across multiple social forms' (Shilling and Mellor 2014, 618). It is not easy to attain and maintain anonymity online. Supposedly anonymised individuals can be de-anonymised using metadata with relative ease (Ohm 2010) or through the normal workings of internet service providers. Currently there are concerted attempts by some states and corporations to collapse multiple online personas into one traceable identity. However, users' deniability practices can disrupt de-anonymising techniques (Spitter et al. 2015).

As well as challenging the representation of anonymity as deceitful, we can also challenge the representation of its opposite as trustworthy. Various governments have sought to establish the measure of trust as the permanence and openness to surveillance of an individual's identity. Governments and private actors seek to link individuals' online personae with their offline identity. These developments are part of the generalisation and privatisation of surveillance and securitisation of everyday life. More and more private organisations are expected to be involved in immigration control, tracking and monitoring extremism and so on. Though this has been represented as privatisation, it might be better to call it nationalisation of the internet and associated technologies by various states from the USA to Russia.

Despite its significance in public discussion of the darknet, anonymity is not a necessary condition for online drug trading (Watters and Phair 2012) and many forms of drug trading go on using the internet, and especially social media, without those involved going to great lengths to disguise their real-world identities from each other or possible third parties. Darknet markets are far from the only way of buying and selling drugs online. While not exactly comparable, evidence from peer-to-peer file-sharing suggests that threats of deanonymisation and prosecutions have only a limited deterrent effect (Lysonski and Durvasula 2008). The development of files-haring was a key moment in the spread of mass, routine lawbreaking using online technology. File-sharing did not initially rely on deep anonymity; users could be and were identified simply by subpoenaing the internet service provider. More recently encryption has been employed by file-sharers to provide more robust security for their activities (Larsson et al. 2013). File-sharing also drove technological innovation (Larsson and Svensson 2010) and it is likely that the need to operate online in an anonymous mode will continue to generate new communities, interaction forms and technological infrastructures. Anonymising communities have moved on from the 'cypherpunk' ethos—highly skilled, demonstrating technical ability—to a more pragmatic and less ideologically framed encryption practice where users concerned with privacy for various reasons employ these techniques to protect themselves. We suggest a politics of anonymity would look to protect these varied aspects of anonymous practice. If we understand anonymity as composed of different elements which become more or less salient in different contexts (such as unlinkability and deniability) we can then focus on how those elements can be supported through a combination of technology, law and social practice (Fischer-Hübner 1998).

Conclusion

There is a tension in the digital world between bureaucratic and legal requirements that users are consistently traceable to a singular, real-world self, and the creation of multiple identities to suit different platforms and aspects of one's persona. Systematised knowledge about populations is the key resource on which others are built. A lot of the focus recently has been on personal data as an economic asset but it does not need to be so. It is an asset of states and as big data has grown so has the power of nation states especially the new powers of Russia and China. During the twentieth century this knowledge was central to state power because populations can be militarised and states used mass identification. In the twenty-first century with the advent of the internet this can become much more fine grained and persistent and now involves the resource of attention. It could be that the main conflict over identity will be between persistent and transitory memory.

References

Abbink, K., & Sadrieh, A. (2009). The pleasure of being nasty. *Economics Letters, 105*(3), 306–308.

Amoore, L., & Hall, A. (2010). Border theatre: On the arts of security and resistance. *Cultural Geographies, 17*(3), 299–319.

Bajc, V. (2007). Surveillance in public rituals. *American Behavioral Scientist, 50*(12), 1648–1673.

Barlow, J. P. (1996). *A declaration of the independence of cyberspace.* Retrieved from http://homes.eff.org/~barlow/Declaration-Final.html.

Barratt, M. J. (2011). Discussing illicit drugs in public internet forums: Visibility, stigma, and pseudonymity. In *Proceedings of the 5th International Conference on Communities and Technologies* (pp. 159–168). https://doi.org/10.1145/2103354.2103376.

Beer, D., & Burrows, R. (2010). Consumption, prosumption and participatory web cultures. *Journal of Consumer Culture, 10*(1), 3–12.

Branwen, G. (2015). *Silk Road: Theory & practice.* Retrieved from http://www.gwern.net/Silk%20Road.

Çalışkan, E., Minárik, T., & Osula, A.-M. (2015). *Technical and legal overview of the tor anonymity network.* Tallinn: NATO Cooperative Cyber Defence Centre of Excellence.

Cobb, N. (2007). Governance through publicity: Anti-social behaviour orders, young people, and the problematization of the right to anonymity. *Journal of Law and Society, 34*(3), 342–373.

Coleman, E. G., & Golub, A. (2008). Hacker practice. *Anthropological Theory, 8*(3), 255–277.

Department of Electronics and Information Technology. (2015). *Draft national encryption policy.* New Delhi: The Indian Ministry of Communications and Information Technology.

Durkheim, E. (2013). *Durkheim: The division of labour in society.* Macmillan International Higher Education, 1893.

Fischer-Hübner, S. (1998). Privacy and security at risk in the global information society. *Information, Communication & Society, 1*(4), 420–441.

Flint, J., & Nixon, J. (2006). Governing neighbours: Anti-social behaviour orders and new forms of regulating conduct in the UK. *Urban Studies, 43*(5–6), 939–955.

Froomkin, A. M. (1999). Legal issues in anonymity and pseudonymity. *The Information Society, 15*(2), 113–127.

Froomkin, A. M. (2015). From anonymity to identification. *Journal of Self-Regulation and Regulation, 1*, 121–138.

Gans, H. (1962). *The urban villages.* New York: Free Press.

Garrett, R. K. (2006). Protest in an information society: A review of literature on social movements and new ICTs. *Information, Communication & Society, 9*(2), 202–224.

Geser, H. (2007). *Me, my self and my Avatar: Some microsociological reflections on "second life."* Working Paper.

Gilman, N., Goldhammer, J., & Weber, S. (Eds.). (2011). *Deviant globalization: Black market economy in the 21st century.* A&C Black.

Haggerty, K. D., & Ericson, R. V. (2000). The surveillant assemblage. *The British Journal of Sociology, 51*(4), 605–622. https://doi.org/10.1080/00071310020015280.

Hales, T. C. (2014). The NSA back door to NIST. *Notices of the AMS, 61*(2), 190–192.

Holt, T. J., Smirnova, O., Chua, Y. T. C., & Copes, H. (2015). Examining the risk reduction strategies of actors in online criminal markets. *Global Crime, 16*(2), 81–103.

Julian. (2015). *Deanonymizing darknet data @atechdad.* Available at: http://atechdad.com/deanonymizing-darknet-data/.

Karp, D. A. (1973). Hiding in pornographic bookstores: A reconsideration of the nature of urban anonymity. *Urban Life and Culture, 1*(4), 427–451.

Kennedy, H. (2006). Beyond anonymity, or future directions for internet identity research. *New Media & Society, 8*(6), 859–876.

Larsson, S., & Svensson, M., (2010). Compliance or obscurity? Online anonymity as a consequence of fighting unauthorised file-sharing. *Policy & Internet, 2*(4), 75–103.

Larsson, S., Svensson, M., & Kaminski, M. D. (2013). Online piracy, anonymity and social change. *Convergence: The International Journal of Research into New Media Technologies, 19*(1), 95–114.

Lee, A., & Cook, P. S. (2015). The conditions of exposure and immediacy: Internet surveillance and Generation Y. *Journal of Sociology, 51*(3), 674–688.

Lysonski, S., & Durvasula, S. (2008). Digital piracy of MP3s: Consumer and ethical predispositions. *Journal of Consumer Marketing, 25*(3), 167–178.

Maddox, A., Barratt, M. J., Allen, M., & Lenton, S. (2016). Constructive activism in the dark web: Cryptomarkets and illicit drugs in the digital 'demimonde'. *Information, Communication & Society, 19*(1), 111–126. https://doi.org/10.1080/1369118X.2015.1093531.

Martin, J. (2014). *Drugs on the dark net: How cryptomarkets are transforming the global trade in illicit drugs.* London: Palgrave Macmillan.

Marx, G. T. (1999). What's in a name? Some reflections on the sociology of anonymity. *The Information Society, 15*(2), 99–112.

Milgram, S. (1963). Behavioral study of obedience. *The Journal of Abnormal and Social Psychology, 67*(4), 371–378.

Natanson, M. (1990). Anonymity: A study in the philosophy of Alfred Schutz. *Human Studies, 13*(1), 97–101.

O'Brien, J. (2001). Putting a face to a (screen) name: The first amendment implications of compelling ISPs to reveal the identities of anonymous internet speakers in online defamation cases. *Fordham Law Review, 70*, 2745.

Ohm, P. (2010). Broken promises of privacy: Responding to the surprising failure of anonymization. *UCLA Law Review, 57*, 1701–1777.

Pfitzmann, A., & Hansen, M. (2010). *A terminology for talking about privacy by data minimization: Anonymity, unlinkability, undetectability, unobservability, pseudonymity, and identity management.*

Pratt, L. H. (1988). *Lying and poetry from Homer to Pindar: Falsehood and deception in archaic Greek poetics.* University of Michigan Press.

Reader, B. (2012). Free press vs. free speech? The rhetoric of "civility" in regard to anonymous online comments. *Journalism & Mass Communication Quarterly, 89*(3), 495–513.

Reid, F., & Harrigan, M. (2013). An analysis of anonymity in the bitcoin system. In Y. Altshuler, Y. Elovici, & B. A. Cremers, et al. (Eds.), *Security and privacy in social networks* (pp. 197 223). New York, NY: Springer New York.

Rogaway, P. (2015). The moral character of cryptographic work. *IACR Cryptology ePrint Archive, 2015*, 1162.

Ruppert, E., Law, J., & Savage, M. (2013). Reassembling social science methods: The challenge of digital devices. *Theory, Culture & Society, 30*(4), 22–46. https://doi.org/10.1177/0263276413484941.

Schreier, F., & Caparini, M. (2005). *Privatising security: Law, practice and governance of private military and security companies.* Geneva: Centre for the Democratic Control Armed Forces. Accessed 27 August 2015, http://www.dcaf.ch/content/download/34919/525055/version/1/file/op06_privatising-security.pdf.

Simmel, G. (1906). The sociology of secrecy and of secret societies. *American Journal of Sociology, 11*(4), 441–498.

Shilling, C., & Mellor, P. A. (2014). For a sociology of deceit: Doubled identities, interested actions and situational logics of opportunity. *Sociology, 49*(4), 607–623.

Spitter, M., Klaver, F., & Koot. G., et al. (2015). Authorship Analysis on Dark Marketplace Forums. In *Proceedings of the IEEE European Intelligence & Security Informatics Conference (EISIC).* Manchester.

Thompson, E. P. (1975). The crime of anonymity. In D. Hay, P. Linebaugh, J. G. Rule, E. Thompson, & C. Winslow (Eds.), *Albion's fatal tree: Crime and society in eighteenth-century England* (pp. 255–344). London: Allen Lane.

U. N. Broadband Commission for Digital Development. (2015). *Cyber violence against women and girls: A world-wide wake-up call.* Geneva: Broadband Commission for Sustainable Development.

Van Hout, M. C., & Bingham, T. (2013a). 'Silk Road', the virtual drug marketplace: A single case study of user experiences. *International Journal of Drug Policy, 24*(5), 385–391.

Van Hout, M. C., & Bingham, T. (2013b). 'Surfing the Silk Road': A study of users' experiences. *International Journal of Drug Policy, 24*(6), 524–529.

Van Hout, M. C., & Bingham, T. (2014). Responsible vendors, intelligent consumers: Silk Road, the online revolution in drug trading. *International Journal of Drug Policy, 25*(2), 183–189. https://doi.org/10.1016/j.drugpo.2013.10.009.

Watters, P. A., & Phair, N. (2012). Detecting illicit drugs on social media using automated social media intelligence analysis (ASMIA). In Y. Xiang, J. Lopez, & C.-C. J, Kuo, et al. (Eds.), *Cyberspace Safety and Security* (pp. 66–76). Accessed 27 July 2015, http://link.springer.com/chapter/10.1007/978-3-642-35362-8_7. Berlin, Heidelberg: Springer.

Wirth, L. (1938). Urbanism as a way of life. *American Journal of Sociology, 44*(1), 1–24.

11

Why Digital Crime Works

How many illegal objects do you have in your home? I would guess many are either illicit drugs, or digital objects such as pirated films. Here we see where changes in the digital economy have transformed crime. Often people in search of illegal content stream content rather than 'own' it so the demand for digital goods of that sort has fallen. Even digital objects lose their permanence.

Cryptomarket participants, law enforcement agencies and security analysts employ several assumptions what drives technical and organisational change and how new techniques and technologies are evaluated by them. These are: law enforcement activity is a major source of disruption; technology is adapted based on its technical qualities; new financial opportunities such as new drugs drive new market actors. In fact, markets are quite resilient to law enforcement takedowns. A major source of disruption is hosting failure, hacking and breakdown of trust between participants. Criminals may rely on older, tried and tested technology even if it presents risks to them. They often seek status opportunities as much as or more than financial ones. Finally, those involved in drug markets often show a strong ideological commitment to the cryptomarkets as a socially beneficial way of obtaining drugs.

© The Author(s) 2020   **197**
A. Bancroft, *The Darknet and Smarter Crime*, Palgrave Studies
in Cybercrime and Cybersecurity, https://doi.org/10.1007/978-3-030-26512-0_11

Cybercriminals and Law Enforcement Imagine Crime and so Shape What Crime Is

In a world of deep fakes, the evidence chain is more reliant on human trust. Perhaps the blockchain could be agreed on as impermeable social memory, with hashing to preserve secrecy. Law enforcement use parallel construction or parallel evidencing to disguise the real source of information on cybercriminal activity. In the case of Silk Road, the official story much repeated around the world is that a badly configured server was leaking IP information. The reality may have been a full scan of the internet by the National Security Agency. New methodological concepts are needed to keep space with the growing capacities of criminals and states: ransomware can be understood by epidemiology, following vulnerability vectors.

'Semi-crime' like captcha-solving by captcha farms can facilitate illicit activities. It uses vast amounts of human labour. Automatic software started to replace captcha farms so then we have tests that are harder for computers to solve which involve categorisation of hills and zebra crossings and so on. Matching this tells us a lot about machine learning as computer scientist teams try and break captcha. Eventually machine learning is good enough to beat new captcha. Now there is a version 3 which is behavioural and involves no direct test.

Social media fraud is a great way of pumping one's reputation (Paquet-Clouston et al. 2018). They found that clients for SMF services were would-be social media celebrities, actors, shops and others who wanted to inflate their reputation. There are legal ways of achieving the same outcome (using click-farm reputation services) and illegal ones (using botnets). As ever the problem comes when someone pays a service to achieve an outcome without caring too much about the means used, so a starlet's agent pays a service to fluff her popularity on instagram and that service uses a botnet. Who is enabling and permitting the crime? It's a chain of demand which creates normal crime. There is not much incentive to any actor in the crime creation chain to actually fight it. Instagram, the actor, the agent, are not threatened by it.

The digital enables both forms of crime and association that do not have direct offline analogues (e.g. swarming, mobbing, automated crime etc.) and that enable meatspace crime in new ways. So there shouldn't be a binary between the real and the virtual. The real/virtual binary creates several problems: cops, victims and bystanders don't take cyberattacks as seriously as they would real-world harassment. It is viewed as both 'not real' and 'too terrifying to contemplate'. There are significant features of cybercrime in terms of its cultural performance, transgression and signification. Part of the pleasure of using cryptomarkets is the enjoyment of transgression and performing oneself as a responsible person with agency, in charge of their drug use purchasing and use. Most important, lots of labour goes into making these things work.

A lot of changes that we attribute to the digital happened long before digitalisation. The flattening of drug trafficking chains, much reduced middle market and so on all happened as a result of globalisation not the ability to use digital technology. Sharing knowledge about new drugs happened via Alexander Shulgin's books and other chemists, it used paper not bits. There are some changes which are made possible through digital systems such as providing reasonably reliably third party mediation, providing more real time intelligence, and new drugs introduced through the cryptomarkets such as nootropics. New drugs and new ways of using them come into being as there is more rapid sharing of knowledge and products. We see how there has to be a strong substrate of shared knowledge, habits and priorities in order for this to happen. Criminal markets are also driving technological change.

Crime Has Logics, not Only Rationality

Illegal markets like any other market would not work if everyone behaved rationally. As in much else it does not really work if we seek to explain human behaviour in terms of calculative rationality. That is not how humans think. We have come to recognise that markets do not work as advertised. The impression of a frictionless, buyer responsive free market in illicit products is illuminating and attractive to but incomplete and in some ways incorrect. Illegal markets are not just black markets that prey on the legal, they are one and the same, central to capital accumulation and resource allocation (Beckert and Dewey 2017).

The second some illegal behaviour is uncovered in an otherwise legal market the first response everyone involved reaches for is that the boundary between legal and illegal was so blurred. Criminals are reasonable, in that they are prepared to give reasons and act according to a logic. It just better be one that you get. Markets exist on shared logics and expectations, shared norms and shared expectations of outcomes, shared procedures and shared commensurability—the assessment of value and whether one has gained or lost value. This is a kind of procedural rationality.

With cryptomarkets, they rapidly became dominated by a very few vendors who can choose their customers. They might say, you only buy from us if you buy more than a certain amount, or we know you. The power shifts from the customer to the vendor. The logic of the supply chain, rather than consumer demand, begins to dominate. This mimics digital markets where increasingly it is the customer being rated along with the seller. For Uber and Airbnb, you have to show you are a worthy customer of their brand. The market is not one of free choice but one where the customer has to demonstrate that they are a good citizen and a good consumer, which increasingly mean the same thing.

What Is Happening to the Cryptomarkets

Even well coordinated cross-jurisdictional law enforcement operations such as 'Onymous' covering multiple agencies and markets have at best short term impact (Soska and Christin 2015). The effect of law enforcement interventions is subject to rapid decay. It is a combination of: highly motivated participants, quasi-trust relationships and mechanisms, extensive weak social network ties and a well maintained underlying infrastructure. At one point it appeared that cryptomarkets were highly resilient in part due to their reproduction of similar factors as the rest of the illicit drug market—a distributed organisational structure and low barriers to entry at even high levels (Reuter and Haaga 1989).

In 2019 the main markets started to go offline. Dreammarket was closed by its administrators. Wall Street was subject to an exit scam, then an administrator began blackmailing users before posting login information on a popular discussion site, before finally being seized by law enforcement.

Wallstreet market was seized after an exit scam, following which one of the site moderators, Med3l1n tried to blackmail users and ended up posting his access information to the site's server on Dread, a discussion forum. The ecosystem is starting to eat itself. Law enforcement is also becoming more adept at cutting out the supporting limbs of the ecosystem, where information is shared about cryptomarkets.

Another development is that markets are seeking new darknets as Tor does not protect them well against DDoS attacks. One market, Libertas, was the first to set up on the i2p darknet for that reason. This may be a last throw of the dice, or presage a larger shift away from Tor.

This All Matters Because as a Society We Are Far More Constrained Than at Any Time in the Past

The great squatters movements of the post-Second World War era, the social movements of the Deep South, the anti-colonial movements all relied on what was annoying not being illegal: they went on being annoying until they got what they wanted. It was recognised that being a responsible citizen and breaking the law could be quite compatible, indeed necessary. Squatters just wanted a home. Those gaps have been slammed shut. Our public forums are private. Our movements are monitored and any step out of line is criminalised.

There are some spaces where communities can form around their own rules and with minimal platform effects. Psychedelic IRC discussions, darknet groupings, discord servers and other corners of the internet allow for communities to form without having to worry too much about the constraints of Big Tech. These spaces matter if digital life is going to be anything other than centralised and algorithmically governed.

It also matters because we live in a world where states and corporations operate strategic lawlessness. There are much softer lines between 'state' 'criminal networks' and politics. Society is becoming more digitally criminal in that sense, of crime being strategically employed as a part of the working of power. Crime therefore stops living in the dark spaces, and occupies the grey spaces—where bitcoin codes can be used to pass along child pornography, where rating systems can be fixed to deliver monetised likes, and where dating apps can be used to deal illicit drugs.

Communities are generally successful when they are communities of shared practice, where members agree on grounds rules of interaction, safety, and where they are not over reliant on the technology. A simple infrastructure can be more resilient than an opaque one. Digital has effects beyond the commission of crime. In some cases it generates community or emerges from new communities, it prioritises trust and resilience, is disorganised but monopolistic, and is information and expertise creating

Conclusion

Illegal markets are not just about the stuff they provide. In the favelas of Rio, drug trafficking is resilient, politically connected criminal activity (Arias 2009). In the Rio favela Santa Ana, traffickers deliver services to Santa Ana residents. They are able to gain legitimacy because violence comes both from police and drug gangs, and state violence is the more dangerous. Residents are not faced with the choice between peace and violence but between two sources of violence, one of which appears far more arbitrary. Those who live in the grey zone much make choices like that. A combination of politics and power shapes the drug economy. In the digital crime economy, we have seen themes of structural violence; contested political authority; state failure; justice; marginalisation; and the connection between the drug trade and globalisation. Criminal networks are structured and located various by territory, or by the social strata they can occupy and claim. Illegal networks are destructive and constructive, spreading norms and technology, creating communities and also intensifying harm. They are more and more tied into the technically embedded logics of modern informational capitalism and the nation-state focused power structures of the fractured internets.

References

Arias, E. D. (2009). *Drugs and democracy in Rio de Janeiro: Trafficking, social networks, and public security.* Chapel Hill: University of North Carolina Press.

Beckert, J., & Dewey, M. (2017). Introduction: The social organization of illegal markets. In J. Beckert & M. Dewey (Eds.), *The architecture of illegal markets: Towards an economic sociology of illegality in the economy* (pp. 1–34). Oxford: Oxford University Press. Retrieved from http://www.oxfordscholarship.com.ezproxy.is.ed.ac.uk/view/10.1093/oso/9780198794974.001.0001/oso-9780198794974.

Paquet-Clouston, M., Décary-Hétu, D., & Morselli, C. (2018). Assessing market competition and vendors' size and scope on AlphaBay. *International Journal of Drug Policy, 54,* 87–98.

Reuter, P., & Haaga, J. (1989). *The organization of high-level drug markets: An exploratory study.* U.S. Department of Justice.

Soska, K., & Christin, N. (2015). Measuring the longitudinal evolution of the online anonymous marketplace ecosystem. In *Proceedings of the 22nd USENIX Security Symposium.* Presented at the USENIX Security 2015, Washington, DC.

Stratton, G., Powell, A., & Cameron, R. (2017). Crime and justice in digital society: Towards a 'digital criminology'? *International Journal for Crime, Justice and Social Democracy, 6*(2), 17–33. https://doi.org/10.5204/ijcjsd.v6i2.355.

References

Abbink, K., & Sadrieh, A. (2009). The pleasure of being nasty. *Economics Letters, 105*(3), 306–308.

Abel, G. M., & Fitzgerald, L. J. (2012). 'The street's got its advantages': Movement between sectors of the sex industry in a decriminalised environment. *Health, Risk & Society, 14*(1), 7–23. https://doi.org/10.1080/13698575.2011.640664.

Afilipoaie, A., & Shortis, P. (2015). *The growing industry of darknet marketing.* Swansea: Global Drug Policy Observatory.

Afilipoaie, A., & Shortis, P. (2018). *Crypto-market enforcement—New strategy and tactics.* Swansea: Global Drug Policy Observatory.

Agar, M. H. (1971). Folklore of the heroin addict: Two examples. *The Journal of American Folklore, 84*(332), 175–185. https://doi.org/10.2307/538988.

Akerlof, G. A. (1978). The market for "lemons": Quality uncertainty and the market mechanism. In *Uncertainty in economics* (pp. 235–251). New York: Elsevier.

Alazab, M., Venkatraman, S., Watters, P., Alazab, M., & Alazab, A. (2011). Cybercrime: The case of obfuscated malware. In *Global security, safety and sustainability & e-Democracy* (pp. 204–211). Berlin: Springer.

Aldridge, J., & Askew, R. (2017). Delivery dilemmas: How drug cryptomarket users identify and seek to reduce their risk of detection by law enforcement.

International Journal of Drug Policy, 41(Suppl. C), 101–109. https://doi.org/
10.1016/j.drugpo.2016.10.010.

Aldridge, J., & Décary-Hétu, D. (2014). *Not an 'e-Bay for drugs': The cryptomarket 'Silk Road' as a paradigm shifting criminal innovation.* Rochester, NY: Social Science Research Network.

Aldridge, J., & Décary-Hétu, D. (2016a). Hidden wholesale: The drug diffusing capacity of online drug cryptomarkets. *International Journal of Drug Policy, 35,* 7–15. https://doi.org/10.1016/j.drugpo.2016.04.020.

Aldridge, J., & Décary-Hétu, D. (2016b). Cryptomarkets and the future of illicit drug markets. In *Internet and drug markets, EMCDDA insights* (pp. 23–30). Luxembourg: Publications Office of the European Union.

Amoore, L., & Hall, A. (2010). Border theatre: On the arts of security and resistance. *Cultural Geographies, 17*(3), 299–319.

Ananthaswamy, A. (2011). Age of the splinternet. *New Scientist, 211*(2821), 42–45.

Ancrum, C., & Treadwell, J. (2017). Beyond ghosts, gangs and good sorts: Commercial cannabis cultivation and illicit enterprise in England's disadvantaged inner cities. *Crime, Media, Culture, 13*(1), 69–84. https://doi.org/10.1177/1741659016646414.

Anderson, R., Barton, C., Böhme, R., Clayton, R., Van Eeten, M. J., Levi, M., et al. (2013). Measuring the cost of cybercrime. In *The economics of information security and privacy* (pp. 265–300). Berlin: Springer.

Anderson, T. L., & Levy, J. A. (2003). Marginality among older injectors in today's illicit drug culture: Assessing the impact of ageing. *Addiction, 98*(6), 761–770. https://doi.org/10.1046/j.1360-0443.2003.00388.x.

Andersson, J. (2011). The origins and impacts of the Swedish file-sharing movement: A case study. *Critical Studies in Peer Production (CSPP), 1*(1), 1–18.

Antonopoulos, G. A., & Hall, A. (2016). The financial management of the illicit tobacco trade in the United Kingdom. *British Journal of Criminology, 56*(4), 709–728. https://doi.org/10.1093/bjc/azv062.

Arias, E. D. (2009). *Drugs and democracy in Rio de Janeiro: Trafficking, social networks, and public security.* Chapel Hill: University of North Carolina Press.

Askew, R. (2016). Functional fun: Legitimising adult recreational drug use. *International Journal of Drug Policy, 36,* 112–119. https://doi.org/10.1016/j.drugpo.2016.04.018.

Badawy, A., Ferrara, E., & Lerman, K. (2018). Analyzing the digital traces of political manipulation: The 2016 Russian interference Twitter campaign. In *2018 IEEE/ACM International Conference on Advances in Social Networks Analysis and Mining (ASONAM)* (pp. 258–265). IEEE.

Bajc, V. (2007). Surveillance in public rituals. *American Behavioral Scientist, 50*(12), 1648–1673.

Bancroft, A., & Scott Reid, P. (2017). Challenging the techno-politics of anonymity: The case of cryptomarket users. *Information, Communication & Society, 20*(4), 497–512. https://doi.org/10.1080/1369118X.2016.1187643.

Barlow, J. P. (1996). *A declaration of the independence of cyberspace.* Retrieved from http://homes.eff.org/~barlow/Declaration-Final.html.

Barratt, M. J. (2011). Discussing illicit drugs in public internet forums: Visibility, stigma, and pseudonymity. In *Proceedings of the 5th International Conference on Communities and Technologies* (pp. 159–168). https://doi.org/10.1145/2103354.2103376.

Barratt, M. J. (2012). The efficacy of interviewing young drug users through online chat. *Drug and Alcohol Review, 31*(4), 566–572.

Barratt, M. J., & Aldridge, J. (2016). Everything you always wanted to know about drug cryptomarkets* (*but were afraid to ask). *International Journal of Drug Policy, 35,* 1–6. https://doi.org/10.1016/j.drugpo.2016.07.005.

Barratt, M. J., Allen, M., & Lenton, S. (2014a). "PMA sounds fun": Negotiating drug discourses online. *Substance Use and Misuse, 49*(8), 987–998. https://doi.org/10.3109/10826084.2013.852584.

Barratt, M. J., Ferris, J. A., & Winstock, A. R. (2014b). Use of Silk Road, the online drug marketplace, in the United Kingdom, Australia and the United States. *Addiction, 109*(5), 774–783. https://doi.org/10.1111/add.12470.

Barratt, M. J., Ferris, J. A., & Winstock, A. R. (2016a). Safer scoring? Cryptomarkets, social supply and drug market violence. *International Journal of Drug Policy, 35,* 24–31. https://doi.org/10.1016/j.drugpo.2016.04.019.

Barratt, M. J., Ferris, J. A., Zahnow, R., Palamar, J. J., Maier, L. J., & Winstock, A. R. (2017). Moving on from representativeness: Testing the utility of the global drug survey. *Substance Abuse: Research and Treatment, 11.* https://doi.org/10.1177/1178221817716391.

Barratt, M. J., & Lenton, S. (2010). Beyond recruitment? Participatory online research with people who use drugs. *International Journal of Internet Research Ethics, 3*(1), 69–86.

Barratt, M. J., Lenton, S., & Allen, M. (2013). Internet content regulation, public drug websites and the growth in hidden internet services. *Drugs: Education, Prevention and Policy, 20*(3), 195–202. https://doi.org/10.3109/09687637.2012.745828.

Barratt, M. J., Lenton, S., Maddox, A., & Allen, M. (2016b). 'What if you live on top of a bakery and you like cakes?'—Drug use and harm trajectories before, during and after the emergence of Silk Road. *International Journal of Drug Policy, 35*, 50–57. https://doi.org/10.1016/j.drugpo.2016.04.006.

Barratt, M. J., Potter, G. R., Wouters, M., Wilkins, C., Werse, B., Perälä, J., et al. (2015). Lessons from conducting trans-national internet-mediated participatory research with hidden populations of cannabis cultivators. *International Journal of Drug Policy, 26*(3), 238–249. https://doi.org/10.1016/j.drugpo. 2014.12.004.

Becher, T., & Trowler, P. R. (2001). *Academic tribes and territories*. New York: McGraw-Hill.

Becker, G. S. (1968). Crime and punishment: An economic approach. In *The economic dimensions of crime* (pp. 13–68). https://doi.org/10.1007/978-1-349-62853-7_2.

Becker, H. S. (1953). Becoming a marihuana user. *American Journal of Sociology, 59*(3), 235–242.

Beckert, J. (2009). The social order of markets. *Theory and Society, 38*(3), 245–269. https://doi.org/10.1007/s11186-008-9082-0.

Beckert, J., & Dewey, M. (2017). Introduction: The social organization of illegal markets. In J. Beckert & M. Dewey (Eds.), *The architecture of illegal markets: Towards an economic sociology of illegality in the economy* (pp. 1–34). Oxford: Oxford University Press. Retrieved from http://www.oxfordscholarship.com.ezproxy.is.ed.ac.uk/view/10.1093/oso/9780198794974.001.0001/oso-9780198794974.

Beckert, J., & Wehinger, F. (2012). In the shadow: Illegal markets and economic sociology. *Socio-Economic Review, 11*(1), 5–30.

Beer, D. (2016). *Metric power*. London: Palgrave Macmillan.

Beer, D., & Burrows, R. (2010). Consumption, prosumption and participatory web cultures. *Journal of Consumer Culture, 10*(1), 3–12.

Bilgrei, O. R. (2018). Broscience: Creating trust in online drug communities. *New Media & Society, 20*(8), 2712–2727. https://doi.org/10.1177/1461444817730331.

Bilgrei, O. R. (2019). Community-consumerism: Negotiating risk in online drug communities. *Sociology of Health & Illness, 41*(5), 852–866.

Birchall, C. (2011). Introduction to 'secrecy and transparency' the politics of opacity and openness. *Theory, Culture & Society, 28*(7–8), 7–25.

Blake, D. (2018). How lotto scammers defraud elderly Americans and fuel gang wars in Jamaica. *The Conversation*. Retrieved from http://theconversation.com/how-lotto-scammers-defraud-elderly-americans-and-fuel-gang-wars-in-jamaica-90676.

Botoeva, G. (2014). Hashish as cash in a post-Soviet Kyrgyz village. *International Journal of Drug Policy, 25*(6), 1227–1234. https://doi.org/10.1016/j.drugpo. 2014.01.016.

Boucher, L. M., Marshall, Z., Martin, A., Larose-Hébert, K., Flynn, J. V., Lalonde, C., et al. (2017). Expanding conceptualizations of harm reduction: Results from a qualitative community-based participatory research study with people who inject drugs. *Harm Reduction Journal, 14*, 18. https://doi.org/10. 1186/s12954-017-0145-2.

Bourgois, P. (1998). The moral economies of homeless heroin addicts: Confronting ethnography, HIV risk, and everyday violence in San Francisco shooting encampments. *Substance Use and Misuse, 33*(11), 2323–2351. https://doi. org/10.3109/10826089809056260.

Bourgois, P. (2003). Crack and the political economy of social suffering. *Addiction Research & Theory, 11*(1), 31–37. https://doi.org/10.1080/ 1606635021000021322.

Bourgois, P., & Schonberg, J. (2009). *Righteous dopefiend.* University of California Press.

Boyd, D., & Crawford, K. (2011). Six provocations for big data. In *A Decade in Internet Time: Symposium on the Dynamics of the Internet and Society* (Vol. 21). Oxford, UK: Oxford Internet Institute.

Boyer, E. W., Lapen, P. T., Macalino, G., & Hibberd, P. L. (2007). Dissemination of psychoactive substance information by innovative drug users. *CyberPsychology & Behavior, 10*(1), 1–6. https://doi.org/10.1089/cpb.2006.9999.

Branwen, G. (2015). *Silk Road: Theory & practice.* Retrieved from http://www. gwern.net/Silk%20Road.

Branwen, G. (2016). *Darknet market mortality risks.* https://www.gwern.net/ DNM-survival.

Broséus, J., Rhumorbarbe, D., Mireault, C., Ouellette, V., Crispino, F., & Décary-Hétu, D. (2016). Studying illicit drug trafficking on darknet markets: Structure and organisation from a Canadian perspective. *Forensic Science International, 264*, 7–14. https://doi.org/10.1016/j.forsciint.2016.02.045.

Bruneel, C.-A., Lakhdar, C. B., & Vaillant, N. G. (2014). Are "legal highs" users satisfied? Evidence from online customer comments. *Substance Use and Misuse, 49*(4), 364–373. https://doi.org/10.3109/10826084.2013.841243.

Bucher, T. (2012). Want to be on the top? Algorithmic power and the threat of invisibility on Facebook. *New Media & Society, 14*(7), 1164–1180. https:// doi.org/10.1177/1461444812440159.

Caleb. (2019, May 7). *What do we know about the DeepDotWeb seizure?* Retrieved 8 May 2019, from Caleb website: https://medium.com/@c5/what-do-we-know-about-the-deepdotweb-seizure-98ca45de9987.

Çalışkan, E., Minárik, T., & Osula, A.-M. (2015). *Technical and legal overview of the tor anonymity network.* Tallinn: NATO Cooperative Cyber Defence Centre of Excellence.

Calo, R., & Rosenblat, A. (2017). The taking economy: Uber, information, and power. *Columbia Law Review, 117,* 1623.

Cameron, D., Smith, G. A., Daniulaityte, R., Sheth, A. P., Dave, D., Chen, L., et al. (2013). PREDOSE: A semantic web platform for drug abuse epidemiology using social media. *Journal of Biomedical Informatics, 46*(6), 985–997. https://doi.org/10.1016/j.jbi.2013.07.007.

Campbell, H. (2000). The glass phallus: Pub(lic) masculinity and drinking in rural New Zealand. *Rural Sociology, 65*(4), 562–581. https://doi.org/10.1111/j.1549-0831.2000.tb00044.x.

Campbell, N. D., & Shaw, S. J. (2008). Incitements to discourse: Illicit drugs, harm reduction, and the production of ethnographic subjects. *Cultural Anthropology, 23*(4), 688–717.

Cárdenas, A., Radosavac, S., Grossklags, J., Chuang, J., & Hoofnagle, C. J. (2009). *An economic map of cybercrime* (SSRN Scholarly Paper No. ID 1997795). Retrieved from Social Science Research Network website: https://papers.ssrn.com/abstract=1997795.

Carnwath, T., & Smith, I. (2002). *Heroin century.* London: Routledge.

Carrier, N., & Klantschnig, G. (2017). Quasilegality: Khat, cannabis and Africa's drug laws. *Third World Quarterly, 39*(2), 1–16. https://doi.org/10.1080/01436597.2017.1368383.

Caudevilla, F., Ventura, M., Fornís, I., Barratt, M. J., Vidal, C., lladanosa, C. G., et al. (2016). Results of an international drug testing service for cryptomarket users. *International Journal of Drug Policy.* http://dx.doi.org/10.1016/j.drugpo.2016.04.017.

Chiauzzi, E., & Wicks, P. (2019). Digital trespass: Ethical and terms-of-use violations by researchers accessing data from an online patient community. *Journal of Medical Internet Research, 21*(2), e11985. https://doi.org/10.2196/11985.

Choo, K.-K. R. (2008). Organised crime groups in cyberspace: A typology. *Trends in Organized Crime, 11*(3), 270–295. https://doi.org/10.1007/s12117-008-9038-9.

Christin, N. (2013). Traveling the Silk Road: A measurement analysis of a large anonymous online marketplace. In *Proceedings of the 22nd International Conference on the World Wide Web* (pp. 213–224). Rio de Janeiro, Brazil: WWW 2013.

Clarke, R. V. G. (1980). Situational crime prevention: Theory and practice. *British Journal of Criminology, 20,* 136–147.

Cobb, N. (2007). Governance through publicity: Anti-social behaviour orders, young people, and the problematization of the right to anonymity. *Journal of Law and Society, 34*(3), 342–373.

Coleman, E. G., & Golub, A. (2008). Hacker practice. *Anthropological Theory, 8*(3), 255–277.

Coles, N. (2001). It's not what you know—It's who you know that counts: Analysing serious crime groups as social networks. *British Journal of Criminology, 41*(4), 580–594. https://doi.org/10.1093/bjc/41.4.580.

Collins, R. (2004). *Interaction ritual chains/Randall Collins.* Princeton, NJ and Oxford: Princeton University Press [2004], ©2004. (Main Library (STANDARD LOAN)—2nd floor HM1111 Col.).

Coomber, R. (1997a). Dangerous drug adulteration—An international survey of drug dealers using the internet and the World Wide Web (WWW). *International Journal on Drug Policy, 8,* 71–81.

Coomber, R. (1997b). The adulteration of drugs: What dealers do to illicit drugs, and what they think is done to them. *Addiction Research and Theory, 5*(4), 297–306.

Coomber, R. (2003). There's no such thing as a free lunch: How 'freebies' and 'credit' operate as part of rational drug market activity. *Journal of Drug Issues, 33*(4), 939–962.

Coomber, R., Moyle, L., & South, N. (2015). The normalisation of drug supply: The social supply of drugs as the "other side" of the history of normalisation. *Drugs: Education, Prevention and Policy, 23*(3), 255–263. https://doi.org/10.3109/09687637.2015.1110565.

Coward, M. (2017). Against network thinking: A critique of pathological sovereignty. *European Journal of International Relations.* https://doi.org/10.1177/1354066117705704.

Critchlow, B. (1985). The blame in the bottle: Attributions about drunken behavior. *Personality and Social Psychology Bulletin, 11*(3), 258–274. https://doi.org/10.1177/0146167285113003.

Cubrilovic, N. (2014). *Large number of tor hidden sites seized by the FBI in operation onymous were clone or scam sites.* Retrieved from https://www.nikcub.com/posts/onymous-part1/.

Cunliffe, J., Martin, J., Décary-Hétu, D., & Aldridge, J. (2017). An island apart? Risks and prices in the Australian cryptomarket drug trade. *International Journal of Drug Policy, 50*(Suppl. C), 64–73. https://doi.org/10.1016/j.drugpo. 2017.09.005.

Curtis, B. (2002). *The politics of population: State formation, statistics, and the census of Canada, 1840–1875.* Toronto: University of Toronto Press.

Cusack, B., & Ward, G. (2018). *Points of failure in the ransomware electronic business model.* Twenty-fourth Americas Conference on Information Systems. New Orleans.

Czajka, J. L., & Beyler, A. (2016). *Declining response rates in federal surveys: Trends and implications (background paper)* (Mathematica Policy Research).

Davey, Z., Schifano, F., Corazza, O., Deluca, P., & Psychonaut Web Mapping Group. (2012). e-Psychonauts: Conducting research in online drug forum communities. *Journal of Mental Health, 21*(4), 386–394. https://doi.org/10. 3109/09638237.2012.682265.

Davis, D. E. (2011). Irregular armed forces, shifting patterns of commitment, and fragmented sovereignty in the developing world. In M. Hanagan & C. Tilly (Eds.), *Contention and trust in cities and states* (pp. 249–265). https://doi.org/10.1007/978-94-007-0756-6_17.

De Filippi, P., & Hassan, S. (2016). Blockchain technology as a regulatory technology: From code is law to law is code. *First Monday, 21*(12). https://doi.org/10.5210/fm.v21i12.7113.

Décary-Hétu, D., & Dupont, B. (2013). Reputation in a dark network of online criminals. *Global Crime, 14,* 175–196. https://doi.org/10.1080/17440572.2013.801015.

Décary-Hétu, D., & Leppänen, A. (2016). Criminals and signals: An assessment of criminal performance in the carding underworld. *Security Journal, 29*(3), 442–460. https://doi.org/10.1057/sj.2013.39.

Décary-Hétu, D., Paquet-Clouston, M., & Aldridge, J. (2016). Going international? Risk taking by cryptomarket drug vendors. *International Journal of Drug Policy, 35,* 69–76. https://doi.org/10.1016/j.drugpo.2016.06.003.

Decorte, T. (2001). Quality control by cocaine users: Underdeveloped harm reduction strategies. *European Addiction Research, 7*(4), 161–175.

Decorte, T. (2011). Blinding ourselves with science: The chronic infections of our thinking on psychoactive substances. In G. Hunt, M. Milhet, & Henri Bergeron (Eds.), *Drugs and culture: Knowledge, consumption and policy* (pp. 33–51). Farnham: Ashgate.

Decorte, T., Malm, A., Sznitman, S. R., Hakkarainen, P., Barratt, M. J., Potter, G. R., et al. (2019). The challenges and benefits of analyzing feedback comments in surveys: Lessons from a cross-national online survey of small-scale cannabis growers. *Methodological Innovations, 12*(1). https://doi.org/10.1177/2059799119825606.

Dennis, F. (2016). Encountering "triggers". *Contemporary Drug Problems, 43*(2), 126–141.

Dennis, F. (2017). Conceiving of addicted pleasures: A 'modern' paradox. *International Journal of Drug Policy, 49,* 150–159. https://doi.org/10.1016/j.drugpo.2017.07.007.

Dennis, F., & Farrugia, A. (2017). Materialising drugged pleasures: Practice, politics, care. *International Journal of Drug Policy, 49,* 86–91. https://doi.org/10.1016/j.drugpo.2017.10.001.

Department of Electronics and Information Technology. (2015). *Draft national encryption policy.* New Delhi: The Indian Ministry of Communications and Information Technology.

Dickinson, T., & Wright, R. (2015). Gossip, decision-making and deterrence in drug markets. *British Journal of Criminology, 55*(6), 1263–1281. https://doi.org/10.1093/bjc/azv010.

Dingledine, R., Mathewson, N., & Syverson, P. (2004). *Tor: The second-generation onion router.* Retrieved from DTIC Document website: http://oai.dtic.mil/oai/oai?verb=getRecord&metadataPrefix=html&identifier=ADA465464.

Dittus, M., Wright, J., & Graham, M. (2017). *Platform criminalism: The 'last-mile' geography of the darknet market supply chain.* ArXiv: 1712.10068 [Cs]. Retrieved from http://arxiv.org/abs/1712.10068.

DoctorX. (2019). *Use and abuse of drug checking by cryptomarkets vendors.* International Energy Control. Retrieved 17 April 2019, from https://energycontrol-international.org/use-and-abuse-of-drug-checking-by-cryptomarkets-vendors/.

Dodd, N. (2018). The social life of bitcoin. *Theory, Culture & Society, 35*(3), 35–56. https://doi.org/10.1177/0263276417746464.

Dodge, A. (2016). Digitizing rape culture: Online sexual violence and the power of the digital photograph. *Crime, Media, Culture, 12*(1), 65–82. https://doi.org/10.1177/1741659015601173.

Dourish, P. (2016). Algorithms and their others: Algorithmic culture in context. *Big Data & Society, 3*(2). https://doi.org/10.1177/2053951716665128.

Drumm, R. D., McBride, D., Metsch, L., Neufield, M., & Sawatsky, A. (2005). "I'm a health nut!" street drug users' accounts of self-care strategies. *Journal of Drug Issues, 35*(3), 607–629.

Du Toit, B. (1977). *Drugs, rituals and altered states of consciousness.* Rotterdam: AA Balkema.

Duff, C. (2011). Networks, resources and agencies: On the character and pro-duction of enabling places. *Health & Place, 17*(1), 149–156. https://doi.org/10.1016/j.healthplace.2010.09.012.

Duff, C. (2014). The place and time of drugs. *International Journal of Drug Policy, 25*(3), 633–639. https://doi.org/10.1016/j.drugpo.2013.10.014.

Dupont, B., Côté, A.-M., Savine, C., & Décary-Hétu, D. (2016). The ecology of trust among hackers. *Global Crime, 17*(2), 129–151. https://doi.org/10.1080/17440572.2016.1157480.

Durkheim, E. (2013). *Durkheim: The division of labour in society*. Macmillan International Higher Education, 1893.

Duxbury, S. W., & Haynie, D. L. (2017). The network structure of opioid distribution on a darknet cryptomarket. *Journal of Quantitative Criminology*, 1–21. https://doi.org/10.1007/s10940-017-9359-4.

Duxbury, S. W., & Haynie, D. L. (2018). The network structure of opioid distribution on a darknet cryptomarket. *Journal of Quantitative Criminology, 34*(4), 921–941.

Edgley, C., & Kiser, K. (1982). Polaroid sex: Deviant possibilities in a techno-logical age. *The Journal of American Culture, 5*(1), 59–64.

Epstein, S. (1996). *Impure science: AIDS, activism, and the politics of knowledge*. Berkeley: University of California Press.

Faulkner-Gurstein, R. (2017). The social logic of naloxone: Peer administration, harm reduction, and the transformation of social policy. *Social Science & Medicine, 180,* 20–27. https://doi.org/10.1016/j.socscimed.2017.03.013.

Fischer-Hübner, S. (1998). Privacy and security at risk in the global information society. *Information, Communication & Society, 1*(4), 420–441.

Fleetwood, J. S. (2009). *Emotional work: Ethnographic fieldwork in prisons in Ecuador*. Glasgow: University of Glasgow.

Fleetwood, J. S. (2014). *Drug mules: Women in the international cocaine trade*. London: Springer.

Fligstein, N. (2002). *The architecture of markets: An economic sociology of twenty-first-century capitalist societies*. Princeton: Princeton University Press.

Flint, J., & Nixon, J. (2006). Governing neighbours: Anti-social behaviour orders and new forms of regulating conduct in the UK. *Urban Studies, 43*(5–6), 939–955.

Fox, N. J., & Alldred, P. (2015). Inside the research-assemblage: New materialism and the micropolitics of social inquiry. *Sociological Research Online, 20*(2), 1–19. https://doi.org/10.5153/sro.3578.

French, M., & Smith, G. J. (2016). Surveillance and embodiment: Dispositifs of capture. *Body & Society, 22,* 3–27. https://doi.org/10.1177/1357034x16643169.

Friedman, S. R., de Jong, W., Rossi, D., Touzé, G., Rockwell, R., Des Jarlais, D. C., et al. (2007). Harm reduction theory: Users' culture, micro-social indigenous harm reduction, and the self-organization and outside-organizing of users' groups. *International Journal of Drug Policy, 18*(2), 107–117. https://doi.org/10.1016/j.drugpo.2006.11.006.

Froomkin, A. M. (1999). Legal issues in anonymity and pseudonymity. *The Information Society, 15*(2), 113–127.

Froomkin, A. M. (2015). From anonymity to identification. *Journal of Self-Regulation and Regulation, 1,* 121–138.

Full Text. (n.d.). Retrieved from https://www.researchgate.net/profile/Mamoun_Alazab/publication/230554535_Cybercrime_The_Case_of_Obfuscated_Malware/links/0912f5014a105a254c000000.pdf.

Furst, R. T. (2000). The re-engineering of heroin: An emerging heroin "cutting" trend in New York City. *Addiction Research, 8*(4), 357–379.

Gambetta, D. (2011). *Codes of the underworld: How criminals communicate.* Princeton: Princeton University Press.

Gangadharan, S. P. (2017). The downside of digital inclusion: Expectations and experiences of privacy and surveillance among marginal internet users. *New Media & Society, 19*(4), 597–615. https://doi.org/10.1177/1461444815614053.

Gans, H. (1962). *The urban villages.* New York: Free Press.

Garrett, R. K. (2006). Protest in an information society: A review of literature on social movements and new ICTs. *Information, Communication & Society, 9*(2), 202–224.

Geser, H. (2007). *Me, my self and my Avatar: Some microsociological reflections on "second life."* Working Paper.

Gilbert, M., & Dasgupta, N. (2017). Silicon to syringe: Cryptomarkets and disruptive innovation in opioid supply chains. *International Journal of Drug Policy, 46,* 160–167. https://doi.org/10.1016/j.drugpo.2017.05.052.

Gillespie, A. A. (2012). Twitter, jokes and the law: Chambers v DPP [2012] EWHC 2157 (QB). *The Journal of Criminal Law, 76*(5), 364–369. https://doi.org/10.1350/jcla.2012.76.5.790.

Gilman, N., Goldhammer, J., & Weber, S. (Eds.). (2011). *Deviant globalization: Black market economy in the 21st century.* A&C Black.

Giommoni, L., & Gundur, R. V. (2018). An analysis of the United Kingdom's cannabis market using crowdsourced data. *Global Crime, 19*(2), 85–106. https://doi.org/10.1080/17440572.2018.1460071.

Goldschlag, D. M., Reed, M. G., & Syverson, P. F. (1996, May 30). Hiding routing information. In *Information hiding* (pp. 137–150). Berlin, Heidelberg: Springer. https://doi.org/10.1007/3-540-61996-8_37.

Goldschlag, D., Reed, M., & Syverson, P. (1999). Onion routing. *Communications of the ACM, 42*(2), 39–41. https://doi.org/10.1145/293411.293443.

Gomart, E. (2002). Methadone: Six effects in search of a substance. *Social Studies of Science, 32*(1), 93–135.

Goucher, W. (2010). Being a cybercrime victim. *Computer Fraud & Security, 2010*(10), 16–18. https://doi.org/10.1016/S1361-3723(10)70134-2.

Gowan, T., Whetstone, S., & Andic, T. (2012). Addiction, agency, and the politics of self-control: Doing harm reduction in a heroin users' group. *Social Science & Medicine, 74*(8), 1251–1260. https://doi.org/10.1016/j.socscimed.2011.11.045.

Granovetter, M. (1973). The strength of weak ties. *American Journal of Sociology, 78*(6), 1360–1380.

Granovetter, M. (1983). The strength of weak ties: A network theory revisited. *Sociological Theory, 1*(1), 201–233.

Grund, J. P. C. (1993). *Drug use as a social ritual.* Rotterdam: Instituut voor Verslavingsonderzoek, Erasmus University Rotterdam.

Gusfield, J. R. (1987). Passage to play: Rituals of drinking time in American society. In M. Douglas (Ed.), *Constructive drinking: Perspectives on drink from anthropology* (pp. 73–90). Cambridge: Cambridge University Press.

Gusfield, J. (1997). The culture of public problems: Drinking-driving and the symbolic order. In *Morality and health* (pp. 201–229). New York: Routledge.

Haggerty, K. D., & Ericson, R. V. (2000). The surveillant assemblage. *The British Journal of Sociology, 51*(4), 605–622. https://doi.org/10.1080/00071310020015280.

Haines, R. J., Johnson, J. L., Carter, C. I., & Arora, K. (2009). "I couldn't say, I'm not a girl"—Adolescents talk about gender and marijuana use. *Social Science & Medicine, 68*(11), 2029–2036.

Hales, T. C. (2014). The NSA back door to NIST. *Notices of the AMS, 61*(2), 190–192.

Hall, S., Winlow, S., & Ancrum, C. (2013). *Criminal identities and consumer culture: Crime, exclusion and the new culture of narcissm.* London: Willan.

Haller, M. H. (1990). Illegal enterprise: A theoretical and historical interpretation. *Criminology, 28*(2), 207–236.

Hamilton, K. (2017, September 26). *Jamaican lottery scammers suspected in slaying of retired U.S. teacher*. Retrieved 26 May 2019, from Vice News website: https://news.vice.com/en_us/article/mb9588/jamaican-lottery-scammers-suspected-in-slaying-of-retired-u-s-teacher.

Hammersvik, E., Sandberg, S., & Pedersen, W. (2012). Why small-scale cannabis growers stay small: Five mechanisms that prevent small-scale growers from going large scale. *International Journal of Drug Policy, 23*(6), 458–464. https://doi.org/10.1016/j.drugpo.2012.08.001.

Hammond, L. (2016). *Obliged to give: Remittances and the maintenance of transnational networks between Somalis at home and abroad, 10,* 27.

Haritavorn, N. (2014). Surviving in two worlds: Social and structural violence of Thai female injecting drug users. *International Journal of Drug Policy, 25*(1), 116–123. https://doi.org/10.1016/j.drugpo.2013.09.008.

Harris, M., & Rhodes, T. (2012). Venous access and care: Harnessing pragmatics in harm reduction for people who inject drugs. *Addiction, 107*(6), 1090–1096.

Harris, M., & Rhodes, T. (2013). Methadone diversion as a protective strategy: The harm reduction potential of 'generous constraints'. *International Journal of Drug Policy, 24*(6), e43 e50. https://doi.org/10.1016/j.drugpo.2012.10.003.

Hearn, J. (2012). *Theorizing power.* Macmillan International Higher Education.

Hine, C. (2015). *Ethnography for the internet: Embedded, embodied and everyday.* London: Bloomsbury Academic.

Holt, T. J. (2013). Exploring the social organisation and structure of stolen data markets. *Global Crime, 14,* 155–174. https://doi.org/10.1080/17440572.2013.787925.

Holt, T. J., Smirnova, O., & Hutchings, A. (2016). Examining signals of trust in criminal markets online. *Journal of Cybersecurity, 2*(2), 137–145. https://doi.org/10.1093/cybsec/tyw007.

Holt, T. J., Smirnova, O., Chua, Y. T. C., & Copes, H. (2015). Examining the risk reduction strategies of actors in online criminal markets. *Global Crime, 16*(2), 81–103.

Hornsby, R., & Hobbs, D. (2007). A zone of ambiguity. *British Journal of Criminology, 47*(4), 551–571. https://doi.org/10.1093/bjc/azl089.

Horton-Eddison, M., & Cristofaro, M. D. (2017). *Hard interventions and innovation in crypto-drug markets: The escrow example.* Swansea: Global Drug Policy Observatory.

Hunt, G., & Frank, V. A. (2016). Reflecting on intoxication. In T. Kolind, B. Thom, & G. Hunt (Eds.), *The SAGE handbook of drug and alcohol studies.* London: Sage.

Hunt, G., Milhet, M., & Bergeron, H. (Eds.). (2011). *Drugs and culture: Knowledge, consumption and policy.* Avebury: Ashgate.

Hutchings, A., & Holt, T. J. (2016). The online stolen data market: Disruption and intervention approaches. *Global Crime,* 1–20. https://doi.org/10.1080/17440572.2016.1197123.

Iginio, G., Danit, G., Thiago, A., & Gabriela, M. (2015). *Countering online hate speech.* Paris: UNESCO.

Iglesias, R. M., Szklo, A. S., de Souza, M. C., & de Almeida, L. M. (2017). Estimating the size of illicit tobacco consumption in Brazil: Findings from the global adult tobacco survey. *Tobacco Control, 26*(1), 53–59. https://doi.org/10.1136/tobaccocontrol-2015-052465.

Jaros, D. M. (2012). Perfecting criminal markets. *Columbia Law Review, 112,* 1947–1991.

Jauffret-Roustide, M. (2009). Self-support for drug users in the context of harm reduction policy: A lay expertise defined by drug users' life skills and citizenship. *Health Sociology Review, 18*(2), 159–172. https://doi.org/10.5172/hesr.18.2.159.

Jensen, C., Forlini, C., Partridge, B., & Hall, W. (2016). Australian university students' coping strategies and use of pharmaceutical stimulants as cognitive enhancers. *Frontiers in Psychology, 7.* https://doi.org/10.3389/fpsyg.2016.00277.

Johansen, P., & von Lampe, K. (2002). *Is there honor among crooks? On the importance of trust in criminal relations.* Chicago: American Society of Criminology.

Joossens, L., & Raw, M. (2012). From cigarette smuggling to illicit tobacco trade. *Tobacco Control, 21*(2), 230–234.

Jordan, T., & Taylor, P. (1998). A sociology of hackers. *The Sociological Review, 46*(4), 757–780. https://doi.org/10.1111/1467-954X.00139.

Julian. (2015). *Deanonymizing darknet data @atechdad.* Available at: http://atechdad.com/deanonymizing-darknet-data/.

Kamat, P., & Gautam, A. S. (2018). Recent trends in the era of cybercrime and the measures to control them. In *Handbook of e-business security* (pp. 243–258). New York: Auerbach Publications.

Karp, D. A. (1973). Hiding in pornographic bookstores: A reconsideration of the nature of urban anonymity. *Urban Life and Culture, 1*(4), 427–451.

Karstedt, S., & Farrall, S. (2006). The moral economy of everyday crime markets, consumers and citizens. *British Journal of Criminology, 46,* 1011–1036. https://doi.org/10.1093/bjc/azl082.

Keane, H. (2003). Critiques of harm reduction, morality and the promise of human rights. *International Journal of Drug Policy, 14*(3), 227–232.

Keegan, B., Ahmad, M. A., Williams, D., Srivastava, J., & Contractor, N. S. (2011). What can gold farmers teach us about criminal networks? *ACM Crossroads, 17*(3), 11–15.

Kennedy, H. (2006). Beyond anonymity, or future directions for internet identity research. *New Media & Society, 8*(6), 859–876.

Kenney, M. (2007). The architecture of drug trafficking: network forms of organisation in the Colombian cocaine trade. *Global Crime, 8*(3), 233–259. https://doi.org/10.1080/17440570701507794.

Kleemans, E. R. (2012). Organized crime and the visible hand: A theoretical critique on the economic analysis of organized crime. *Criminology & Criminal Justice, 13*(5), 615–629. https://doi.org/10.1177/1748895812465296.

Kraemer-Mbula, E., Tang, P., & Rush, H. (2013). The cybercrime ecosystem: Online innovation in the shadows? *Technological Forecasting and Social Change, 80*(3), 541–555. https://doi.org/10.1016/j.techfore.2012.07.002.

Krebs, B. (2016a). *Source code for IoT botnet 'Mirai' released.* Retrieved 13 May 2019, from Krebs on Security website: https://krebsonsecurity.com/2016/10/source-code-for-iot-botnet-mirai-released/.

Krebs, B. (2016b). *The democratization of censorship—Krebs on security.* Retrieved 13 May 2019, from https://krebsonsecurity.com/2016/09/the-democratization-of-censorship/.

Kroneberg, C., Heintze, I., & Mehlkop, G. (2010). The interplay of moral norms and instrumental incentives in crime causation. *Criminology, 48*(1), 259–294. https://doi.org/10.1111/j.1745-9125.2010.00187.x.

Kruithof, K., Aldridge, J., Décary-Hétu, D., Sim, M., Dujso, E., & Hoorens, S. (2016). *Internet-facilitated drugs trade: An analysis of the size, scope and the role of the Netherlands.* Santa Monica, CA: RAND Corporation.

Kshetri, N. (2010). *The global cybercrime industry: Economic, institutional and strategic perspectives.* Berlin: Springer Science & Business Media.

Kücklich, J. (2005). Precarious playbour: Modders and the digital games industry. *Fibreculture, 5*(1).

Ladegaard, I. (2017). "I pray that we will find a way to carry on this dream": How a law enforcement crackdown united an online community. *Critical Sociology.* https://doi.org/10.1177/0896920517735670.

Ladegaard, I. (2018). We know where you are, what you are doing and we will catch you: Testing deterrence theory in digital drug markets. *The British Journal of Criminology, 58*(2), 414–433. https://doi.org/10.1093/bjc/azx021.

Larsson, S., & Svensson, M., (2010). Compliance or obscurity? Online anonymity as a consequence of fighting unauthorised file-sharing. *Policy & Internet, 2*(4), 75–103.

Larsson, S., Svensson, M., & Kaminski, M. D. (2013). Online piracy, anonymity and social change. *Convergence: The International Journal of Research into New Media Technologies, 19*(1), 95–114.

Law, J. (1990). Introduction: Monsters, machines and sociotechnical relations. *Sociological Review, 38,* 1–23. https://doi.org/10.1111/j.1467-954X.1990.tb03346.x.

Lee, A., & Cook, P. S. (2015). The conditions of exposure and immediacy: Internet surveillance and Generation Y. *Journal of Sociology, 51*(3), 674–688.

Leukfeldt, E. R., Kleemans, E. R., & Stol, W. P. (2016). Cybercriminal networks, social ties and online forums: Social ties versus digital ties within phishing and malware networks. *British Journal of Criminology, 57*(3), 704–722. https://doi.org/10.1093/bjc/azw009.

Leukfeldt, E. R., Kleemans, E. R., & Stol, W. P. (2017). A typology of cyber-criminal networks: From low-tech all-rounders to high-tech specialists. *Crime, Law and Social Change, 67*(1), 21–37.

Levi, M., & Osofsky, L. (1995). *Investigating, seizing and confiscating the proceeds of crime.* London: Home Office Police Research Group London.

Lévi-Strauss, C. (1969). *The raw and the cooked: Introduction to a science of mythology* (Vol. 1). New York: Harper & Row.

Lewis, S. J. (2016). *Untangling the dark web: Unmasking onion services.* Presented at the HackFest 2016, Quebec City.

Lewis, S. J. (Ed.). (2017). *Queer privacy: Essays from the margins of society.* http://leanpub.com/queerprivacy.

Lum, C. (2008). The geography of drug activity and violence: Analyzing spatial relationships of non-homogenous crime event types. *Substance Use and Misuse, 43*(2), 179–201.

Lupton, D. (2015). *Lively data, social fitness and biovalue: The intersections of health self-tracking and social media.* New York: Social Science Research Network.

Lupton, D. (2016). *The quantified self: A sociology of self-tracking cultures.* Cambridge: Polity.

Lusthaus, J. (2013). How organised is organised cybercrime? *Global Crime, 14*(1), 52–60. https://doi.org/10.1080/17440572.2012.759508.

Lusthaus, J. (2015, August 5). *All's fair in love and war?* Retrieved 11 July 2018, from Industry of Anonymity website: https://industryofanonymity.com/2015/08/05/alls-fair-in-love-and-war/.

Lysonski, S., & Durvasula, S. (2008). Digital piracy of MP3s: Consumer and ethical predispositions. *Journal of Consumer Marketing, 25*(3), 167–178.

MacKenzie, D., Beunza, D., Millo, Y., & Pardo-Guerra, J. P. (2012). Drilling through the Allegheny mountains. *Journal of Cultural Economy, 5*(3), 279–296. https://doi.org/10.1080/17530350.2012.674963.

Mackenzie, S. (2014). Conditions for guilt-free consumption in a transnational criminal market. *European Journal on Criminal Policy and Research, 20*(4), 503–515. https://doi.org/10.1007/s10610-013-9229-z.

MacNeill, K. (2017). Torrenting game of thrones: So wrong and yet so right. *Convergence, 23*(5), 545–562.

Maddox, A., Barratt, M. J., Allen, M., & Lenton, S. (2016). Constructive activism in the dark web: Cryptomarkets and illicit drugs in the digital 'demimonde'. *Information, Communication & Society, 19*(1), 111–126. https://doi.org/10.1080/1369118X.2015.1093531.

Manderson, D. (1995). Metamorphoses: Clashing symbols in the social construction of drugs. *Journal of Drug Issues, 25*(4), 799–816. https://doi.org/10.1177/002204269502500410.

Mansfield, D. (2002). *The economic superiority of illicit drug production: Myth and reality—Opium poppy cultivation in Afghanistan.* In International conference on drug control and cooperation, Feldafing, January 7–12.

Mansfield, D. (2018). Turning deserts into flowers: Settlement and poppy cultivation in southwest Afghanistan. *Third World Quarterly, 39*(2), 331–349. https://doi.org/10.1080/01436597.2017.1396535.

Marres, N., & Weltevrede, E. (2013). Scraping the social? *Journal of Cultural Economy, 6*(3), 313–335. https://doi.org/10.1080/17530350.2013.772070.

Martin, E. (2006). The pharmaceutical person. *BioSocieties, 1*(3), 273–287.

Martin, J. (2014a). *Drugs on the dark net: How cryptomarkets are transforming the global trade in illicit drugs.* London: Palgrave Macmillan.

Martin, J. (2014b). Lost on the Silk Road: Online drug distribution and the 'cryptomarket'. *Criminology and Criminal Justice, 14*(3), 351–367.

Marx, G. T. (1999). What's in a name? Some reflections on the sociology of anonymity. *The Information Society, 15*(2), 99–112.

Masson, K., & Bancroft, A. (2018). 'Nice people doing shady things': Drugs and the morality of exchange in the darknet cryptomarkets. *International Journal of Drug Policy, 58,* 78–84.

Mathews, P. W. (2017). Cam models, sex work, and job immobility in the Philippines. *Feminist Economics, 23*(3), 160–183. https://doi.org/10.1080/13545701.2017.1293835.

Maurer, B., Nelms, T. C., & Swartz, L. (2013). "When perhaps the real problem is money itself!": The practical materiality of bitcoin. *Social Semiotics, 23*(2), 261–277.

Mauss, M. (1954). *The gift: The form and reason for exchange in archaic societies.* London: Routledge.

Maxwell, D., Speed, C., & Pschetz, L. (2017). Story blocks: Reimagining narrative through the blockchain. *Convergence: The International Journal of Research into New Media Technologies, 23*(1), 79–97. https://doi.org/10.1177/1354856516675263.

May, T., & Hough, M. (2004). Drug markets and distribution systems. *Addiction Research & Theory, 12*(6), 549–563. https://doi.org/10.1080/16066350412331323119.

Mayhew, P., Clarke, R. V. G., Sturman, A., & Hough, J. M. (1976). *Crime as opportunity* (Vol. 34). London: HM Stationery Office.

Mba, G., Onaolapo, J., Stringhini, G., & Cavallaro, L. (2017). Flipping 419 cybercrime scams: Targeting the weak and the vulnerable. In *Proceedings of the 26th International Conference on World Wide Web Companion* (pp. 1301–1310). International World Wide Web Conferences Steering Committee.

Measham, F., & Brain, K. (2005). 'Binge' drinking, British alcohol policy and the new culture of intoxication. *Crime, Media, Culture, 1*(3), 262–283. https://doi.org/10.1177/1741659005057641.

Measham, F., & Shiner, M. (2009). The legacy of 'normalisation': The role of classical and contemporary criminological theory in understanding young people's drug use. *International Journal of Drug Policy, 20*(6), 502–508. https://doi.org/10.1016/j.drugpo.2009.02.001.

Merton, R. K. (1938). Social structure and anomie. *American Sociological Review, 3*(5), 672.

Milgram, S. (1963). Behavioral study of obedience. *The Journal of Abnormal and Social Psychology, 67*(4), 371–378.

Moeller, K. (2012). Costs and revenues in street-level cannabis dealing. *Trends in Organized Crime, 15*(1), 31–46. https://doi.org/10.1007/s12117-011-9146-9.

Moeller, K., Munksgaard, R., & Demant, J. (2017). Flow my FE the vendor said: Exploring violent and fraudulent resource exchanges on cryptomarkets for illicit drugs. *American Behavioral Scientist, Early Online*(v). https://doi.org/10.1177/0002764217734269.

Moeller, K., & Sveinung, S. (2016). Debts and threats: Managing inability to repay credits in illicit drug distribution. *Justice Quarterly, 34*(2), 272–296.

Moore, D. (2008). Erasing pleasure from public discourse on illicit drugs: On the creation and reproduction of an absence. *International Journal of Drug Policy, 19*(5), 353–358.

Morselli, C., Décary-Hétu, D., Paquet-Clouston, M., & Aldridge, J. (2017). Conflict management in illicit drug cryptomarkets. *International Criminal Justice Review*. https://doi.org/10.1177/1057567717709498.

Morselli, C., & Roy, J. (2008). Brokerage qualifications in ringing operations*. *Criminology, 46*(1), 71–98. https://doi.org/10.1111/j.1745-9125.2008.00103.x.

Morstatter, F., Pfeffer, J., Liu, H., & Carley. K. M. (2013). Is the sample good enough? Comparing data from Twitter's streaming API with Twitter's firehose. In *Seventh International AAAI Conference on Weblogs and Social Media*.

Moyle, L., Childs, A., Coomber, R., & Barratt, M. J. (2019). #Drugsforsale: An exploration of the use of social media and encrypted messaging apps to supply and access drugs. *International Journal of Drug Policy, 63*, 101–110. https://doi.org/10.1016/j.drugpo.2018.08.005.

Munksgaard, R., & Demant, J. (2016). Mixing politics and crime—The prevalence and decline of political discourse on the cryptomarket. *International Journal of Drug Policy, 35*, 77–83. https://doi.org/10.1016/j.drugpo.2016.04.021.

Munksgaard, R., Bakken, S., & Demant, J. (2017). Risk perception in emerging markets for illicit substances in Scandinavia-The effect of available information through online communities. *The Scandinavian Research Council for Criminology*.

Natanson, M. (1990). Anonymity: A study in the philosophy of Alfred Schutz. *Human Studies, 13*(1), 97–101.

National Centre for Cyber Security. (2017). *The cyber-threat to UK business*. London: NCSC.

Netherland, J., & Hansen, H. B. (2016). The war on drugs that wasn't: Wasted whiteness, "dirty doctors", and race in media coverage of prescription opioid misuse. *Culture, Medicine, and Psychiatry, 40*(4), 664–686.

Newmeyer, K. P. (2014). *Cybersecurity strategy in developing nations: A Jamaica case study* (PhD thesis). Walden University.

Noble, S. U. (2018). *Algorithms of oppression: How search engines reinforce racism*. New York: New York University Press.

Nugent, P. (2014). Modernity, tradition, and intoxication: Comparative lessons from South Africa and West Africa. *Past & Present, 222*(Suppl. 9), 126–145.

O'Brien, J. (2001). Putting a face to a (screen) name: The first amendment implications of compelling ISPs to reveal the identities of anonymous internet speakers in online defamation cases. *Fordham Law Review, 70*, 2745.

Ohm, P. (2010). Broken promises of privacy: Responding to the surprising failure of anonymization. *UCLA Law Review, 57*, 1701–1777.

Orsolini, L., Papanti, G., Francesconi, G., & Professor Schifano, F. (2015). 'Navigating in the virtual mind of the web': The E-psychonauts' profiling. *European Psychiatry, 30,* 1045. https://doi.org/10.1016/S0924-9338(15)30822-1.

Paquet-Clouston, M., Décary-Hétu, D., & Morselli, C. (2018). Assessing market competition and vendors' size and scope on AlphaBay. *International Journal of Drug Policy, 54,* 87–98.

Parkin, S. G. (2013). *Habitus and drug using environments: Health, place and lived-experience.* Farnham, Surrey, England: Ashgate. https://www.dawsonera.com/abstract/9781409464938.

Passas, N. (2003). Cross-border crime and the interface between legal and illegal Actors. *Security Journal, 16*(1), 19–37.

Pauly, B. (2008). Harm reduction through a social justice lens. *International Journal of Drug Policy, 19*(1), 4–10. https://doi.org/10.1016/j.drugpo.2007.11.005.

Pearson, G., & Hobbs, D. (2003). King pin? A case study of a middle market drug broker. *The Howard Journal of Criminal Justice, 42*(4), 335–347.

Pennay, A. (2012). Carnal pleasures and grotesque bodies: Regulating the body during a 'big night out' of alcohol and party drug use. *Contemporary Drug Problems; London, 39*(3), 397–428, 346.

Pfitzmann, A., & Hansen, M. (2010). *A terminology for talking about privacy by data minimization: Anonymity, unlinkability, undetectability, unobservability, pseudonymity, and identity management.*

Pfitzmann, A., & Köhntopp, M. (2001). Anonymity, unobservability, and pseudonymity—A proposal for terminology. In H. Federrath (Ed.), *Designing privacy enhancing technologies* (pp. 1–9). Berlin: Springer. https://doi.org/10.1007/3-540-44702-4_1.

Powell, A., & Henry, N. (2017). *Sexual violence in a digital age.* London: Springer.

Powell, A., Stratton, G., & Cameron, R. (2018). *Digital criminology: Crime and justice in digital society.* https://doi.org/10.4324/9781315205786.

Pratt, L. H. (1988). *Lying and poetry from Homer to Pindar: Falsehood and deception in archaic Greek poetics.* University of Michigan Press.

Qiang, X. (2019). The road to digital unfreedom: President Xi's surveillance state. *Journal of Democracy, 30*(1), 53–67. https://doi.org/10.1353/jod.2019.0004.

Raab, J., & Milward, H. B. (2003). Dark networks as problems. *Journal of Public Administration Research and Theory, 13*(4), 413–439.

Reader, B. (2012). Free press vs. free speech? The rhetoric of "civility" in regard to anonymous online comments. *Journalism & Mass Communication Quarterly, 89*(3), 495–513.

Read, M. (2018). How much of the internet is fake? *Intelligencer*. Retrieved 7 January 2019, from http://nymag.com/intelligencer/2018/12/how-much-of-the-internet-isfake.html.

Reid, F., & Harrigan, M. (2013). An analysis of anonymity in the bitcoin system. In Y. Altshuler, Y. Elovici, & B. A. Cremers, et al. (Eds.), *Security and privacy in social networks* (pp. 197–223). New York, NY: Springer New York.

Reuter, P. (1983). *Disorganized crime: The economics of the visible hand*. Cambridge and London: MIT Press.

Reuter, P., & Caulkins, J. P. (2004). Illegal 'lemons': Price dispersion in cocaine and heroin markets. *Bulletin on Narcotics, 56*(1–2), 141–165.

Reuter, P., & Haaga, J. (1989). *The organization of high-level drug markets: An exploratory study*. U.S. Department of Justice.

Reuter, P., & Kleiman, M. A. (1986). Risks and prices: An economic analysis of drug enforcement. *Crime and Justice, 7*, 289–340.

Rhodes, T. (1997). Risk theory in epidemic times: Sex, drugs and the social organisation of 'risk behaviour'. *Sociology of Health and Illness, 19*(2), 208–227.

Rhumorbarbe, D., Staehli, L., Broséus, J., Rossy, Q., & Esseiva, P. (2016). Buying drugs on a darknet market: A better deal? Studying the online illicit drug market through the analysis of digital, physical and chemical data. *Forensic Science International, 267*, 173–182.

Robbins, T. (1969). Eastern mysticism and the resocialization of drug users: The Meher Baba cult. *Journal for the Scientific Study of Religion, 8*, 308–317.

Robins, S. (2004). 'Long live Zackie, long live': AIDS activism, science and citizenship after apartheid. *Journal of Southern African Studies, 30*, 651–672. https://doi.org/10.1080/0305707042000254146.

Rodriguez, S., Fernandez, M., Cepedabenito, A., & Vila, J. (2005). Subjective and physiological reactivity to chocolate images in high and low chocolate cravers. *Biological Psychology, 70*(1), 9–18.

Rogaway, P. (2015). The moral character of cryptographic work. *IACR Cryptology ePrint Archive, 2015*, 1162.

Ronen, S. (2010). Grinding on the dance floor. *Gender & Society, 24*(3), 355–377.

Rosenberg, C. E. (2002). The tyranny of diagnosis: Specific entities and individual experience. *The Milbank Quarterly, 80*(2), 237–260. https://doi.org/10.1111/1468-0009.t01-1-00003.

Rossow, C., Andriesse, D., Werner, T., Stone-Gross, B., Plohmann, D., Dietrich, C. J., & Bos, H. (2013). SoK: P2PWNED—Modeling and evaluating the resilience of peer-to-peer botnets. In *2013 IEEE Symposium on Security and Privacy* (pp. 97–111). https://doi.org/10.1109/SP.2013.17.

Ruggiero, V., & South, N. (1997). The late-modern city as a bazaar: Drug markets, illegal enterprise and the 'barricades'. *The British Journal of Sociology, 48*(1), 54. https://doi.org/10.2307/591910.

Ruppert, E., Law, J., & Savage, M. (2013). Reassembling social science methods: The challenge of digital devices. *Theory, Culture & Society, 30*(4), 22–46. https://doi.org/10.1177/0263276413484941.

Sadowski, J., & Pasquale, F. A. (2015). *The Spectrum of control: A social theory of the smart city* (SSRN Scholarly Paper No. ID 2653860). Retrieved from Social Science Research Network website: https://papers.ssrn.com/abstract=2653860.

Sandberg, S. (2013). Cannabis culture: A stable subculture in a changing world. *Criminology and Criminal Justice, 13*(1), 63–79. https://doi.org/10.1177/1748895812445620.

Sandberg, S., & Copes, H. (2013). Speaking with ethnographers: The challenges of researching drug dealers and offenders. *Journal of Drug Issues, 43*(2), 176–197.

Schreier, F., & Caparini, M. (2005). *Privatising security: Law, practice and governance of private military and security companies.* Geneva: Centre for the Democratic Control Armed Forces. Accessed 27 August 2015, http://www.dcaf.ch/content/download/34919/525055/version/1/file/op06_privatising-security.pdf.

Schüll, N. D. (2012). *Addiction by design: Machine gambling in Las Vegas.* Princeton: Princeton University Press.

Scott, S. (2010). Revisiting the total institution: Performative regulation in the reinventive institution. *Sociology, 44*(2), 213–231.

Seddon, T. (2016). Inventing drugs: A genealogy of a regulatory concept. *Journal of Law and Society, 43*(3), 393–415. https://doi.org/10.1111/j.1467-6478.2016.00760.x.

Shilling, C., & Mellor, P. A. (2014). For a sociology of deceit: Doubled identities, interested actions and situational logics of opportunity. *Sociology, 49*(4), 607–623.

Simmel, G. (1906). The sociology of secrecy and of secret societies. *The American Journal of Sociology, 11*(4), 441–498.

Smith, G. J. D., Bennett Moses, L., & Chan, J. (2017). The challenges of doing criminology in the big data era: Towards a digital and data-driven approach. *The British Journal of Criminology, 57*(2), 259–274. https://doi.org/10.1093/bjc/azw096.

Snapshot. (n.d.). Retrieved from https://link.springer.com/chapter/10.1007/978-3-642-33448-1_28.

Soska, K., & Christin, N. (2015). Measuring the longitudinal evolution of the online anonymous marketplace ecosystem. In *Proceedings of the 22nd USENIX Security Symposium*. Presented at the USENIX Security 2015, Washington, DC.

Sparrow, M. K. (1991). The application of network analysis to criminal intelligence: An assessment of the prospects. *Social Networks, 13*(3), 251–274.

Spitter, M., Klaver, F., & Koot. G., et al. (2015). Authorship Analysis on Dark Marketplace Forums. In *Proceedings of the IEEE European Intelligence & Security Informatics Conference (EISIC)*. Manchester.

Squirrell, T. (2017). Linguistic data analysis of 3 billion Reddit comments shows the alt-right is getting stronger. *Quartz*. https://Qz.Com/1056319/What-Is-the-Alt-Righta-Linguistic-Data-Analysis-of-3-Billion-Reddit-Comments-Shows-a-Disparate-Group-Thatis-Quickly-Uniting/.

Steinmetz, K. F. (2015). Craft(y)ness an ethnographic study of hacking. *The British Journal of Criminology, 55*(1), 125–145. https://doi.org/10.1093/bjc/azu061.

Stevens, A. (2007). Survival of the ideas that fit: An evolutionary analogy for the use of evidence in policy. *Social Policy and Society, 6*(1), 25–35. https://doi.org/10.1017/S1474746406003319.

Stevens, A. (2011). *Drugs, crime and public health: The political economy of drug policy*. Abingdon: Routledge.

Stokes, J. K. (2014). The indecent internet: Resisting unwarranted internet exceptionalism combating revenge porn cyberlaw. *Berkeley Technology Law Journal, 29,* 929–954.

Strang, J., Griffiths, P., & Gossop, M. (1997). Heroin in the United Kingdom: Different forms, different origins, and the relationship to different routes of administration. *Drug and Alcohol Review, 16*(4), 329–337.

Stratton, G., Powell, A., & Cameron, R. (2017). Crime and justice in digital society: Towards a 'digital criminology'? *International Journal for Crime, Justice and Social Democracy, 6*(2), 17–33. https://doi.org/10.5204/ijcjsd.v6i2.355.

Szabo, N. (1997). Formalizing and securing relationships on public networks. *First Monday, 2*(9). https://doi.org/10.5210/fm.v2i9.548.

Taylor, A. (1993). *Women drug users: An ethnography of a female injecting community*. Oxford: Clarendon Press.

Thanki, D., & Frederick, B. J. (2016). Social media and drug markets. In *Internet and drug markets* (pp. 115–123). Luxembourg: Publications Office of the European Union.

The Economist. (2014, November 1). The Amazons of the dark net: Business is thriving on the anonymous internet, despite the efforts of law enforcers. *The Economist.*

The Economist. (2016, June 16). Shedding light on the dark web: The drug trade is moving from the street to online cryptomarkets. Forced to compete on price and quality, sellers are upping their game. *The Economist.*

Thomas, S. (2006). The end of cyberspace and other surprises. *Convergence, 12*(4), 383–391. https://doi.org/10.1177/1354856506068316.

Thompson, E. P. (1975). The crime of anonymity. In D. Hay, P. Linebaugh, J. G. Rule, E. Thompson, & C. Winslow (Eds.), *Albion's fatal tree: Crime and society in eighteenth-century England* (pp. 255–344). London: Allen Lane.

Tzanetakis, M., Kamphausen, G., Werse, B., & von Laufenberg, R. (2016). The transparency paradox: Building trust, resolving disputes and optimising logistics on conventional and online drugs markets. *International Journal of Drug Policy, 35,* 58–68. https://doi.org/10.1016/j.drugpo.2015.12.010.

U.N. Broadband Commission for Digital Development. (2015). *Cyber violence against women and girls: A world-wide wake-up call.* Geneva: Broadband Commission for Sustainable Development.

Valverde, M. (2014). Studying the governance of crime and security: Space, time and jurisdiction. *Criminology & Criminal Justice, 14*(4), 379–391. https://doi.org/10.1177/1748895814541899.

Van Buskirk, J., Naicker, S., Bruno, R., Burns, L., Breen, C., & Roxburgh, A. (2016). *Drugs and the internet.* Sydney: National Drug and Alcohol Research Centre.

Van Buskirk, J., Bruno, R., Dobbins, T., Breen, C., Burns, L., Naicker, S., & Roxburgh, A. (2017). The recovery of online drug markets following law enforcement and other disruptions. *Drug and Alcohol Dependence, 173,* 159–162.

Van Buskirk, J., Roxburgh, A., Farrell, M., & Burns, L. (2014). The closure of the Silk Road: What has this meant for online drug trading? *Addiction, 109*(4), 517–518.

van der Gouwe, D., Brunt, T. M., van Laar, M., & van der Pol, P. (2017). Purity, adulteration and price of drugs bought on-line versus off-line in the Netherlands. *Addiction, 112*(4), 640–648. https://doi.org/10.1111/add.13720.

Van Hout, M. C., & Bingham, T. (2013a). 'Silk Road', the virtual drug marketplace: A single case study of user experiences. *International Journal of Drug Policy, 24*(5), 385–391.

Van Hout, M. C., & Bingham, T. (2013b). 'Surfing the Silk Road': A study of users' experiences. *International Journal of Drug Policy, 24*(6), 524–529.

Van Hout, M. C., & Bingham, T. (2014). Responsible vendors, intelligent consumers: Silk Road, the online revolution in drug trading. *International Journal of Drug Policy, 25*(2), 183–189. https://doi.org/10.1016/j.drugpo.2013.10.009.

Van Hout, M. C., & Hearne, E. (2017). New psychoactive substances (NPS) on cryptomarket fora: An exploratory study of characteristics of forum activity between NPS buyers and vendors. *International Journal of Drug Policy, 40*, 102–110.

Wang, X., & Gu, B. (2016). The communication design of WeChat: Ideological as well as technical aspects of social media. *Communication Design Quarterly Review, 4*(1), 23–35. https://doi.org/10.1145/2875501.2875503.

Watters, P. A., & Phair, N. (2012). Detecting illicit drugs on social media using automated social media intelligence analysis (ASMIA). In Y. Xiang, J. Lopez, & C.-C. J, Kuo, et al. (Eds.), *Cyberspace safety and security* (pp. 66–76). Accessed 27 July 2015, http://link.springer.com/chapter/10.1007/978-3-642-35362-8_7. Berlin, Heidelberg: Springer.

Wendel, T., & Curtis, R. (2000). The heraldry of heroin: "Dope stamps" and the dynamics of drug markets in New York City. *Journal of Drug Issues, 30*(2), 225–259. https://doi.org/10.1177/002204260003000201.

Williams, M. L., Burnap, P., & Sloan, L. (2017). Towards an ethical framework for publishing Twitter data in social research: Taking into account users' views. *Online Context and Algorithmic Estimation, Sociology, 51*(6), 1149–1168. https://doi.org/10.1177/0038038517708140.

Winstock, A., Barratt, M. J., Maier, L. J., & Ferris, J. A. (2018). *Global drug survey 2018: Key findings report.* London: Global Drug Survey.

Winter, H. (2008). *The economics of crime: An introduction to rational crime analysis.* London: Routledge.

Wirth, L. (1938). Urbanism as a way of life. *American Journal of Sociology, 44*(1), 1–24.

Yang, X., & Luo, J. (2017). Tracking illicit drug dealing and abuse on Instagram using multimodal analysis. *ACM Transactions on Intelligent Systems and Technology, 8*(4), 1–58, 15. https://doi.org/10.1145/3011871.

Yar, M. (2005). The novelty of 'cybercrime': An assessment in light of routine activity theory. *European Journal of Criminology, 2*(4), 407–427. https://doi.org/10.1177/147737080556056.

Yip, M., Shadbolt, N., & Webber, C. (2012). Structural analysis of online criminal social networks. In *ISI 2012: IEEE International Conference on Intelligence and Security Informatics* (pp. 60–65). IEEE.

Yip, M., Webber, C., & Shadbolt, N. (2013). Trust among cybercriminals? Carding forums, uncertainty and implications for policing. *Policing and Society, 23*, 516–539. https://doi.org/10.1080/10439463.2013.780227.

Zabyelina, Y. G. (2016). Can criminals create opportunities for crime? Malvertising and illegal online medicine trade. *Global Crime*, 1–18. https://doi.org/10.1080/17440572.2016.1197124.

Zinberg, N. (1986). *Drug, set, and setting: The basis for controlled intoxicant use.* New Haven, CT: Yale University Press.

Zwick, A. (2018). Welcome to the Gig Economy: Neoliberal industrial relations and the case of Uber. *GeoJournal, 83*(4), 679–691.

Index

© The Editor(s) (if applicable) and The Author(s) 2020
A. Bancroft, *The Darknet and Smarter Crime*, Palgrave Studies
in Cybercrime and Cybersecurity, https://doi.org/10.1007/978-3-030-26512-0

Druck:
Customized Business Services GmbH
im Auftrag der
KNV Zeitfracht GmbH
Ein Unternehmen der Zeitfracht - Gruppe
Ferdinand-Jühlke-Str. 7
99095 Erfurt